META-CATION VOLUMES. I, II & III

Education about Education
with
Neuro-Linguistic Programming

by
Sid Jacobson

AN AUTHORS GUILD BACKINPRINT.COM EDITION

AN AUTHORS GUILD BACKINPRINT.COM EDITION

Published by iUniverse.com, Inc.

For information address:
iUniverse.com, Inc.
5220 S 16th, Ste. 200
Lincoln, NE 68512
www.iuniverse.com

Originally published by Meta Publications

ISBN: 0-595-15388-7

Printed in the United States of America

META-CATION VOLUME I

Prescriptions For Some
Ailing Educational
Processes

by
Sid Jacobson

DEDICATION

This book is dedicated to my parents, Joe and Joanne, my brothers Steve and Dick, and my entire family for inventing me.

To Richard Bandler and John Grinder for inventing NLP.

To some very important teachers, parents, and, especially, some real special children. They're doing the best they can.

And most of all, to Judy Schuler who is so special to me. Thanks for patience above and beyond the call of sanity.

I love you all

CONTENTS

PART I

PART II

For me, after fifty years of pushing these ideas about, it has slowly become clear that muddleheadedness is not necessary.

Gregory Bateson*

*Bateson, Gregory, *Mind and Nature* (New York: E.P. Dutton, 1979), p. 209.

ACKNOWLEDGEMENTS

The author wishes to acknowledge the following people and sources, without which this volume would have been considerably less interesting, or, perhaps, not even written:

Illusions: The Adventures of a Reluctant Messiah by Richard Bach, copyright © 1977 by Creature Enterprises, Inc. Used by permission of Delacorte Press/Eleanore Friede.

Frogs Into Princes by Richard Bandler and John Grinder, copyright © 1979 by Real People Press.

Mind and Nature: A Necessary Unity by Gregory Bateson, copyright © 1979 by E.P. Dutton, Inc. Used by permission of the publisher.

NLP Vol. I by Robert Dilts, John Grinder, Richard Bandler, Leslie Cameron-Bandler, and Judith DeLozier, copyright © 1979 by Meta Publications.

Robert Dilts for permission to adapt his excellent computer programs: *Spelling Strategy* and *Math Strategy* for use in this book as well as for writing appendices II and III.

Growing Up Absurd by Paul Goodman, copyright © 1956 by Random House, Inc. (Vintage Books). Used by permission of the publisher.

The Politics of Experience & The Bird of Paradise by R.D. Laing, published by Penguin Books, Ltd. Copyright © 1967 by R.D. Laing, p. 71, reprinted by permission of Penguin Books, Ltd.

The Human Zoo by Desmond Morris, copyright © 1969, McGraw Hill Book Co. Reprinted by permission of the publisher and Jonathan Cape Ltd. on behalf of Desmond Morris.

Awareness by John O. Stevens, copyright © 1971 by Real People Press.

My warmest thanks go to Nancy Hakala for her wonderful illustrations of my cartoons.

In addition I would like to make a special acknowledgement to Richard Bandler and John Grinder for developing NLP, and therefore all of the concepts presented in this book. They are the best teachers in the world.

PUBLISHER'S NOTE

The following book by Sid Jacobson is an example of the growing fulfillment of the dream called Neuro-Linguistic Programming. As far back as 1975, there were attempts to provide teachers access to the tools of NLP; however, none of those projects reached that goal. Some became much broader publications while others were just left undone. Since that time NLP seemed to develop and change so rapidly, that books took too long to write for the NLPers to share. At last, by my request, one of us settled down to provide a book for teachers. What follows in this book represents what I hope is only the beginning for Sid. It shares NLP and does so with humor and practicality that is sorely needed in NLP literature. NLP offers choices to make your work easier, faster, and more satisfying.

Richard Bandler

INTRODUCTION: (NOT SO) RANDOM THOUGHTS

I have always been intrigued by paradoxes: the more confusing, the better. I'm sure that this has something to do with my having become a psychotherapist. Oddly enough, the most confusing paradoxes I have encountered involve the rather obscured borderline between psychology and education. The wives of two well-respected clinical psychologists—both have Ph.Ds—have asked me not to discuss learning disabilities with their spouses. Both women gave the same reasons: their husbands had been diagnosed as learning disabled when they were young. The wives felt that my "radical" views on this subject would dredge up unpleasant memories of early school years and that their husbands would become defensive.

Were the difficulties that these men faced in school because of their own disabilities or the schools'? I suspect and fear the latter; though their wives—both experienced psychotherapists—accept the former. R.D. Laing, psychiatrist and communication theorist, once pointed out the following:

A child born today in the United Kingdom stands a ten times greater chance of being admitted to a mental hospital than to a university, and about one fifth of mental hospital admissions are diagnosed schizophrenic. This can be taken as an indication that we are driving our children mad more effectively than we are genuinely edu-

1

cating them. Perhaps it is our way of educating them that is driving them mad.[1]

That's a hell of a thought.

Until I began working with school children, I took education (with the exception of my own) largely for granted: a necessary and unavoidable evil, somewhat like death and taxes. As I became more intimately involved with education, I found the analogy to be even more fitting, except that (1) Education seems more confused and less personal than either death or taxes though (2) one has a slightly better chance of overcoming its effects.

Just like health care, government, and many other "organized" human experiences, education is somewhat intangible. It should, therefore not be expected to operate as Ford's assembly line where all the cars are delivered to the end of the line in the same manner and with consistent results. Yet the assembly line is becoming the model for educating children. Why?

One reason is that we don't know, or don't ask for, what we want. If you order eggs in a diner, but fail to specify how you want them, they will probably come back scrambled. That's the fastest and easiest way.

Try to define "educated person:" A person with vast amounts of knowledge, regardless of value? Perhaps a person who is capable of integrating and organizing difficult concepts? An individual who is well rounded and has a broad perspective of the world? Someone trained to do something efficiently and effectively? I'm afraid that to most people "educated person" means a person with an education and that's all. I am convinced that—at least in the human-service professions—the number of letters following one's name means more than either the name or the knowledge gained in the letter-collection process. Whether the knowledge is useful or even relevant seems totally unimportant.

At times I have wondered if some of the assumptions at the root of our present plight in education don't have some merit.

After all, one could argue, with all of our acheivements and abilities, we *should* be able to take certain human services for granted. Couldn't we rely on the assembly-line process? Wouldn't this free us to pursue higher goals? To reach our true human potential? Well, maybe. But if so, we certainly got side-tracked somewhere along the line. We hardly seem to be heading swiftly toward our higher potentials or even effective human services. Come to think of it, maybe the assembly line never has been all it was cracked up to be (I sure wouldn't own a Pinto).

Perhaps, with all our other societal problems, it shouldn't be surprising that most of us only notice education in its grimmest moments: When a national magazine, the newspaper, or the evening news point out that a significant number of kids are graduating from high school unable to read (count, talk, think, and so forth), many of us righteously stand up and shout our most scathing indictments of the educational system in all of its non-glory. Then we forget.

Two decades ago, Paul Goodman told us: ". . . people put up with a system because 'there are no alternatives.' And when one cannot think of anything to do, soon one ceases to think at all."[2] The reverse is also true and may have come first.

At any rate, surrendering to the system is the dilemma in which we are placing much of the current generation of school children. Even if we stop blaming the system, we still will find someone and/or something to blame. That is how human beings work. Forgetting the system, we still have teachers, money, or the lack thereof, public attitudes (meaning everyone else's), social changes, the "family," and as many other favorite targets as there are people to aim at them. We have in general as much influence over those things as we have over the "system." Back to square one.

In the meantime, what happens to Johnny who can't read? He certainly has fewer choices than we do. He's stuck in a system and the system's stuck as well. We have, however, developed some extremely clever and elaborate ways to spend time and money to amuse ourselves over poor Johnny: Johnny gets screened, referred, tested, evaluated, diagnosed, and categorized until some fool finds out what *Johnny's* problem *really* is.

It is somewhat axiomatic among cynics like myself that once you begin looking for "the problem," you will certainly find it. It matters little whether it is there or not. And, it is easy to attach a very sticky label once you find "IT." Once that is done, all further difficulties can be attributed to the "disease" (deficit, syndrome, or whatever is popular that week). Besides, the label itself is often enough to give the poor kid the ailment it describes. In his book *Illusions*, Richard Bach reminds us: "Argue for your limitations, and, sure enough, they're yours."[3]

This entire process is endemic (read epidemic if you wish) among psychotherapists, educators, researchers, and others. Many insist that they are aware of the dangers inherent in labels. Then they will tell you how important it is to gather a great deal of information on each "case" in order to form a good, solid diagnosis before proceeding with treatment. That, by the way, is not a paradox. It's just plain dumb. Often, all that is ever done is further refinement of the diagnosis, ad infinitum. In some instances, treatment never begins. What is worse is that therapists and researchers teach this double-speak to educators under the guise of "expertise." The labels go everywhere. How could so many "smart" people invent such a stupid trap for themselves? It was pretty easy. Human beings are marvelously creative and flexible even in stifling their own creativity and flexibility. That isn't a paradox either. It just is.

At the heart of my highly refined cynicism (which comes and goes) is a sentiment, highly touted among cynics, that states: 90% of everything is crap. So, it is easy for me to accept the miserable state of our social institutions as inevitable. In fact, I often think the 90% figure is far too generous. In my more positive moments, however, I find the status quo not at all acceptable. But I don't want to be a guru. Just a commentator. I like the role of instigator/provoker. I love to introduce change and watch it perpetuate itself. In plain English, I think that means jump in, say my piece, jump out, and move to higher ground.

"Change" is an interesting word. Or, rather, what is interesting is its common use. Though regularly uttered by everyone, few people ever stop to think what it really means. Those who have studied the elements of change have been limited pretty much to some (but not all) systems theorists and analysts, political scientists and games theorists, logicians, communication theorists, a (painfully) few psychotherapists, epistemologists and philosophers of science, and some other not so run-of-the-mill intellectual types. Too bad. Making decisions without understanding the processes of change is somewhat like dressing in the dark. . . .

The most pervasive and useful changes always seem to be the ones that develop out of an alternative framework or viewpoint. These usually grow out of some dissatisfaction with the status quo or a major stumbling block of some sort. This is true for philosophies, theologies, sciences, societies, organizations, families, and on and on. In my circles, we call it creating alternate realities (cognitive revolutions, mental gymnastics, and other catch phrases also come to mind). But the mere thought of alternate realities is confusing for most people. When people get confused, they get scared. When they get scared, they get angry. And when they get angry in numbers, they often choose up sides for a fight: polarization, the idea that "it" has got to be "either this or that." The funny part is that "this or that" is seldom the issue. More often it is in the "either-or." How about "both," "neither," or a combination of the two?

Anthropologist Desmond Morris once wrote that the ". . . human animal is remarkably good at blinding itself to the obvious if it happens to be particularly unappealing, and it is this self-blinding process that has caused so many of the present difficulties."[4]

There seems to be an unfortunate circular truth there: Belief systems die hard, sometimes only with the believer (or not even then). When what is necessary is a new belief system, we often get stuck. And it isn't always the new system that is scary. Sometimes it is the change itself, or even just the thought of change. How do we make it so damned hard?

Attachments. Eastern philosophy has become fascinating to many people in our culture because it is so full of obvious truths. Yet that also seems to be what makes it difficult to grasp. Typically, the Zen master says to his student, "Let go, empty your mind, you don't need 'attachments' of any kind."[5] The good, American student asks for a statistical analysis that will show him the relative value of all of his attachments as well as a detailed explanation of why he should bother in the first place. He wants to formulate his next argument (that is, figure a way out of THIS one) and show the master that he is really pretty smart, too.

The master can wait. HE isn't stuck. He cracks the student on top of the head with his hand to stop the needless figuring-out process. The hardest attachments to let go of always seem to be the ones we least need, like pain and foolishness.

If we could teach our kids to painlessly switch belief systems to make their lives work, we'd all be a lot better off. On second thought, maybe they should teach us. Kids adopt alternate realities with phenomenal grace and fluidity. We call it playing (pretending). I wonder how we manage to do such a good job of teaching them to lose that important natural talent.

Wouldn't it be interesting to adopt a belief system in which learning disabilities, hyperactivity, and behavioral disorders didn't exist? The next logical step would be to get on with the task at hand: teaching kids. That would be an unusual outcome. It seems there is a woman in the inner city of Chicago who already did just that. Her ten-year-olds read and understand Dostoevsky (probably better than I do). Even the people at 60 MINUTES liked her. What a relief that was. For a while I didn't think they liked anybody. They must have thought that she was someone special. They must also have thought there was something worthwhile to be learned from her. I wonder if it was her convictions about the dignity, worth, and abilities inherent in her children?

This book is about trains of thought that result in certain belief systems. Also about certain belief systems that result in specific trains of thought. It also teaches how to avoid certain stuck belief systems. The upshot is how to help children and, just as important, how not to. Theories of development, psychopathology, traditional learning theory, and other standard fare are conspicuously absent. The reason is that much of that stuff is irrelevant. That's a pretty good reason. Besides, there is SO MUCH of that information available that the real difficulty isn't in finding it, but in avoiding it.

What follows in the first part of this book are some true stories. People who understand how human beings learn know that they learn best from stories. It's how children are taught about life at bedtime. It's how religion, morals, and other influential and important information is passed on from one generation to the next. Like most stories, the ones that follow have much in them to be found. I hope you'll grow and enjoy yourself in the search. Mostly, I let the stories speak for themselves. Occasionally I speak for them a little, hopefully in ways that enrich them. Happy exploring.

Notes

Introduction

1. R.D. Laing, *The Politics of Experience* (New York: Pantheon Books, A Division of Random House, Inc., 1967), p. 71.
2. Paul Goodman, *Growing Up Absurd* (New York: Vintage, A Division of Random House, Inc. 1956), p. xi.
3. Richard Bach, *Illusions: The Adventures of a Reluctant Messiah* (New York: Delacorte Press/Eleanore Friede, 1977), p. 75.
4. Desmond Morris, *The Human Zoo* (New York: McGraw-Hill Book Co. 1969), p. 241.
5. Part of learning Zazen, or Zen Meditation, is the practice of "emptying" one's thoughts. This is almost impossible to begin with, but even more so with intellectually oriented people. The master will often smack the student when he feels the student is too much "in his head," i.e., thinking when he should be experiencing something. It works. Almost anyone can be conditioned to do anything if you know how to interrupt the old patterns, and then replace them with new ones.

CHAPTER 1

KEEPING IT SIMPLE

Long, long ago, and far, far away, (not really but I love that beginning) I was working as a social worker in a rather traditional, family-oriented agency. Every agency has at least one or two misfits—I was about three of them. I'm a Gestalt therapist/Neuro-linguistic Programmer who dabbles in body therapy, martial arts, Eastern/Western models of integrated thought, and thinks a lot like a physicist. Got it?

Neither did many of my colleagues. Let's just say that my work was very different from traditional social work (or traditional anything).

One day a sweet little old lady (really) brought her twelve-year-old grandson in for some help. His name was Pendleton (not really). Grandma told me Pen's story. He was in special education class, and had been for six years because his I.Q. was supposedly about 50. Lately he'd been getting into a lot of fights in class. She had also noticed him fighting with other kids in the neighborhood more than usual. As she talked, I noticed that Pen was smiling. Both he and his grandma looked relaxed and at ease.

The concept of I.Q. has always triggered (and always will) the same reaction in me: I wish schools would find a more accurate measurement for placing kids—they'd probably do better using shoe size. I also found myself consciously reverting to my classical training: thinking of developmental stages, puberty, endocrinology, broken homes (he was with grandma, not ma) oedipal conflicts, and other nonsense that was still with me back in those good old days.

I told that little, nagging voice in my head to: "shut up, watch, listen, and feel or you'll miss the point." The little voice would grumble a bit, but it knew I was right. After these little internal dialogues, I would always do the same thing anyway: ask the right questions.

Me: What happens in class, Pen, when you get in fights?
Pen: They be messin' with me.
Me: Then what?
Pen: I hit 'em.
Me: Then what?
Pen: I get in trouble.
Me: But if they started it, what happens to them?
Pen: Nothin'!
Me: They don't get caught?
Pen: The teacher don't see 'em.
Me: How come?
Pen: I don't know.

I believed that, at this point, Pen really did feel like the victim and that he really wanted to talk about his predicament. I was sure I was not being conned, and my heart went out to him.

As we talked, I watched Pen's body movements. His body and his words seemed to "agree" with each other.

Bodies talk, just as words do. Usually, when people tell what they believe to be the truth their facial expressions, mannerisms, and other actions match what they are saying. Great liars can also do this but my gut reaction was that Pen was telling the truth.

As he talked, I visualized Pen in his his classroom. Visualizing people in their usual settings is important for two reasons: First, it gives me a perspective on the whole situation, not just one element, Pen. Second, it is important to design changes

that will work in an individual's environment. If I help someone to change, but that change causes more problems, I haven't done my job. A useful change should fit the person and
his or her situation. In NLP, we call this concept ecology.

I thought of other kids I had worked with who also got set
up to look stupid. Children really can be cruel to one another.
Once they find a sucker, watch out. I chuckled, cryptically,
remembering how often, as a child, the sucker had been me.
Later on, I had realized that it was just one more game to play
to fight the drudgery of compulsory education. I wished I was
flexible enough to counteract the set-ups when I was twelve
though. I'd sure have felt better about myself. Being stuck,
angry, unhappy, and predictable was really a drag. I figured
that was what Pen was feeling. I decided to keep things real
simple and to help Pen find a solution other than fighting.

> Me: Pen, can you think of anything else you could do with
> the other kids, besides hittin' 'em,[1] when they mess with
> you?
> Pen: Make friends with 'em?
> Me: (stunned) Great idea! Did anyone ever tell you that, or
> did you just think of it?
> Pen: (triumphant) I just thought of it.
> Me: Good thinkin'! It's a great idea! But do you have any
> ideas about how to do it?
> Pen: (with the wind gone from his sails) Nope.
> Me: Well let's see. . . .

I put my hand under my chin and looked a little stuck, as
Pen looked. I hadn't disagreed with anything he said. I was
startled when he suggested making friends with the other kids
though, because of the way he said it. Kids usually express
lines like that one with the enthusiasm of listening to a broken
record. In their facial expressions, they say, "If I hear 'make
friends' one more time from some adult, I shall be forced to
commit irrational acts of violence. . . ."

With Pen it was totally different. When he said that he just thought of the idea himself, he was deadly earnest. I had not experienced this before in a child and it struck me as unusual. I always look for such unusual qualities when I work with people. They're what's important.

At this point I was pretty sure that Pen would do just about anything I asked. I had already decided what I was going to try, but I wanted to motivate him while I did it. I spent the next couple of minutes pretending to painfully figure out some way to help him.

I remembered a lecture I heard in graduate school. The lecturer was one of those not so run-of-the-mill intellectual types I mentioned earlier. He was into hypnosis, brief therapy, and paradoxical interventions—essentially the art of telling someone to do something stupid, hoping that they will resist by doing something clever and productive instead. He told us what he did with children who fight in class and what he did not do with them. He told us we could do a couple of years of nondirective play therapy, talk to the parents and teachers about oedipal conflicts, or a massive variety of other garbage, depending upon our individual orientations to therapy. Then he suggested a much better idea: He would teach them to make crazy faces at the other kids rather than punch them out. I decided to try this with Pen.

Me: Pen, do you know how to make crazy faces?
Pen: Yeah.
Me: (goading) Nah, I'll bet you don't.
Pen: Yes I do!
Me: All right, let's see your best stuff.
Pen: (makes face)
Me: Not too bad, but you'll have to do a lot better than that for what I've got in mind.
Pen: What?
Me: If you can make really good faces, I'll bet you can get the other kids in trouble with the teacher.
Pen: Yeah?
Me: Sure! Cause I got an idea . . . but uh . . . (goading) nah it probably won't work, forget it.

Pen: Come on!

Me: Well, OK but we're gonna have to practice.

We, not him.

I wanted him to know that we were in this together. We both practiced making funny faces, for about five minutes. I told him which ones I liked the best for this particular project. Then I interrupted him, catching him off guard, and said: "I wonder if you could make these silly faces at kids right when they start messin' with ya." I watched Pen closely immediately after I said it. His face went blank, his eyes glazed over, I noticed his pupils dilate slightly. He appeared to be visualizing something in his head. I assumed he was imagining himself doing what I had just suggested: that he make faces at his classmates when they give him a hard time. Before he had a chance to finish the thought, or interrupt himself by saying anything, I said, "Let's practice a different way for a couple of minutes. Pretend you're in class. I'll be one of the guys giving you some trouble." I stood up and pretended to walk by him. When I was close to him, I gave him a good hard shove. In fact, I almost knocked him out of the chair. He (and grandma) stiffened up and immediately looked angry.

Me: Wait, make a face!

Pen: Oh yeah! (makes ridiculous face, laughs)

We repeated the sequence several times. I approached him from different angles. I pushed him, pinched him, and pretended to knock work from his desk. Soon his face making was just as automatic as his anger and hitting had been.

I asked him to sit back and relax. Talking very slowly and carefully, I told him what I thought would happen in class from then on. I matched the tempo of my voice to the pace of his breathing. I described the classroom: other kids, the teacher, activities, and so on. I used vague generalities, mentioning things that are standard in every classroom. I again watched him carefully. He appeared to be visualizing everything I described.

When I thought he was really experiencing the scene internally, I added what would happen the next time somebody started messin' with him. I asked him to guess just how surprised that other kid would be when he made a crazy face instead of getting angry, and how good he was going to feel that he was clever enough to outsmart the other kids like that, and what a difference it would make . . .

Then I spent a few minutes alone with grandma. I explained that all I wanted was to change the way Pen played the game in class, nothing more. I also promised her what I promise parents of almost every child I work with: "It will either work or it won't." Then I told her she would have to watch him, and listen to him, closely, to see and hear if it worked. Also, I suggested that, in a few days she ask Pen's teacher for a report.

When I saw them the next week, Pen had a big grin on his face. He said, "I made four friends this week!" Grandma told me that she had watched him closely in the playground outside their building and had seen a great difference in the way Pen handled himself with the other kids. He had not had a single fight. Both Grandma and Pen were delighted. So was I. Then Grandma said, "But if only . . ." Ah, but that is a story for yet another chapter. In the meantime, enjoy the following experiments and the next story.

Experiment #1: To Blame, Or Not

We all get stuck sometimes. We wouldn't be human otherwise. Unfortunately, we often tend to blame someone else when we are stuck. I remember consulting with a group of teachers who were complaining about one child in particular. When they were at the height of their agony, I noticed a teacher in the back of the room with a disgusted look on his face. I knew at once what was going on. After we were done, I took that teacher aside and said, "I'll bet you don't have any trouble with that kid at all." His response was, "Of course not, there is just this one, little, simple thing I noticed . . ."

Think of that one child you know that no one can handle. Then find the person who really *can*. Ask him or her how it's done. Be specific. You may really learn some easy, little approach. Then go try it! See what happens. That extra effort may really pay off.

Experiment #2: Complicated?

Teaching a child to make faces rather than fight is one of those simple, little twists that clever people have been using for years. I can not count the times I have been stuck and confused by trying to figure out some grand plan to change the course of some person, place, or thing. Then somebody came by with an obvious solution that left me feeling like an idiot. Such is life, not to mention learning.

Spend a few minutes remembering times in your life when this has happened. It's part of growing up. When you have thought of two or three examples, think of some children who could benefit from your experience. Then go, benefit them.

Once upon a time a mother brought me her ten-year-old son. Let's call him Josh. Josh's mother briefly told me that his problem was that he kept running away—from both school and home: He would just bolt out the door and be gone for hours at a time.

She knew where he went. He would go to the bus depot and hang around there. Apparently, he knew one of the drivers. Mother described this man as a big brother/father figure. He was also a friend of the family, though I never did find out what kind. There was a whole lot I never found out. Mother seemed to be playing dumb to avoid answering some of my rather pointed questions. At the time, though, I was not sure whether she was dumb or just played the role well. She also told me that Josh was retarded or at least a "slow learner." That was supposed to settle everything, I think. She wasn't clear about what she meant. But neither are those labels so I really didn't care anyway.

As she described Josh, I was watching him. He seemed detached, somehow. He was also a little fidgety—he kept looking around—but not in a way that struck me as particularly nervous. It was more exploratory: he was getting a feel for my office. Each time he saw something new (I had posters, pictures, and so forth in my office) his body would physically register the visual information. Every now and then I would interrupt his mother to ask him if what she just said was true. Fidgeting, he would nod yes, but that was all. He almost never made eye contact with me. He also never disagreed with his mother.

In these first few minutes I felt uneasy. I knew that his mother—either fully intentionally, or in part—was giving me incomplete or inaccurate information. Then she got a little more cryptic: She told me the address she had given me was for mail only. They didn't really live there. She had no telephone. If I wanted to reach her, I would have to write. I asked what to do in case of an emergency (sometimes you just have to go fishing for whatever information you can get). She told me there was an outreach worker at the project where she lived who could get a message to her. None of this stuff was *that* unusual for the clientele I was used to working with (prisons teach you a lot). But, still, I felt uneasy. There was something about the way she communicated . . .

Since Josh was not talking and his mother was being a bit hard on him, as well as generally weird, I decided to switch things up a bit. I asked her to leave so that I could spend some time alone with Josh. I was hoping that, with his mother out of the room, he would open up or at least give me some better clues.

Whenever I send parents out of my office for the foregoing reasons, I perform a little "dance." With great affect, I breathe a huge sigh of relief and say, "Whew! Now that SHE'S gone we can REALLY find out what's going on here" (I know I'm going to get letters on that one). Kids usually loosen up physically and verbally. This time my technique fell absolutely flat. Josh made it painfully and quietly clear that he was not talking. I even pulled out my "OK, I know I'm just another, dumb, white, pain-in-the-ass social worker, but c'mon, kid, give me a break . . ." routine. Nothing.

This little voice in my head would tell me all sorts of stupid things at times like this, such as, "Well, maybe he and his mother are both retarded, and this will just have to wait a few years so they can both grow out of it. . . ." Or, "He has a right to be silent. Why not play nonverbal games together for three to six months and see if he works out his oedipal problems . . ." Or, "Maybe you could give him a phobia of buses. It could be a bit of a problem later on, but at least . . ." I told the little voice to knock it off unless it could come up with something useful.

When I get really stuck, I play a little game in my head. I think of someone I know who is really clever. Then I ask myself what that person would do at a time like this. So I imagined my NLP instructor, Richard. Then I had the answer.

Richard once told a group of us that one of the reasons he learned some of the techniques he had was to avoid having to gather much verbal information. He had developed techniques whereby he could gather a minimal amount of information, and then do the rest of the talking himself. This opened up a number of avenues for me. I was pretty thoroughly trained in these techniques and tools. And I had ways of using them while, at the same time, developing a really special relationship with whomever I worked.

Establishing rapport with someone you're trying to help is a necessary and obvious first step. With someone who is verbal and willing it's easy. With Pen, for example, I just avoided arguing with him and lead him to an agreeable solution. With someone who won't talk, like Josh, the whole idea of rapport, or even agreement, gets a little cloudy, unless you have the knowledge and skills I spoke of.

I knew that if I could pace, or accurately match, some portion of Josh's ongoing experience continuously for a few minutes, I would get to a level of rapport adequate for my purposes. His whole thinking about me, and the situation, would change once he knew that I understood how he experienced himself at that moment. I know this sounds a bit sticky. To put it another way, if I could convince him that we were on a similar wavelength for at least some of the time, he would be more open to me. Hopefully, he would hear and consider whatever suggestions I came up with.

All I really wanted at that point was a chance to air my ideas about his problem and to offer alternatives. To pace some portion of his experience was really a pretty easy task. I simply decided to "feed back" to him whatever he was overtly doing with his body (This technique is called biofeedback.) But I wanted to do it in a way that would gain and hold his attention. So I started with a story.

"Josh, you remind me of another kid, just about your age, I saw not too long ago. In fact, he looked a lot like you. And you know what? This kid was really CRAZY! I wonder if you are too."

At this point Josh lit up like a Christmas tree. He looked really startled, then confused. That's what I wanted. Confusion is a very useful tool in general, but especially at times like this. I sure as hell had his attention. Pretending to talk about this "other" kid, I just started to comment on what he was doing. I also matched the pace of my voice with the rise and fall of his chest as he breathed in and out.

"Yeah, Josh, that crazy kid sat in *that very chair* where you're sitting now. And he would look up at the ceiling (as Josh looked up at the ceiling), then look down (as Josh looked down), then slide back in his chair (as Josh did)," and so forth.

After about five minutes of this, Josh was showing the signs I was looking for. His body had become a little rigid, but relaxed, his pupils were slightly dilated, and his movements looked as if he had gone onto "automatic pilot."

I wanted to know if I had paced his experience well enough to lead him to new ones. I tried suggesting something to find out if I had.

"And, Josh, as that kid looked up (as Josh did), and wiggled his feet, (as Josh did), he found himself getting *very very tired."*

When I said that Josh's shoulders slumped slightly, his eyes half closed, and he yawned. I figured I was on the right track, so I continued. I kept commenting on what he was doing, within the story, and interspersed what he was doing with comments about how tired that other kid had gotten. It seemed to work better as I continued. I decided it was time for the really important suggestions.

"And, Josh, you know what I found out about that other kid? He wasn't crazy after all! He had just made some mistakes he had to fix. Like stayin' where he was s'posed to. Yep, he found out he would *feel a lot better, Josh,* when he stayed with his momma and stayed in class. And he got a lot happier, too."

For several minutes I repeated this part of the story, and embellished it. After I had told it in several different ways, I stopped. The entire process had taken about twenty to twenty-five minutes.

"Josh, that was some story, huh? Well I know you're still real tired, so I'm gonna let you go home with your momma in a couple of minutes. And, by the way, as you walk out the door of my office, you'll be wide awake."

I opened the door for him. As soon as he passed through the door he stopped suddenly in the middle of the hallway. He looked around, a bit frantically, as if he were lost. I led him back to where his mother was waiting. He looked confused but not upset.

I spent a few minutes talking with his mother. I observed her closely as we talked, because I again had those feelings of something being very wrong. I still didn't know what, though. We scheduled another appointment, and she left.

I saw her and Josh about three or four weeks after that initial session. Josh had run away twice: once from school and once from his mother, the day after I had seen them. Then he stopped completely. He hadn't run away for almost a month, whereas it had been an almost daily ritual before. Mother said he was OK now, and she didn't want to come back. I told her I wanted to stay in touch, though. I still felt funny about the whole thing. And I had come up with some really nasty hunches shortly after the first session.

Whenever a child is into running away, there is a reason. It isn't just a bad habit. It can be treated that way, which is essentially what I had done. But I knew it was only a start. The only reason I had treated it that way at all was that I didn't see many other choices at the time. I knew that if the running stopped, which it had, the reasons for it would soon show themselves in some other way. Sooner or later I would have to get reinvolved. That's why I wanted to stay in touch.

This was one of those uncomfortable times when there is nothing else to do but wait a while. For an action-oriented guy like me, it was almost torture. But that goes with the territory. It was especially hard because of my scary suspicions. But we need to set this story aside for a while and go on to other things. While you wait patiently for the continuation of this story, do the following experiment.

Experiment #3: As If . . . [2]

Have you ever found yourself enjoying someone for their talents? (If not, see a doctor!) There are many people who can make the hardest things look effortless. We wonder how they do it. Then we pass it off to brilliance, genetics, hormones, or luck. But we don't have to.

Think of someone with a special talent for communicating with children. Pretend for a few minutes that *you are that person*. Stand or walk the way that person does. Steal their posture, carriage, voice, thoughts. Now think of some problem you are having with a child. Imagine what you would do *as that talented special person*. How would you see or hear this child? How would you feel about the child as this other person? When you think you have the idea, approach that child *as if you were* that other person. See what happens.

Notes

Chapter 1

1. Imitating diction is one technique used in pacing.
2. This experiment is based on "The *As If Frame,*" a concept introduced to NLP by John Grinder, one of the co-founders of NLP. Presented in numerous workshops.

CHAPTER 2
WEIGHING ANCHORS

It came to pass that a friend of mine got a part-time job, working with an autistic child. She was babysitter, companion, big sister, and tutor to this little girl. She told me about it one evening after a class we were taking together. She asked if I knew anything about autism and if I had any advice. I said, "Yes and yes." Then I asked her what, exactly, she wanted to accomplish with this little girl.

She said the little girl could do some things, some times. The girl was in a special school program and had some work to do that my friend wanted to help her with. She figured that would be a good start. She also told me that she knew people did all sorts of fancy behavior modification with autistic children and that it sometimes worked. I responded that that was especially true with errorless learning paradigms[1] (she looked at me as if I were speaking Martian). I also added that, even though it was often successful work, it was extremely tedious. My friend admitted having little experience with this type of behavioral work, other than having read about it. She was a little hesitant, but willing.

I asked her if she knew about "anchoring." She said, "No." I told her that it was an NLP way of talking about classical (Pavlov's) conditioning, but it made a lot more sense. She said she knew about "pairing," or conditioning one thing to another, but she wasn't sure what to connect with what (why, when, or how). I told her that it was a lot easier to do than she thought. She could establish a signal (an "anchor") that would immediately bring the little girl to a mood (or state of consciousness/awareness) in which she was able to perform at her level best. It was a way of bringing all the little girl's internal resources, strengths, and abilities to bear. I told her we call this a resource anchor. My friend was highly skeptical. I proposed that she try the following experiment.

I asked her to pick a time and place in which the little girl was doing something really well *and* enjoying herself. She replied that, each afternoon, she sits with the child and does homework (of a sort). Sometimes the little girl would do fine and enjoy herself. But, at the slightest sign of difficulty or pressure, she would blow up and throw a semivolcanic tantrum. So far my friend had been unable to find or establish any consistent pattern. As a result, homework, and almost everything else, was a totally hit-or-miss proposition. I responded that her description was typical of children described as autistic. That was the reason that errorless learning, in effect guiding all behavior to correct responses, was developed. Frustration never occurs. But, if she did what I told her, she could take the whole idea a quantum leap farther.

I told her that, the next time the little girl was in that initial efficient and enjoyable state of mind, she should reach around her and calmly and naturally place her hand on the girl's shoulder. She was to pay special attention to the exact location and pressure of the touch, so that she could duplicate it, precisely, at will.

I explained that this touch would become a part of the little girl's internal experience of herself while she was in that positive state of mind. And it would be most effective if she repeated it when they sat in the same room doing the same task: homework. If she used this technique properly the little girl should be able to maintain that same positive mood. Hopefully, this would lead to the consistency she had been lacking. I suggested that the term consistency should be used only to describe the little girl's state of mind and abilities. None of this vague reward-and-punishment, robotic thinking. That would lead her astray. My friend agreed, albeit with great skepticism, to try the experiment.

I saw her a week later. She reported the following:

> I did exactly what you said. Each day we sat down in the same place in the room and I put my hand on her shoulder, like you said. She seemed fine each day, but I figured she was just feeling good that week. So the fifth day, I just sat down next to her and did nothing. I had already decided you were crazy for devising an experiment like this, anyway, and I was going to prove it. But as I sat there, nothing happened. The little girl sat there doing nothing at all. It was like she was waiting for something to happen. She gave me a couple of strange looks. After a couple of minutes of this she reached over, picked up my hand, and put it on her own shoulder, just as I had been doing. Then she smiled, sighed, and started her work. I COULDN'T BELIEVE IT.

I could.

Experiment #4: Do You Believe . . .

Reality is a tough concept. Truth is even worse. Both are incredibly elusive and totally dependent on your frame of reference besides. Isn't it strange that most of our arguments with one another really come down to, who is right? What an incredible waste of time and energy! And what a useless way to hurt each other's feelings.

Just fifty years ago, the idiom in the English language to describe the ridiculously impossible was: "Why, that's as crazy as trying to put a man on the moon!"[2] Funny how the impossible becomes the mundane in a few short years. Expecially in all the fields of technology. But isn't education a set of technologies? Spend some time thinking about things that you were absolutely sure were impossible. But they happened anyway. Do any of them involve school children? If not, think harder.

I once had an adult client with whom I was doing essentially nothing-on a monthly basis. His name was Russ. The reason we had undertaken this Herculean task was that there was nothing else we wanted to do. Social workers sometimes have clients assigned to them by the courts or some related institution just to "keep an eye on" them. Russ was one such client. Such is life in the legal/medical/social systems we live in.

After some time, though, Russ confided in me that there was something in his life that bothered him. He could barely read. This surprised me. His verbal ability and his memory for auditory detail were remarkable. He could recite whole portions of comedy albums (one of my favorite pastimes as well). As he had with his previous worker, we had been sharing stories for months. It really is a fine way to pass the time when you have nothing else to pass. After he told me about his reading problem, we had the following conversation:

Me: What happens when you read?
Ru: I just can't.
Me: Not at all?
Ru: Well no. I can read a little. I can get through a few things in the newspaper. And they gave me a test once on reading. They said I read about like a second grader.
Me: So you can read some. What happens when you do?
Ru: I get mixed up. I mess up a lot of words.

I then pointed to a poster on the wall and said, "Read that for me." Russ craned his neck, stiffened up, held his breath, squinted his eyes, and (after some coaxing) plunged ahead. He did all right on the shorter words. On the longer ones, he tended to reverse parts of the words. If the word was more than three or four syllables long, he would transpose the last couple of syllables, delete one and reverse another, or some other combination of deletion and reversal. The most notable thing, however, was that he was frustrated, tense, and worn out after about five minutes. And pretty disgusted with himself.

I told him to relax for a couple of minutes. I taught him how to breathe properly and deeply by directing his breath to the lowest part of his abdomen first and then to fill up his chest.

I told him to shake out the tension in his neck and shoulders by wiggling his hands and arms and rolling his head around in slow circles. Then I told him to sit quietly for a few moments. He felt much better.

I then asked him to try again, very slowly, but only to go as fast as he could and still feel comfortable. He immediately did much better. Once I told him what the longer words *sounded* like, he was much more comfortable with them. While he was doing this, I spoke to him in a slow, relaxed, and care-free voice. And the tone of my voice was lower and "softer" in feeling as well as volume. I wanted the calm tone of my voice to become an anchor for his calm feelings. So I asked him— always speaking in the same, calm tone—to do a few more things. As I did so, he remained calm and relaxed.

I suggested that, from now on, he could do this on his own. Each time he picked up something to read, or learn, he could first relax, then notice how much easier the material seemed. He said that his wife had been helping him with his reading for years and that he was sure what I taught him would help. He also said that, in the future, he would pay much closer attention to his feelings.

At this point, I flashed back in my mind to some of the training I had had. I thought to myself about the importance of that last step he and I had done together, called future-pacing, in NLP language.

I had learned that many therapists and teachers are very adept at getting someone to be able to do something in the office or classroom. But the person doesn't seem to take what they've learned home. This makes perfect sense when you stop to think about it. Many moods (states of consciousness/awareness) are tied or anchored to a particular setting. Even though Russ could be relaxed with me in my office, he would not necessarily have the same experience at home with his wife, or at work with his boss. Different places (and people) don't look, sound, feel, or smell the same by any means. (That's one of the major reasons that I spend more of my time in Italian restaurants than in sewage-treatment plants.) Most important, psychologists have known for a long time that many things learned and/or experienced in one particular state of consciousness are much better remembered in that same state.[3]

From that point on, each time Russ would read he would pay closer attention to his feelings and get nice and relaxed. In effect, he would go back to the same state he was in at my office, as much as possible. He was a capable and well-motivated adult who could, and would, learn rapidly with the proper instruction. It's really that way most of the time.

I used a similar—but more complex—process with little Pen. I wanted him to enjoy school and feel good in class. This usually isn't too hard as long as there isn't some good reason for a kid to be uncomfortable. As I said earlier, getting Pen to make faces and relax at the right time simply took a little role playing, as practice. Future pacing required another step called guided fantasy.

A guided fantasy is simply an imagined experience containing sights, sounds, feelings, smells, and tastes (when appropriate). The guide structures it so that anyone having the fantasy will learn something useful. Pen got my standard classroom trip.

I began with a relaxation exercise developed especially for children. It's called the dreaming arm technique. I asked Pen what his favorite TV show was. He said, "Abbott and Costello." Then I asked him if he knew about his dreaming arm. He, of course, looked puzzled and said no. First, I gave him a hard time about it to raise his level of curiosity. Then I told him. I said that if he lifted his left arm in the air just right, he would be able to remember his favorite episode of Abbott and Costello. Then he could let his arm drift down slowly to the arm of his chair, but only as quickly as he watched the whole show in his mind's eye. And I added the suggestion that, by the time he had finished watching the show, his eyes would be closed and he would feel deeply relaxed.

Then I told him to listen to me while I told him what I wanted him to see and hear next. I asked him to make a picture of his classroom in his head. He was to see, clearly, the teacher, the other kids, desks, chairs, blackboard, and so forth. I guided him from object to object, slowly over the next several minutes. I repeatedly suggested that he *see how good he was feeling,* as he looked around. This was sort of a rigged game since he was already feeling really good and relaxed. I had set up the dreaming arm as a permanent anchor to make him feel good whenever we did it. Now the internal pictures of his classroom became anchors for the same set of internal experiences. In essence, whenever he thought of his class, he should feel the same way he did during the fantasy: good and comfortable.

Then I continued to guide him through his classroom, noting sounds. I told him to pay attention to the rustle of papers, scratching of pencils, movement of chairs, chalk on the board, the teacher's voice, other kids' voices as well as his own, and so forth. Again, interspersed with these were reminders of how good he was feeling.

I repeated this exercise again, emphasizing special feelings associated with the classroom. I asked him to notice if he could feel the wooden chair and desk, the pencil in his hand, the temperature (I threw in the smell as well) of the air, and so forth. Again, all of this portrayed against the background of his good feelings.

The entire fantasy took about fifteen to twenty minutes. The structure, again, was to create new anchors. These were all objects, sounds, and feelings found in the classroom. They were the sum of things that made up the "atmosphere" of his class. Provided that he was really relaxed and comfortable while I took him through the fantasy, he should feel that way in the classroom as well.

The obvious question was, how could you ever know for sure that he would go into that same exact state of mind when he went to class. The obvious answer is that you can never know for sure. Ideally, he would go in feeling and experiencing his classroom with at least some of the positives I had suggested. Would he be exactly the same as in the office? No. He would probably develop a state of mind with most of the features of that fantasy, but because the fantasy couldn't possibly be *the same as* the classroom, his state of mind wouldn't be exactly the same either. What he would have would be an experience unique to him, a unique human being. And experience tells those of us who do this kind of work that it would be uniquely useful to him as a person.

Experiment #5: Experiencing the Obvious[4]

When is the last time you were in a school classroom? Even if it is recent, did you try it from a child's point of view? Go, sit alone in a classroom somewhere, at a student's desk. Look around. Let your eyes wander and see what attracts, or distracts, your attention. Listen to your own internal dialogue for a few moments. What are you telling yourself? What memories come back? Are they fond memories or . . . ? What do you feel as you look around? Most obvious to me about this experiment is that everyone will have their own ideas about what is obvious . . .

Notes

Chapter 2

1. An errorless learning paradigm, as the name implies, is a structure or procedure for working with a person that forces or guides the person to the correct answers all the time. A good example is in teaching a child to put round pegs in round holes on a board. Each time the child would try to place the peg into a hole that was square or into which the peg would not fit, you would push his or her hand over to the correct hole, avoiding the possibility of error. This is effective with so-called autistic children because they generally can't stand to make errors. It avoids frustration, creates constant positive reinforcement, but is extremely tedious.
2. Richard Bandler, "Fabric of Reality," (Paper presented at second annual NLP conference, 1981).
3. This principle is called state-dependent learning or state-specific learning. It is the key to understanding why people cannot remember what they did or what happened to them while they were drunk or under the influence of a drug. These memories are not really lost. To recall them, one must take the same drug or drink, in other words, re-enter that same state of consciousness. This principle is also the basis for the phenomenon known as post-hypnotic suggestion.
4. This is a standard Gestalt-Therapy experiment.

CHAPTER 3

THE EYES HAVE IT

Come back now to a time when Pen and his grandmother and I left off (Chapter 2). We were all delighted with Pen's progress in making friends and avoiding fights. He had seemingly licked those problems. Then she and I had the following conversation:

Gr: But if only he could learn. If only somebody could teach him.

Me: What do you mean? What can't he learn? Can he read (most impatiently)?

Gr: READ?! He can't even say the alphabet (sadly).

Me: (under my breath "Oh x@!!") How long has he been in special education?

Gr: This is his seventh year.

Me: They did a terrific job (even more disgusted than the words would indicate).

Actually, my head was swimming at this point. I was so angry and disgusted with a system that had failed so miserably that I almost wanted to cry. I was also bound and determined to do whatever repair work was necessary. Pen was going to get something out of school besides frustration. I figured that since he was feeling better in class, and making friends, now was the best time to help him. I also knew that, with my NLP skills, I could teach rings around just about any teacher in any school.

I began, as always, by finding out exactly what Pen did when attempting to recite the alphabet. In NLP, we call this process "strategy elicitation." That's a fancy way of saying, "finding out what he does." I then said the magic words, "Pen, say the alphabet for me."

Pen looked almost straight up, and slightly to his left. He then began to recite, in a dull, slow monotone, "A,B,C,D," and so forth. When he got to the sequence L,M,N,O,P he faltered and stopped. He was unable to continue, so I watched closely as he went back to the beginning. His eyes and head actually shifted back to the left, then he started again. His repetition was in the same tone, and he faltered in the same spot. He tried a third time—it was identical to the first two. He failed at L,M,N,O,P. Each time his eyes and head went through the same movements. Each time his voice echoed the same dull, slow monotone. I glanced over at grandma who said, "It's always the same. And it's funny, his sister sings it right off."

It was clear to me that I had more than enough information to help Pen. First of all, Pen had the alphabet arranged as a picture in his head, from left to right. I knew this, because his eyes shifted up and to his left. For most people, eye movement in the direction of up and to their left indicates that they are visualizing a memory, whether they are aware of it or not. The following section, taken from *Neuro Linguistic Programming: Vol. I,* will give you an adequate summary of eye-movement patterns that are useful in this process.

3.231 Eye Movements as Accessing Cues

We have noticed that the eye movements people make as they are thinking and processing information provide a remarkably accurate index for sensory specific neurological activity. We introduced these patterns in *Patterns II:*

"When each of us selects the words we use to communicate to one another verbally, we typically select those words at the unconscious level of functioning. These words, then, indicate which portions of the world of internally and externally available experience we have access to at that moment in time. More specifically, the set of words known as predicates (verbs, adjectives and adverbs) are particularly indicative. Secondly, each of us has developed particular body movements which indicate to the astute observer which representational system we are using. Especially rich in significance are the eye scanning patterns which we have developed. Thus, for the student of hypnosis, predicates in the verbal system and eye scanning patterns in the nonverbal system offer quick and powerful ways of determining which of the potential meaning making resources—the representational systems—the client is using at a moment in time, and therefore how to respond creatively to the client. Consider, for example, how many times you have asked someone a question and they have paused, said "Hmmmmm, let's see" and accompanying this verbalization they move their eyes up and to the left. Movement of the eyes up and to the left stimulates (in right handed people) eidetic images located in the non-dominant hemisphere. The neurological pathways that come from the left side of both eyes (left visual fields) are represented in the right cerebral hemisphere (non-dominant). The eye scanning movement up and to the left is a common way people use to stimulate that hemisphere as a method for accessing visual memory. Eye movements up and to the right conversely stimulate the left cerebral hemisphere and constructed images—that is, visual representations of things that the person has never seen before (see *Patterns,* volume I, page 182).

"Developing your skill in detecting the client's most highly valued representational system will give you access to an extremely powerful utilization tool for effective hypnotic communication. There are two principal ways which we have found effective in teaching people in our training seminars to refine their ability to detect representational systems:

(1) attending to accessing cues which may be detected visually. Specifically (for the right-handed person):

accessing cue	representational system indicated	
eyes up and to the left . . .	eidetic imagery	(V)
eyes up and to the right . . .	constructed imagery	(V)
eyes defocused in position . . .	imagery	(V)
eyes down and to the left . . .	internal dialogue	(A)
telephone positions . . .	internal dialogue	(A)
eyes left or right, same level of gaze . . .	internal auditory	(A)
eyes down and to the right . . .	body sensations	(K)
hand[s] touching on midline . . .	body sensations	(K)

I knew Pen well enough to know that he fit this scheme perfectly. It only takes a couple of minutes to determine this, anyway. You just have to ask the right questions, as always.

Also, it was clear that he was "reading" his picture from left to right, because I could see his eyes (and head) scanning that way. I was also pretty sure that he had almost no corresponding awareness of the sounds of the letters, or even his voice, as he recited. The monotone he recited the alphabet in was very different from his normal speaking voice. I knew that, normally, this strategy should be adequate for reciting the alphabet. But for some reason it didn't work for Pen.

Next, I wanted to verify all of my ideas. So I asked Pen if he was actually seeing the alphabet in his head. He said he was. I also asked him if he was having some kind of trouble with the picture when he got to L,M,N,O,P. He said yes, again.

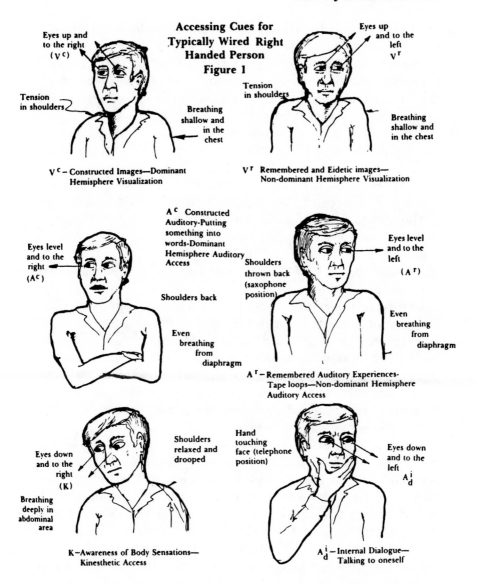

Accessing Cues for
Typically Wired Right
Handed Person
Figure 1

Eyes up and
to the right
(V^c)

Tension
in shoulders

V^c – Constructed Images—Dominant
Hemisphere Visualization

Eyes up
and to the
left
V^r

Tension
in shoulders

Breathing
shallow and
in the
chest

Breathing
shallow and
in the chest

V^r Remembered and Eidetic images—
Non-dominant Hemisphere Visualization

A^c Constructed
Auditory-Putting
something into
words-Dominant
Hemisphere Auditory
Access

Eyes level
and to the
right
(A^c)

Shoulders back

Even
breathing
from
diaphragm

Shoulders
thrown back
(saxophone
position)

Eyes level
and to the
left
(A^r)

Even
breathing
from
diaphragm

A^r – Remembered Auditory Experiences-
Tape loops—Non-dominant Hemisphere
Auditory Access

Eyes down
and to the
right
(K)

Breathing
deeply in
abdominal
area

Shoulders
relaxed and
drooped

Hand
touching
face (telephone
position)

Eyes down
and to the
left
A_d^i

K –Awareness of Body Sensations—
Kinesthetic Access

A_d^i – Internal Dialogue—
Talking to oneself

I asked if he became uncomfortable when the picture got
scrambled. He said, and his body showed me, absolutely yes.

I then thought for a moment about why this strategy could
possibly be ineffective here. I decided that I really didn't care;

I just needed to help Pen change it. And Grandma had already told me how. Pen needed to either, "sing it right off," just as his sister or at least *hear* it inside his head while he said it. I was convinced that expanding his awareness by adding in the "soundtrack" to his silent movie would be enough. I still didn't know quite why.

I decided to keep it as simple as possible. I asked Pen to use his dreaming arm to get as relaxed and comfortable as he could. When he felt comfortable, I asked him to let his head be clear of any distractions. (Actually I said, "Make a blank movie screen in your head.") Then I asked him to look at the alphabet in his head "only as I sing it to you." I began to sing the alphabet song to him while I carefully watched him watching his internal picture. When I got to the problem sequence, *L,M,N,O,P,* I slowed down and exaggerated each of the sounds.

I continued normally. I did this to mark out that sequence as one that needed special attention.[1] I also wanted him to go slow enough to remain comfortable and relaxed, even in the hard parts. Again, we started off with the method we always used to get him comfortable. It was also connected to his classroom, through anchoring. This was to insure that he "took it to school with him." I repeated the alphabet two or three times, the same way each time.

I then asked him to open his eyes and stay relaxed. He did. Then I said, "Pen, say the alphabet for me." He started with a much more relaxed and pleasant voice, sort of halfway between my singing and his monotone. He comfortably glided right through *L,M,N,O,P* with no trouble. Then a strange (not really) thing happened. When he got to *S,* he said, "X," floundered, got lost, and had to start over. He repeated it the same way twice. He knew he was making a mistake, but he was just as stuck as before.

By this point, he had reversed his strategy to a totally auditory one. *S* and *X* sound almost the same, though they look quite different. I asked Pen if he could see that part of the alphabet in his head. He said it was hard. I remembered that he could recite the first half of the alphabet fine all along, but he hadn't gotten this far before. At least not with me, and not enough to have formed a good internal picture of it.

I wrote out the alphabet on a small piece of paper. I asked Pen to do the dreaming-arm technique again. I told him we were going to do it the same way, except that, this time, I wanted him to look at *my* picture of the alphabet, which I had drawn on a piece of paper. I sang it again, two or three times, and pointed to *S* and *X,* when I got to them. (This emphasized these two letters separately from the rest.)

I then asked him to take a breath and recite the alphabet. He did so perfectly three times in a row. It was the first time in his life. The three of us were rather ecstatic.

Next, I did more of the future pacing that I talked about earlier. I took him through another guided fantasy of his classroom. This time, however, I added important suggestions. I told him that since he now knew the alphabet, it would be much easier for him to learn to read: it would be comfortable, and he would really enjoy it. From that point on, he was going to begin to learn important and fun things. All this was going to make him a more interesting, better, and happier person: one both he and his grandmother could be proud of. And it was all because he worked so hard in a really fun and relaxed way.

I always add suggestions like those to all the work I do with people. I think it is important to do more than just solve problems—though that is certainly worthwhile. These suggestions put problems into a framework of growth and personhood. I organize the suggestions so that each hurdle that is overcome becomes a building block for future growth as well as a solved problem: each solved problem becomes a blueprint for future solutions. (This is certainly my personal value judgement. I keep it because I think it is a worthwhile one to have.)

Another value of mine is to intellectually understand what I do as thoroughly as possible. As I said earlier, it was not necessary for me to know exactly *why* Pen had the particular trouble that he did. I knew I could help him regardless. The whole process only took about forty-five minutes and was effective. This was, in part, because I didn't bother to try to figure it all out. But I am in the business of packaging and teaching strategies that are effective for other people. So I wanted to know. Especially since I had considered Pen's visual representation of the alphabet to be a perfectly good one. Shortly after I finished this piece of work, I spent a few quiet minutes reflecting on the whole set of processes involved here. A better way of putting it might be to say that I was "playing detective." Then it hit me.

In the sequence *L,M,N,O,P*, there is a built-in problem for someone with *only* a visual image of the letters. That is, *M* and *N* look very similar. When someone sees two similar things, their natural tendency is to glance quickly back and forth between them to distinguish between the two. This is a fine way to make subtle distinctions, but it is a really lousy strategy for completing a sequence.

In effect, to complete the sequence *L,M,N,O,P,* you need to visualize the letters in that order. One letter acts as a cue for the next. If you ask people where a particular letter falls in the alphabet, many adults will have to start from the beginning to be able to answer you correctly. This indicates that they have it arranged in order in their minds.

Pen's visual strategy must have been something like this:

$$J \rightarrow K \rightarrow L \rightarrow M \overset{\curvearrowleft}{\underset{\curvearrowright}{}} N$$

The loop between *M* and *N* must have just continued without the proper distinction ever being made. This loop never did cue the subsequent letters of the alphabet. His frustration grew each time this happened until it appeared overwhelming.

A more complete description is: he started with a set of visual images; at the problem sequence, it became difficult to keep the picture clear; he had physical discomfort at this point; the bad feelings became more powerful, that is he was more aware of them than of the visual representation; he could then no longer *see* while he paid attention to how bad he *felt;* the more the picture scrambled, the worse he felt; the task at hand became less important than feeling miserable; he would give up. He really didn't have a choice by the time he felt that way. But, he was still sitting in front of someone who was waiting to hear him say the alphabet. I was convinced that he would try to please that someone until he got exhausted. He would start over and fail at the same point as long as there was someone he wanted to please. Even though he knew he was doing something that didn't work, he didn't have anything else to replace it with.

All of this may sound too complicated. It is. Remember these were just my (not so) random thoughts at the time. And, admittedly, not many people think the way I do, randomly or otherwise. It isn't necessary. The only thing that is necessary is the ability to help someone change something that doesn't work to something that does. Indeed, I didn't consciously think, step by step, of all I just described. Mainly, I was concerned with Pen's visualization at a particular sequence, his lack of auditory awareness, and his discomfort. The other stuff was for my enlightenment.

I once had an experience in a workshop that illustrates how to use visualization. My former partner and I were making a presentation at a school for teachers and parents. As in most introductory NLP demonstrations, we wanted to give them an example of a strategy that works for spelling. We asked for some good spellers in the room to volunteer themselves. We asked the volunteers to spell a couple of words for us. We asked the rest of the group to watch closely. Each one—as do all good spellers—did exactly the same thing: they looked up and to their left, and then spelled the words correctly. By asking them the appropriate questions, we made it clear to everyone present that, as these people looked up and to the left, they were visualizing the word. Then they "read" it to us. They knew they were correct by a feeling they had. (Some people check themselves by the sound of the word rather than the feeling, but almost all good spellers do one or the other.) They all said they knew whether they had it right because it *felt* right or did not. They said they rarely made mistakes.

We then asked if there were any really bad spellers in the

room. The teachers all began to laugh and point at Steve, the physical education teacher. They said he was the worst speller around. Several remarks were passed attesting to his good fortune at getting his own name right the majority of the time. They also said how much fun it was to torment him unmercifully. Especially since he was so capable in many other areas.

When the jokes died down, we asked Steve to spell a couple of words for us. Each time he would look down and to the right, then to the left, back and forth, and everywhere but up. He became tense and really uncomfortable and was, essentially, unable to spell.

We asked him to take a couple of deep breaths and to relax for a moment. When he felt better, we asked him a couple of questions about how he had managed to get this far in life, as well as in education, without being able to spell. He told us he always had a dictionary nearby. He never hesitated to use it.

My colleague and I looked at each other for about one fourth of a second. Then we explained in detail what we knew about visualization. We told the group that, essentially, we all have photographic memory (technically known as eidetic imagery). In fact our memories are remarkably complete. Many people, including me, choose to believe that everything we have ever experienced, that is, seen, heard, felt, tasted, or smelled, is stored intact in our brains.[2] We automatically store information that comes in through our senses. Effective "retrieval," on the other hand, has to be taught and learned. Understanding more about *how* retrieval works, in experiential terms, can improve us tremendously.

Understanding eye-movement patterns is important. Since most people look up and to their left to retrieve visual-stored information, it stands to reason that it is a natural phenomenon of some sort (even without the supporting neurological evidence). We assumed that Steve, after years of exposure to the dictionary, probably had most of it stored. He just didn't have a way of getting to that stored memory.

My colleague went over to Steve and helped him relax by doing a quick exercise. Then she asked him to spell some words. He was to visualize the dictionary. He was then to imagine opening it, turning the pages while simultaneously watching the guide words at the top of each page, finding the page with the word on it, looking down the page to find the word, then reading us the word. For the first word he took a breath and began looking around as before. We both said, "No, up and left, with your eyes." He looked up and began again. His face brightened. I said, "Now look carefully at the guide words, then look down the page." He said, "I don't have to. It is the guide word." He then spelled it smoothly, easily, and correctly, just by reading his own internal dictionary. When he finished the word, he immediately looked forward, wide-eyed, as if stunned and said, "I'll be damned." We practiced a couple more words until everyone in the room was convinced (especially Steve) that he had almost the entire dictionary at his disposal. He simply had to look in the right place.

We were using much the same strategy and technique that I used with Pen. Relaxation was important, as always. So was the ability to visualize. So was the fact that we used a major strategy already being employed by Steve, and changed it slightly. With Pen, I kept his visualization pretty much intact and added the auditory component. With Steve, we took his external use of the dictionary and "internalized" it. That is we made it faster, easier, less traumatic, and more graceful. Most people have what they need to function, whether they are "retarded" children or competent adults. Sometimes the more subtle approaches are the best.

Experiment #6: How Are You Organized?

You have probably just learned about the importance of eye-movement patterns for the first time. Within the basic pattern, there are a few characteristics that are different in different individuals. For example, some people, myself included, can visualize, regardless of the direction of gaze and equally well with eyes opened or closed. Others can't. It may be interesting to find out more about how you, internally, are organized.

Start by visualizing something, perhaps a difficult word to spell. Where is the picture the clearest? Straight ahead? Up and to the left or to the right?

Once you have established the easiest way for you to visualize, find out if there is a direction of gaze that makes visualizing difficult or impossible. For many people, making an internal picture while looking down is impossible. Find out whether this is true for yourself.

Repeat the above instructions, for sound and feelings. Listen to a tune in your head while looking down and to the left. See if that is the way that you "hear" it most clearly. Then try hearing it while looking in another direction, say up and to the right. Next, pay attention to your feelings. (Probably, this will be easiest if you move your eyes down and to the right, or straight down.) Find out.

The chart and explanation (on page 41) should help you devise some more interesting combinations to explore. Have fun with it!

Once in a while, you run into someone who is doing something in a way that, fundamentally, won't work very well. One example is Russ, who could barely read. Once we worked on his ability to *see* the words (inside as well as out) and relax while reading, there was still more to do. He told me, just as Steve had, that he couldn't spell. He was convinced that, if he could learn to spell, everything else would fall right into place. He said so with such conviction that I believed him. I didn't think that understanding why this was true was particularly relevant to the task at hand. So I didn't bother to try. I felt that believing along with him would suffice.

I asked him how he spelled. He said if he could not sound out a word, he didn't bother to try at all. He also said that some teacher he had had when he was young taught him to spell the word "arithmetic" by using the following mnemonic device: *A R*at *I*n *T*om's *H*ouse *M*ight *E*at *T*om's *I*ce *C*ream. He said this was drummed into his head, and he never forgot it. He had been trying to devise other mnemonics for words he felt he should know.

I told him that this would work well, especially for him since he "listened" so well internally. I also said that he could eventually learn to spell quite adequately in this way. This, however, was only provided that he was willing to spend all of his time doing nothing but this for approximately the next five hundred years. Mnemonic devices can be entertaining as well as helpful when used in a limited way. But they are extremely cumbersome and slow. I insisted that it was totally an illusion that the only way he could spell the word "arithmetic" was by using that device.

I proceeded to tell him what we had told Steve about photographic memory. I then said that all he really had to do was learn to visualize something on which he had seen the word "arithmetic" written. He replied that the last time he could think of must have been the last time he had an arithmetic book, which would have been about sixth grade. He was sure he couldn't possibly remember back that far. I told him he was wrong, and that all he had to do was look up and to his right (left and right were reversed for him) and tell me what color the book was. He said it was red. I then asked him if he could *see* what color the letters were. He said, "Yeah, sort of silver or gray." I said that, if he could see them, he could certainly read them to me from the book cover. He said, "A-R-I-T-H-M-E-T-I-C." Then he looked a little bewildered for a few moments and said, "S---, I got it right? I really *do* have photographic memory! Boy I can't wait to get home and flip out my wife with THIS one!" At that point it was simply a matter of future pacing and practice. Russ felt really good.

Experiment #7: Stretch . . .

Think of a teaching method you know of (or use one that is moderately effective but slow, cumbersome, or difficult). After reading this far, you may be able to think about this method in a new way. Break it down into some logical, component parts. Then, examine these and find out what the problem areas are. Make up replacement parts for these problem areas and reassemble this formerly cumbersome teaching method into a streamlined version.

As an alternative, imagine some totally new and different approach to teaching this subject matter. Use your creativity. Anything that works at least as well or better will provide a viable alternative for teaching. Get in the habit of having as many viable alternatives as possible.

Notes

Chapter 3

1. In NLP, this is called analog marking.
2. In his famous studies of the effects of electrical stimulation of the surface of the brain, Penfield showed that a small amount of electricity applied to the cortex, on conscious patients, caused some of them to recall experiences they thought they had forgotten. And they often remembered them in vivid detail. This does not prove the point I am making here. It simply points to an interesting possibility. For more information see: Penfield, Wilder and T. Rasmussen, *The Cerebral Cortex Of Man: A Clinical Study Of Localization Of Function* (New York: Macmillan Publishing, 1957).

CHAPTER 4

CONNECTIONS

It was a simpler time back in the days when I had a continual flow of children to experiment with. It is easy to use a private practice to practice privately, but you can't do it on as large a scale as in a crowded social services agency. I used to have the most fascinating children and parents come to see me. I used to invent and explore galore. And, using sheer simplicity, I used to get immense pleasure out of stopping bureaucratic bucks. Most of what seems really complicated and depressing is usually really simple and can be made pleasurable. (That sounds a lot like the last fortune cookie I read.)

I'll never forget a phone call I had from a scared and confused mother. Her little girl Sally had really been through the mill. She was in third grade in the regular class, but her mother told me that that wasn't the right class. Sally's mother was warned about the emotional problems Sally was going to develop any day now because she was supposed to be in the special class and she needed a social worker. That's what the tests said. Sally was flunking everything, and mother was very angry because the tests were so expensive and the psychologist's recommendations were impossible to follow, but they were supposed to be the best ones available.

(If those two sentences got you as short of breath and confused as they did me, you'll have an accurate idea of what that conversation was like.)

I asked Sally's mother to bring Sally in to see me, and we'd see what I could do to help. She said she couldn't do that. She'd have to see me herself, first.

When Sally's mother came in to see me she was rather upset. First, I tried to make her comfortable enough to explain to me, clearly, just what was going on. She wanted me to read the lengthy and very prestigious psychological report that she had brought with her. I refused on the grounds that I could probably write one just like it after spending five minutes with Sally—if I were so inclined. The tests, I told her, may be fairly accurate, but they wouldn't be of much use to me. She would just have to tell me what *she* thought was important. I told her, also, that I might be able to do a lot more than provide emotional support for her "misplaced" child.

She then started at the beginning. Sally had had problems in school from the start. After a while, her teachers discovered that she had real, physical, eye and ear problems. Over a series of months, she had several operations to correct these difficulties. As a result, she could now see and hear normally. But, she was still doing lousy in school. Sally's mother was not satisfied with the handling of the evaluation procedures by the school board. (There was generally a four to five month wait for testing and evaluation, plus a couple of months before the results could come back.) She decided to have the testing and evaluation done privately. It was quite thorough but also quite expensive. The major recommendation was a special education class of no more than eight children. The feeling was that little Sally was emotionally immature and, thus, needed more individual attention than other children. They said she was learning disabled, so there were lots of other complicated recommendations as well. *But,* due to the timing of the evaluation and to the limited choices available in the public schools, Sally was assigned to a *regular* class of twenty-five children. One ill-equipped to provide the unusual services recommended in the evaluation. So Sally's mother was told to *expect* failure, to expect emotional problems for little Sally due to frustrations and so forth. With this glum prognosis, the school suggested that she seek the help of a social worker to provide emotional support and to ease the inevitable pain . . . In other words, she should surrender.

I asked Sally's mother how well Sally *liked* her current class. She said that Sally really enjoyed it. She liked the other kids and her teacher even though she was having a lot of trouble doing the work. At that point, I told her that I had heard all I needed to help Sally. I also said that I thought that as long as Sally liked her class, she should stay there. I would help her catch up. Mother thought I was kidding or nuts. I assured her that I was serious and that I could teach Sally to learn quickly and painlessly. (I was really cocky at that point.) I would also give her some exercises and experiments to do with Sally that would help even more. We made another appointment.

I thought that this work would probably be pretty easy and allow me the freedom to experiment a great deal. I figured that Sally had not had much chance to develop many workable strategies for relating visual, auditory, and kinesthetic kinds of information to each other. I also figured that part of the reason she was enjoying school, even though she had not improved academically, was that she could now at least see and hear decently. (*I* would sure have felt better if I were her.) Third, her "immaturity" was probably just an outgrowth, or artifact, from not having had the opportunity to develop understanding strategies.

I also became whimsically philosophical. One of my hobbies is studying epistemology (essentially the study of the origins and nature of knowledge itself—I have strange hobbies). I remembered the ideas of John Locke and others who believed that a human being begins life as a *tabula rasa,* or "a blank slate." Real humanness, according to this belief, comes only through experience. To take this a step further, human potential really is limited by how much can be packed onto that slate through learning. The better organized, the more he, she, or it will hold. My forte (and my goal with Sally) is to teach the organization: the how, not the how much, of learning. I remembered the old Zen saying that if you give a man a fish, you feed him for a day. But if you teach him to fish, you feed him for a lifetime.

The only surprise I had when Sally came in was her appearance. Her mother was an extremely attractive and outgoing woman. Little Sally was a pudgy little cherub with glasses and a nasal voice. She was clever and funny though. After spending a couple of minutes getting to know her, and vice versa, I asked her a few questions, such as what gave her the most trouble in school. She and her mother both agreed it was spelling. Sally had a spelling test every Friday. She had been getting four or five right each week, which was good solid failure.

Since it was so incredibly easy to teach spelling, I decided to start there and expand to other areas. I explained to Sally and her mother about visualization and how it was necessary in spelling. I also said that I bet the psychological reports said that Sally had "a deficit or inability to 'pair' auditory and visual information." Sally's mother said that was true. The psychologists had told her that was one of the main sources of Sally's problems. I told her that I knew what the report said because every psychological report I had ever read on every child with any learning problem said the same things. And, that was the main reason I didn't bother to read the damn things. I also said the usual recommendation for this "problem" was a whole bunch of games, exercises, and strange devices that were to be administered by teachers and other professionals for a couple of years, in the hope of some improvement or compensation. Mother told me this all sounded sickeningly familiar. She also mentioned something about several hundred dollars, a few all-day trips across town, considerable anguish (and a lot of other stuff that even I consider unprintable) just to find out what I had just told her (for free) in about the five minutes I had mentioned earlier.

While we were talking I was formulating an experiment. I remembered a research study on eidetic imagery (photographic memory) that I had heard about years earlier. I remembered my introductory psychology professor telling us about it, so it must have been about ten years earlier. I often find tidbits from diverse sources incredibly useful. Not because they tell me what to do, but rather, because they lead me to new possibilities.

This particular study made several interesting points. First, many children before the age of five or six have fantastically complete visual memories. Most of them "lose" it after that age.[1] Second, the study revealed something really interesting regarding visual foreground and background (gestalt, for those who are curious). The children were shown a picture on a plain white screen for a few seconds. Then the picture was turned off and they were asked to "hold it" on the screen in their minds's eyes. As long as they looked at the screen, many of them had remarkably complete memory for the picture. They were able to describe very minute details about even very complex pictures. Some of them were questioned for up to twenty minutes on details of pictures they had seen for only a few seconds. They did as well as if the picture itself were still there in front of them, not just their memory of it. But, if they "moved" the picture off the screen, they seemed to lose it. In fact, if they moved the picture toward the edge of the screen, it seemed to fall off the edge. If they moved the picture halfway off the screen, they would lose that half only. That which had remained on the screen would continue to remain.

In Sally's case, I was thinking about this in relation to the eye movement patterns. I knew that most people, when remembering a visual image, move their eyes up and left. I added to this the thought that it is easier to visualize something against a plain white background, as in the study. I also knew that, for most people, when they remember something they have heard, they move their eyes down and left. It helps internal listening. A fourth piece of information I gained from that study was that as long as the picture was held on the white background it would stay. I didn't, and still don't, believe the part about losing the *ability* after six years of age. I believe, rather, that we are taught not to use this wonderful natural ability in favor of much less effective methods of information (mis)processing (I know my cynicism is showing).

Another piece of information is important here. When someone's eyes are aimed up and to their left, though it is easy to visualize, it *can* be very difficult or even impossible to remember (or "access") *sounds*. By the same token, when looking down and left, though it is easy to internally access memories of sounds, it can be difficult or impossible for some people to visualize.

During my NLP training, we experimented with these ideas. I remember particularly some people's difficulty when looking down and to the right (which gets most people in touch with their feelings), remembering simple visual information. One man could not tell me the color of his mother's eyes, or the color of his car, while he was looking down at all. He had to move his eyes up to be able to give me information even this basic. And this has absolutely nothing to do with intelligence or capability as a person.

What does this have to do with little Sally? Everything. On a spelling test a word is spoken by the teacher. The child's job at that point is to *hear* the word, attach a visual image (internal) to the sound—visual/auditory pairing—and write the word.[2] Remember, writing is just a visual representation (a picture) of speech. It just takes a bit of physical motion to perform the transformation from sound to picture, provided there is no problem in the translation on the *inside*. If someone fails, it is usually because he or she did not attach the right picture to the right sound. Of course, if words were spelled the way they sound, they could be "sounded out." This isn't the case in the English language. So the memory of a particular picture (the correct spelling of the word) *must be* attached (anchored) to the sound of that particular word.[3]

Again, this was the knowledge I had to work with, in the context of the difficulties presented to me by Sally and her mother. Next, I asked Sally to spell a few easy words. Each time she looked lost or puzzled. She would move her eyes in several directions as if searching[4] for the answer. She would either guess, usually wrong, or forget what the word was altogether. She just didn't know how to "think" about what she was doing. This was exactly what I expected. Fortunately, she did not become terribly flustered during the process, and she still wanted to know how to do it.

I asked her a few questions to determine exactly what kind of eye movements were normal for her. (Remember, not everyone is the same.) I asked her what color her house was. Then her car, bedroom walls, and so forth. Each time, she looked up and to her left just before answering. Then I asked her about some of her favorite songs and how they sounded to her. Her eyes would go down and to the left each time, just prior to her answer. When I asked her what certain things felt like, she would access that information while looking down and to her right. These questions are pretty standard fare for a novice NLP therapist, which is what I was at the time. But I needed to make sure that I knew her naturally occurring eye movements before I could proceed.

Actually, I knew several ways (ranging from simple, obvious and direct to complex, covert, and vastly indirect) to teach Sally to connect the sounds of words to their visual image (spelling). I wanted one that was fun and simple. Also, I wanted something fast and simple to give to teachers. Third, I wanted to get Sally's mother into the process of helping her, since she was feeling so abused about the entire thing so far. I wanted to simultaneously help them both. I explained to them what Sally needed to be able to do. I explained about the eye movements and what they meant. I offered them a new experimental technique for teaching the proper sequence for spelling. (I told them the reason it was new and experimental was that I had just made it up in my head.)

I took a note pad with a plain white sheet of paper on it. I told Sally we were going to practice using the paper as a movie screen and try to "see" things on it. I also told her that she really did know how to spell, but that she didn't know she knew because nobody had taught her where to look. I said she would be able to see what she needed to on the blank page easiest if her eyes were pointed up and to her left. I had her face directly ahead and move her eyes in that direction. I held the note pad about eighteen inches from her eyes, directly in the line of her gaze. Then I asked her to see letters as I called them out on the page. Then words as I spelled them to her. Within a few minutes, she was comfortable making her own images on the page.

I asked her again to spell a couple of words for me. She began to have trouble: She could generally get the first couple of letters but didn't have the rest of the image of the word. When I asked her to tell me the word, she couldn't: she forgot it. Remember that she didn't have the whole picture of the word, and her eyes were aimed up and left. To hear the word internally, she had to look down and left. So I added another step.

As she looked at those first few letters, I told her to keep the picture on the page. I knew, provided the information in the study was correct, that she should be able to do this fairly easily. I then slowly moved the note pad—her movie screen— downward. Her eyes followed. When the pad was in the proper position for internal hearing (down and to her left) I asked her if she had held the picture. She said, "Yes." I asked her to hear the word inside her head. She was able to say the word with her eyes pointed in this direction. I had her repeat the word. Then I slowly moved the pad back to its original position: up and left. She would generally get more of the picture at this step. I repeated this process several times for each word. I simply started with the note pad at the position she normally visualized in. Then I told her the word and found out how much of it she could see. I moved the pad down to the position where she could best hear inside her head. I would continually move the pad from one spot to the other, while helping her add letters if necessary. I stopped after about twenty to twenty-five minutes because I was convinced it was working and because Sally was a little tired. I had discovered earlier that this work was quite powerful and could cause fatigue quickly. But in the long run . . .

I asked Sally's mother if she would be willing to practice with Sally at home for a couple of weeks. She said of course, but wasn't real sure what she was to do. I told her to take

Sally's spelling list for the week to start with. Sally and her mother would do the following exercise: Sally was to look at the first word carefully. Sally's mother was to hold up a plain white note card or piece of paper, up and to Sally's left, as I had done, then say the word as Sally "held" the picture on the card, and move the card from up and left to down and left. She was then to make sure Sally could hear the word inside her head as well as seeing it spelled correctly on the card. I also told her to experiment with the process.

I explained that this was how most classroom information was stored in memory. So, they were to feel free to play with the procedure as they wished. Sally could hold the card herself when she felt comfortable, while her mother called out the words. The goal of these exercises was for Sally not to need the viewing screen at all. I told them that, if they practiced a half hour each day, they could probably reach that goal in a couple of weeks or less. And that process would spread to other class-room activities as well.

I saw them again about three weeks later. On the first spelling test Sally had after that initial session, she got fourteen of sixteen correct. On the next she got all sixteen correct. I kept track for the next few weeks. She got all of her words right from then on.

As for memorization, Sally did fine from then on. In fact most of her abilities improved along with her spelling. I did no more work with her on anything except one small problem. Several weeks after I had helped her with spelling, her mother brought her in and said, "She's stuck again." I asked what the problem was. Mother said she was stuck in math and couldn't learn anything. I told her that was a bigger statement than I was willing to accept and that she would have to break it down a bit. After some discussion, it turned out that Sally was stuck on long division. Everything else was OK, but the class was spending some time on division. Since Sally wasn't getting it, it looked like she was a lot worse off than she really was.

I gave Sally a couple of problems to do. She couldn't even begin without trouble: she would put the numbers or the lines in the wrong places, making different mistakes each time. This really upset her mother, which really upset Sally. I stopped for a few minutes to calm them both down.

Then I asked Sally if she knew what division was for. She didn't. I asked a few more basic questions to determine if she had any concept about what division was or its relationship to addition, subtraction, and multiplication. She had no idea what I was talking about. As I watched her, I realized that she was again searching around in her head and coming up blank. I decided to draw her a picture.

I thought about pictures of pies with slices taken out, á la Montessori (and Sara Lee—I used to get hungry in math class as a kid). As I thought about it, I decided this wasn't quite to the point. Sally was comfortable with addition, subtraction, and multiplication. Indeed, she was comfortable with numbers as long as her mother didn't get angry or upset.

I also knew that mathematics is really an artificial system, devised by man. But it's a pretty useful one. Once you can understand how different processes within it make up the whole form, it gets easy. This is holistic (from whole) thinking. It is what Sally didn't have for division. She knew what steps to take, that is, the sequence of events. But without the whole picture, the sequence was meaningless to her. Besides, her nervousness kept her from getting the picture.

So I decided to forgo pies and stick with numbers. I wanted to keep her as relaxed as possible the whole time she was learning. I sent mother out of the room. Next I wrote the number 111. I asked Sally if she knew how many ones were in 111. She didn't really understand, which was sort of what I expected. So I drew the following diagram:

$$100$$
$$10$$
$$1$$

I pointed to the one and asked how many ones were there. She said one. Then I pointed to the ten and asked how many ones were there. She looked puzzled for a second then said ten. I repeated with the 100. Then I went on to explain that if you added:

$$
\begin{array}{r}
100 \\
+\ 10 \\
+\ \ 1 \\
\hline
=111.
\end{array}
$$

you got

I then explained to her that I had just shown her a kind of division. We had just divided 111 into hundreds, tens, and ones to see how many ones would fit into it. I saw a glimmer of understanding. I then spent about ten minutes showing her how to add up the ones, tens, and hundreds, how to multiply the ones by tens, tens by tens, and so forth, and what would happen if we subtracted some from the total. I showed her addition, subtraction, and multiplication, based on the number 111. Then I showed her how to divide with other numbers, using some of the same examples. Within a half an hour of work she understood what she was doing. She was able to divide.

Then I spent some time showing her mother what we had done. I asked her if anyone had ever done that for her when she was Sally's age. She said no but she wished they had. I said she could help make up for it by helping Sally with this kind of explanation whenever she needed it. It was at that point that she really understood that Sally was all right. Sally never had suffered from a learning disability.

Notes

Chapter 4

1. Some people associate this loss with the completion of myelinization that occurs in a child's brain at about the same age. "Myelinization" describes a process in which fatty sheaths grow around the cells in the cortex, turning them into white matter instead of gray matter. This speeds up the electrical activity along each cell.

   These theorists do not make the more obvious correlation: the loss of this ability occurs at the same time that formal education, with its prescribed processes of learning, begins.

2. Writing itself is a complex task, but those complexities are not germane here.

3. We usually distinguish similar sounding words from each other by the context in which they appear. On a spelling test this is taken care of ahead of time.

4. This process is called transderivational search.

CHAPTER 5

LATER ON

There are several ways to help or teach someone. You can treat people as if they are on an assembly line in which the same thing is done to everyone in the same way. Results are measured and counted at the end of the line. All that matters are the percentages. If they look good, the process rolls along. If they don't look so good, you change up, retool, and start again. You just keep counting and measuring.

A much better way is to think in individual terms. Then you do what people need, rather than what *you* always do. If each person you meet presents you with a challenge, or a series of challenges, you get to be creative. For each challenge you can set up a new experiment and see what happens.

The nice thing about an experiment is that there are no bad results. Just learning. For each of the people I work with, I set up experiments to see what will happen right in front of me. If the person I am trying to help gets something worthwhile out of the experiment, fine. If not, we set up another experiment. Knowing what won't work is often at least as valuable as knowing what will.

Aside from immediate results in the office, new patterns often stick in the person's behavior. When I was working with the people described in this book, I would do three to six month follow-up calls to make sure the changes lasted for at least that long. Generally, if new behavior lasts past three months, that's good enough. It is seldom that people will slip back into the old patterns unless some major trauma occurs. For Russ, Pen, and Sally, I waited until I had written to this point, to call them for a second followup. I knew that they had done fine for months after I saw them. But now it was several years later. I had no doubt that they would remember me. Also, I was sure they would remember what I had taught them. I was curious, though, to see if what I had taught them had become a normal part of their ongoing behavior. I also wondered what *other* changes were generated by the work we did.

Before we go back to discussing Russ, Pen, and Sally, there is one other person we need to remember: Josh. True, he had stopped running away altogether, but I had many uneasy feelings about the whole affair. I was essentially waiting for what we had done to either backfire completely or not to last. As is often the case, I got sort of a combination.

I wrote Josh's mother a letter, asking her to call me. When she did, she told me he had run away again. I asked her to be more specific, and we had the following conversation:

Her: We went over to the laundromat, and I told him to sit in that chair and be quiet. Then he ran out the door.

Me: Wait a minute. How long did he sit in the chair?

Her: About 20 minutes.

Me: How long did you expect him to?

Her: Well, the laundry takes 2–3 hours.

Me: What did you have for him to do? Did you bring some books, or toys, or something for him?

Her: Nope.

Me: (with probably too irate a tone in my voice) Did you just expect him to sit quietly in a chair for 2–3 hours without anything to keep him occupied?

Her: He's supposed to do what I say.

Me: He lasted longer in that chair than I would have! Twenty minutes is great with a setup like that.

We then had a short, somewhat circular discussion about expectations: reasonable versus ridiculous. I then asked about his behavior in school. Her answer was something like the following:

Her: I don't send him to school now.
Me: Why not?
Her: He'll just run away.
Me: But he hasn't run away from school since I saw him!
Her: It doesn't matter, he will.
Me: But, but . . .

We continued in another short loop until I finally insisted that she send him to school. I told her that she would just have to, that it was the law, and so forth. She agreed that she would. She also agreed that she would arrange things for him to do when she took him places, to see if it helped him stay put.

She called me again a couple of weeks later as we had prearranged. I asked if she had sent Josh to school. She said she was going to take him to school one day but it rained, and she hadn't gotten around to it yet, and the holidays were coming, and . . . We made an appointment for after the holidays. I intended to ask her some pretty direct questions when I saw her in person.

Not only did she fail to show up for her appointment, but she started avoiding me. She answered neither the letters I sent her nor the messages sent through the outreach worker at the project. After several weeks of this, I called the school social worker and the outreach worker. I told them to go over to the place Josh and his mother were living, and *bring* him to school themselves, or whatever they thought was appropriate once they got there.

Two days later, the school social worker called me back with the following report:

Sid, we went out there, but it was real strange. We *knew* she was home with Josh and her baby. But she wouldn't answer the door. We even saw her peeking through the window, so she knew who we were. It was spooky, so we left. What do you think we ought to do?

"Call child protection," was my reply. We had a short discussion and agreed that we had seen enough of the subtle signs of child abuse to call in the authorities. There was nothing else we could do at that point. Josh's mother's refusal to send him to school was grounds enough to do *something,* anyway.

The outreach worker had told me earlier that Josh's mother had complained to her about Josh's behavior at home, particularly with the man she was living with. When I asked her about the conversations they had had, she said that Josh's mother had been letting her know that it was coming down to a choice between the man and Josh. She also made it clear that Josh would lose that battle. We filled in the other pieces of the puzzle in our heads, but they aren't relevant here. The child protection agency handled it from there.

In retrospect, there were several things to learn from working with Josh. My original hypothesis was that if I paced and led Josh properly, I could get him to change his behavior immediately: to stop running away. My hypothesis was correct. My second hypothesis was that there was a good reason for him to be running away and that it would become apparent if I paid attention. This one was also correct. But it took months to confirm it and handle the situation in a useful fashion. I had been advised several times to close the case, because Josh's mother was so uncooperative. But I am an ornery fellow. I felt that it was worthwhile to pursue. I still do.

I visited with Pen and his grandmother the other day. When I first met Pen he was twelve and a half. He is now about seventeen. I had high hopes that in the meantime he had made significant progress in school. I began by asking about his behavior. His grandmother told me that he had been skipping classes the past few months and she was concerned that this was an indication of behavior problems in general. I asked her about her own worries about Pen.

Grandma: And like I tell him, they got nothin' but trouble out there. Boys stealing, using dope, doing everything. He could be coming along the street and just get hurt for nothing!

Sid: Let me ask you something. Has he really gotten into any trouble so far?

Grandma: No, he never did.

Sid: Not a bit, huh?

Grandma: No, he never did.

Sid: Not a bit, huh?

Grandma: Not a bit.

In fact, as we talked further, it became apparent that Pen is unusually well behaved. He hasn't had a single fight since the day I met him. She and I discussed this, and she felt reassured that, since he had so far managed to avoid the fights, crimes, drugs, and trouble that he was surrounded by, he was probably going to continue to do so. Then I wanted to find out about academics.

Sid: (To Pen) You remember when we did all that funny stuff, right? Have you been able to read any better since then?

Pen: Not that good.

Sid: Not that good, huh. Did you do any better than you did before?

Pen: Uh, huh (nods yes).

Sid: But, you still don't read as good as you want to.

Pen: No, I wanna read good.

I then asked him to read the labels on a couple of things on their kitchen table. He couldn't. Pen, his grandma, and I then talked about his frustration in class and about getting help from teachers. He was very clear about his difficulty in reading and his teachers' unwillingness, or inability, to help him. The thought of him going into tenth grade next year without knowing how to read was mind boggling. At that point Grandma handed me some report cards and papers.

Grandma: This is some more, the reports. They're bad, very bad. I be ashamed when it comes. Very, very, very bad. (She shakes her head sadly.)

Sid: Don't be ashamed, now. It sound to me like, you know, when he asks for help, they're not going to give it to him.

Grandma: I know . . . You know, if he could spell, it seems like he could be able to read better. But, he just can't.

Sid: Yes, he can. I can teach him to spell in fifteen minutes.

Grandma: Yeah?

Sid: How long did it take me to teach him the alphabet and how to relax in school?

Grandma: *No* time!

Sid: That's right. Spelling's just as easy.

I then took Pen through the spelling strategy, exactly as it is explained in the tear-out section of this book. He was able to spell words that he hadn't seen, heard, or understood before. He spelled them backwards and forwards, in about five minutes. Then he ran to get his brother, so I could teach him too. We discussed math and the use of the same mechanisms for multiplication tables, and so on.

Grandma: This boy went to start school when he was four years old and eight months. And, I say "darn." It looks like all your life is going to school, and ain't nothing coming out!

Sid: They just don't know how to do it. You know every time I sat down with him and taught him something, he learned it like that!

Grandma: Like that (snaps fingers).

Sid: Do you think he's slow?

Grandma: No.

Sid: He's not slow.

Grandma: I know.

Sid: He's not.

Grandma: They don't want to have the patience, neither.

They just mark him right down "bad." No attention or nothing like that. They don't help the kids.

We then talked about what to do. I told her that the teachers had obviously given up on Pen a long time ago and that none of them had any intentions of sitting down with him and teaching him. We all agreed that it was up to them to make sure Pen learned what he needed. My original sadness and disgust was renewed. It was very painful to tell a sixty-eight-year-old woman that teaching her grandson to read would be *her* responsibility. I told her I would help when I could. (What a shame.)

I went straight from Pen's home over to see Russ and his wife. We talked about old stories and how life was going for them, for a while. Then I told him about this book and what I was doing.

Sid: What I'm interested in is how you're doing with your reading.
Russ: Uh.
Sid: Do you work on it?
Russ: To be honest with you, I haven't had the time to really get into it . . . I can understand some things—like, my brother, he had sent over these, uh (hands me a volume that is a yearbook from a very difficult encyclopedia).
Sid: Can you read this (not believing)?
Russ: No. Some things I can, like, this issue here: Elvis Presley's death is in here, like an obituary . . .

At this point he turned to that section of the volume and began reading to me. He read flawlessly, only faltering over three or four of the longest words. I helped him with those, but it was immediately clear to me that his reading was much better than it had been. He told me that he was able to read the newspaper as well as he wants. He couldn't when I had last seen him. I remarked on his improvement and his wife agreed. He read at a comfortable pace, without tension, breathing normally.

Sid: Sounds pretty good to me.

Russs: Still a little rusty around the edges (wife laughs).

Sid: How much better is that than the way he read 3 years ago?

Wife: You know I've had a seventh grade education, and there's words that I stumble over myself. So everybody's not perfect. You could have a high-school education and you'd still stumble over words.

Russ: I know a word when I *hear* it. She'll say a word, and she won't pronounce it right, and I'll tell her how to pronounce it right, because I've *heard* that word before. Big words.

We spent some time practicing spelling and showing Russ's daughter how to visualize properly. We talked some more about Russ's remarkable auditory memory, and how much fun he has with it.

Russ: . . . I'm doing better, not great, but . . .

Sid: You're pretty hard on yourself, because you're really doing all right.

Russ: Well, I figure if I be hard on myself, I'll do better. The harder I am, the better I'll get.

Sid: All right, I'll go along with that. You might be right.

Russ: If I say to myself, "Now you're doing great," then you tend to relax—a little *too* much. Then you end up right back where you was, and it takes you that much longer to get started again. So this way, you know, I keep it up there, try harder.

Sid: Well, if it makes you try harder, keep it up.

Wife: After he used to come home from seeing you, he'd talk about what you had showed him. It was really remarkable that he could just make a picture in his head and spell. He picked it up like that, right off the bat.

I was thoroughly pleased at this point with the progress Russ had made. His motivation strategy was to be negative and hard on himself. But as long as it worked this well, I left it alone. Russ's parting comments were something about getting drunk together the next time we . . .

I called Sally's mother a couple of weeks ago. It had been nearly three years since I had spoken with her. We talked for a short while and got caught up. The family had had a series of tragedies and a string of deaths, so times have been hard for them. I told her what I was doing and why I had called.

Sid: How is Sally doing in school now? I know things have been tough but I'm wondering if she has been improving.
Mother: Sid, you would be so proud of her, she's really doing well. She's had some problems, of course, but so would you if you couldn't hear or see straight for nine years. (laughs).
Sid: Objectively, how much of a help was I back then?
Mother: Oh, she couldn't have done it without you. I mean, you set her right on the right track. You were exactly what she needed.

She went on to praise the school Sally is in. It really is a model public school. The staff, some of whom I know, are really dedicated. They believe in developing the whole child rather than just pumping children with information.

When I went to visit them, Sally's mother pulled out her files. She had literally journals full of information on everything from her feelings and thoughts, to Sally's school records, test papers, and on and on. She remarked about her own compulsiveness and attention to detail. I praised her for her energy and commented on the amount of stress she could handle. I also suggested she ease up on herself. She told me that she had finally gotten her own high-school diploma in the three years we hadn't seen each other.

I asked her about comments from Sally's teachers. She said that her present teacher is amazed at how well Sally does, considering her history. He said she progresses rapidly and works hard to improve. She reads fluently though she has some problems with comprehension. He is not worried though, because even in that area, she is steadily improving. Overall, he is confident that Sally is doing fine.

We finished our talk with some suggestions from me about experiments for Sally and her mother. Her mother carefully wrote them down and asked pertinent questions. They were really glad that I had come to see them. So was I.

The most interesting thing about doing experiments to me is that you get to ask yourself questions that lead to better questions. With Josh, I asked myself how to make meaningful contact with him. Once I had done that, it brought up the question of how he would deal with my suggestions. That led to the question, what in his environment was precipitating his running away? When the serious family problems surfaced, the question was how best to handle them. The core of his problem was a family that wasn't safe. He screamed for help, silently, by running away. That's what brought him to me in the first place. But he'd been to many therapists, and even "homes" before. I think I was a little more persistent. I had the belief that if you communicate with a child, in terms of what he or she needs, that child will show you where to look.

Hypotheses and questions: most are just educated guesses. When you guess right, it feels good. But the good feelings can be deceptive. Many people who read the story of Josh would tend to generalize: They might say, "You see, you have to work with the entire family. 'It's always in the family.'" That's a good generalization, right?

WRONG. I think Pen's family is terrific. I met his brothers, sisters, cousins, and an aunt as well as his grandma. They're nice people. The kids seem happy and well-behaved. They communicate clearly and directly with one another, and they did so with me as well. They have always cooperated with the school when asked. I expected nothing less from the moment I met Pen and his grandmother.

So what were my hypotheses and questions? Well, as far as his fighting in school, I shared those earlier. He told me every-thing I needed to know. I picked a simple and direct intervention, laid it on him, and watched for the results. They were fine. But with his thinking processes, comfort level in class, the alphabet, and so forth, it took a few more steps. I explained my thought processes and the way I tested each assumption. Everything worked perfectly. Pen still remembers exactly how to do everything I taught him. My last hypothesis, several years ago, was that his new abilities and comfort would expand to other areas and that he would be able to catch up in school. There was, however, an important question I did not pursue: would anyone care about, or even notice, the new abilities?

I knew that you have to alert the people who surround the child to the changes that are made. If you don't, they may not recognize or use them in a useful fashion. In this instance, Pen's grandmother was keeping in touch with the school. Grandma reported to me that it didn't seem to matter much. Her input was pretty much in vain. No teacher has used Pen's abilities since he left my office. A group of people, on hearing Pen's story, might generalize. "See? It's the school system that's to blame for kids not learning properly." That's certainly true, right?

Not exactly. You see, Sally goes to school in the same school district, in the same town, only about a mile and a half away from Pen. But her school is special: the teachers are caring and dedicated. They are willing to spend some of the one-on-one time she needs. And they pay very close attention to her progress.

My original hypothesis was that her only real problems had been medical ones. After she had had surgery, all she needed was to learn to organize the new auditory and visual input on the *inside* as well as the outside. I was right. The only really important question was, would she be able to use those skills to catch up enough? Well, she is not, in all honesty, caught up completely. But her teachers are satisfied that she will be soon. So my question is mostly answered. I guess we can say that what education comes down to is good health, caring, love, and dedication. Right?

Well . . . Russ told me that, when he was growing up, he had some very good persistent teachers. He had one that drummed mnemonic devices into his head like crazy. These can be quite useful. They were probably the best tools available at the time. I applaud that teacher for recognizing Russ's auditory skills and matching his or her approach to Russ's abilities. My hypothesis though was that, with the newer NLP technology, Russ could expand his abilities to include the visuals he needed. I wondered how he would continue on his own once the hypothesis had been confirmed. Obviously, I was quite pleased with the results. So, what it really boils down to is having the most advanced technology. Right?

Uh . . .

CHAPTER 6

TEACHING TEACHING

Recent years have seen some strange priority shifts in the field of education, with some resulting backlash. The Sixties and most of the Seventies were full of early screening programs galore. Immense amounts of money and time were spent trying to find as many medical, psychological, and social problems as anyone could dream up. Grant money went in the direction of diagnostic aids of all types. Teachers and kids shuffled in and out of doctors' and therapists' offices looking for all kinds of deficiencies. After ten or fifteen years of all this progress, things were at least as bad, if not far worse than ever before. So the reactions had to happen. *Back to basics.* In other words, let's do what we did before. But, wait a minute. We stopped doing what we did before because it wasn't real terrific. This is progress?

The victims are as much the teachers as the students. Teacher education is extremely vast, but not that usable: tons of theory, little practicality. And nobody can make up their mind about what is best for kids.

That is why teachers have so much continuing education. About every teacher I have ever met is still in school and attending countless workshops and seminars. As far as I can tell, and I've done an awful lot of asking, they learn the same stuff over and over again! Teachers are supposed to be flexible. They are supposed to make good contact with children and speak the same language as the kids. They are supposed to shape the children's behavior, but only within the limits of whatever developmental model is in vogue. In addition, special education teachers are supposed to keep up with the latest advances, newest screening instruments, teaching aids, games, devices, and so forth. I've asked a bunch of them if they use those thousands of games and things. The last one told me, "No, and the closet is so full of the damn things there is no room for any coats!"

Under this barrage of obvious or useless information and junk, there are countless teachers burning out at an early age. They know their education is inadequate. They know the theories are impractical. They know that 40% of the children aren't brain damaged. They want help.

It seems to me that one of the areas of really weak teacher education is in useful communication skills. I know teachers go to lots of seminars on communication, but that isn't what I'm talking about. Are teachers taught "platform skills" or "stage presence?" Are they taught to organize information in a way that fits in with the sensory/neurological organization of the children? Are they taught foolproof ways of establishing rapport with a child or group? Are they taught group dynamics in a way that will help them get kids to cooperate and help one another? Are they taught ways of heightening their own sensory acuity so that they really perceive what is happening in front of them? Are they taught models of organizing their behavior that will literally teach them how to be flexible? I don't think teachers are taught any of those things. But these are central to teaching effectively.

This chapter is about how to learn those things. This book will not teach you. It will structure your thinking, so that you can learn, however, and you'll learn by doing. You can read this chapter in minutes; *doing* this chapter will take longer. Doing these experiments will make you a better teacher. Much better than the reading of them. This chapter is divided into sections: each is designed to help you learn progressively more useful skills. Each section includes a good deal of explanation and three experiments: the first is quite easy. The second is less easy, the third is the most advanced. None of them is hard. Some take more time than others. Different people will find different things in each. Sounds like life, doesn't it? Happy exploring!

Platform Skills

We have all watched a wide variety of performers in action. We go to concerts, movies, and plays. We watch TV, listen to records, tapes, and the radio, and we know what is entertaining to us personally. Usually, if we watch/listen to a particular performance we have a sense of whether or not we like it, within the first few minutes. I wonder if many of us have ever taken the time to figure out how we make up our minds.

It is interesting to me that there are so many different things certain types of performers have to do. Comedians George Carlin, Rodney Dangerfield, and Joan Rivers have to make people laugh.

Johnny Carson has to do that and much more. He has to be able to interview a variety of people. If he is talking with Rodney Dangerfield, he has to be a straight man. If he is talking with someone who isn't used to being on TV, he has to make them feel comfortable, get them to talk about themselves, and create an attitude in the audience—perhaps curiosity or warmth. If he is interviewing the author of a book (generally in the last few minutes of the show) he may have to first change the pace of the show, then create an attitude of interest and respect for the guest, gather general information about his or her work, and make some pertinent point about the subject. At the same time, he has to sell the book! No matter what's going on, Johnny is still expected to be clever, smooth, and funny. The audience doesn't much care how he's feeling that particular day. They'll expect his best.

The same goes for news people, politicians, actors, and others who communicate directly to an audience. However, there is a whole class of communicators who don't even get the opportunity to confront their audience: a conductor faces his orchestra, but holds his *back* to his audience. He has to trust that his skill at getting a large number of musicians to watch him, listen to themselves, read the music, cooperate with one another, and act as a single entity will convey a message to the audience. The amazing thing is that it's almost always someone else's message! No conductor will ever have the opportunity to check with Beethoven or Mozart to make sure he got it straight.

At least the conductor gets to turn around right after he's finished and find out how he did. Just think of the job of a film director: when he's done shooting, he still has to wait months, or even years, before anyone sees what he's accomplished.

If you are saying to yourself, "I'm beginning to understand some parallels between teaching and performing," congratulations! If not, you're still in luck. You have an opportunity to look at your profession in a fun, new way.

We can start by setting up a framework for comparison. We then pick a type of performer, the stand-up comic, for instance, as a model. To some teachers, the analogy is closer than to others, but we'll just let that stand. Then we can look more closely at the steps each one goes through while performing. To narrow ourselves down, we can compare the delivery of a monologue to the delivery of a lesson, step by step.

The first thing to be aware of is that, even before the comic or teacher starts, many important things have already happened. For the comic, the stage has already been set, literally. The audience comes with a set of expectations. The comic already has his assignment: make people laugh. The same is true for the teacher: the classroom already exists. The children come with a set of expectations also. So the teacher has an assignment as well: help children learn. The extent to which each has the preexisting ability to perform flexibly and effectively and to meet the audience's expectations will determine the extent to which he or she can fulfill the respective assignments.

Once on stage, or in class, the actual task begins. We can break this down into four steps. The first step for each is *building rapport.* This is pacing, as I have described through-

out this book. For the comic telling a joke, it is the "setup." He
or she begins to tell a story that people in the audience can
relate to. As he or she tells this, he or she hopes that expectation, curiosity, and understanding will build in the audience.
For the teacher, the task is quite similar. He or she will begin
to tell some story or explain some process. The steps in a math
problem are a good example of this. Again, there should be a
building of expectation, curiosity, and understanding. These
feelings for both the comic and the teacher bring the watchers,
listeners, or both closer, not only to him or her but also to each
other. It's that group feeling that is so important.

The second step is *leading*. For the comic, this is the punch
line: usually, some twisted conclusion to his story. His purpose
is to be funny enough to get people to laugh. For the teacher,
this is some sort of conclusion drawn from the information he
or she has presented: this can be the point to the story or the
answer to a math problem. The purpose is to be clear enough
so that children understand, know, or can do something new.

The third step is *attending*. At this point, both the comic and
teacher have to pause a moment for their audiences to respond. The comic listens for laughter. He also watches for
facial expression and other cues from the audience. If people
are smiling and appear to be enjoying themselves—big fun; if
they are yawning and looking at their watches—big trouble.
The teacher listens for comments or questions regarding what
he or she has just presented. He or she also watches facial
expressions and other subtle hints from the children. If the
children seem contented, interested, and alert—good job; if
they look confused, worried, and lost—good luck.

The fourth step is further *building*. Here, the comic or
teacher uses the responses, the feedback, to build on what has
been done. For the comic who has gotten a big laugh, he or she
keeps rolling in the same direction. Perhaps more jokes in the
same vein. They will bring the audience even closer and create
more fun. If however, the joke didn't go over, he or she might
slyly comment on the failure in a way that might get a laugh.
Then the experienced comic will try something in a different
vein: go back to step one. The teacher who got his or her

message across can expand on the idea or give further examples or assignments. He or she can answer questions and comments and dialogue in a useful way with students. If, however, the teacher perceives a major lack of understanding or a large amount of head scratching—back to step one. The experienced teacher will explain the problem, or story, in a different way.

We have established, then, a convenient four-step model for both stand-up comedy and teaching (easy, huh?): (1) building rapport, (2) leading, (3) attending, (4) building. We can call this the "BLAB model." The nice thing about models is that you can call them whatever you want when you make them up. BLAB is, after all, what comics and teachers actually do. Some just do it better than others.

You may be saying at this point, "OK, Sid, jokes aside, this four-step pattern seems too simple." Of course it is! All models and analogies are simplifications. That is why we use them. None of them is perfectly accurate, either. In NLP, we constantly remind ourselves that the map is not the territory.

With this limitation in mind, I'll get back up on my high horse for a moment and slyly divulge a major difference between comics and teachers. Any experienced comic who gets no response, even to his best stuff, will take responsibility for it. I've never heard George Carlin accuse anybody in an audience of having "dyshumoria, the dreaded laughter disability." I don't expect to, either. He is much too creative for that!

As I get down off my horse, I am aware that there are lots of other comparisons between teachers and performers. Some are obvious; others are quite subtle. It is always that way when we talk about communication: there are so many ways to explore, understand, and talk about it. As you bear that in mind, the following exercise will give you a chance to try your hand at modeling.

Modeling Experiment #1

Step 1

Pick an entertainer of whom you are particularly fond of. To make it easy on yourself, you might choose someone who is on TV regularly. There are many talk shows that give you the opportunity to watch and listen to the same person at least several times each week. The same is true for newscasters and, to a lesser extent, actors in weekly series. There are also the Sunday morning TV clergymen, some of whom are very interesting, from a purely communication standpoint.

Step 2

As you watch this person, notice unique features in his or her physical behavior. These are the ones, we generally say, that make that person who he or she is. Watch for specific physical movements. For example:

1. unusual postures
2. specific hand movements
3. head turns
4. leaning to one side
5. rocking back and forth or side to side
6. facial expression (mouth and especially eyebrows)
7. movement

(It may help to turn off the sound for a few minutes and just watch.) You will find these to be very obvious most of the time. Remember the way Jack Benny held his arms? Or the way he walked? These were his trademarks. They make up much of our memory of him.

Step 3

Now listen for particularly unique features in the person's voice. Things to listen for include:

1. particular words or phrases
2. unusual sentence structure
3. voice quality and pitch
4. tone
5. volume, inflection
6. resonance (nasal, breathy)
7. speed, tempo (rhythmic, choppy)

Again, it may help to only listen. You can turn away from the set or turn down the picture for a few moments. Try also to pay less attention to what this person is talking about than normal. We're not interested so much in what he or she is saying as in how it is being said. You will undoubtedly find many obviously unique features here as well. Remember the sound of Walter Cronkite, John F. Kennedy, or Martin Luther King, Jr.? These men all had their own unique sound and were immensely powerful and influential.

Step 4

Now comes the tricky part. Here you want to find the patterns into which these sights and sounds are organized. Pick something you have seen or heard that struck you as somehow special. See if this occurs at certain times only and, perhaps, never at all. Maybe several of these features occur simultaneously. You'll know if it is repeated in the same way often, you have found a real pattern. You will know that you understand this pattern well when you can predict it moments before it happens.

This task seems obtuse for some people. An example may help. As Johnny Carson switches topics during his monologue, he generally looks over to his right, where his production staff and Ed McMahon are. He will usually turn to his left and deliver the introductory line of his next joke.

Setting up his joke, he will, almost invariably, alternate his stance: sometimes directing his lines to his right, sometimes to his left. When he gets to the punch line, however, he will often look straight ahead and deliver it directly into the camera. Changes in his hand movements, facial expressions, tone of voice, volume, and inflection all correspond to this pattern as well. When you have played with this experiment for a while, answer the following questions:

1. Was this totally mind boggling? If so, you were probably trying to relate too many things to each other at once. Go back to smaller chunks.
2. Was it easier for you to do the visual portions? Was step 3 easier? What does this tell you about your ability to

attend to one portion of your experience as opposed to
another?

3. Do you have a new appreciation of what we mean when
   we say that someone has a particular style?
4. Do you think this might be a useful and fun experiment
   for other people who are professional communicators?
   How about for school children?

Modeling Experiment #2

When you feel you understand the patterns you have found
in this powerful communicator, duplicate them. Stand in front
of a full-length mirror and see if you can match that person's
precise movements. Do the same with your voice by talking or
reading something into a tape recorder. When you think you
have it, answer the following questions:

1. Can you duplicate these motions and sounds smoothly
   and naturally?
2. How do you feel as you do this: awkward? surprised?
   confident?
3. Can you achieve a comfortable blend of that person's
   style and yours?
4. Does this show you areas in your own style that are rigid
   or limiting in some way?

Modeling Experiment #3

This is where you find out how brave and flexible you can
be. Take this new style to school with you. Try it out on your
classes. Be a bit subtle. If you exaggerate too much, you'll
come across as a caricature of that other person. Leave that
to Rich Little, he gets paid for it. Then, answer the following
questions:

1. Did the children realize or figure out what you were
   doing?
2. Did they respond to you, or each other, differently? Did
   they understand better?

3. Did you notice certain parts of this new style that seemed to effect the class more than others? Did some fall flat?
4. Would you be inclined to use this style more often?
5. Would you like to try it all over again, choosing another performer? Go ahead!

This modeling process is the basis of NLP. It was developed by people who were experts in picking out the details that make up the whole of a person's communication style. They studied very powerful, effective, and influential people to duplicate their styles. They then found they could create the same effect, and of course get the same responses, as those gifted individuals. In NLP, we call this *stealing behavior*. It is not against the law: steal from the best!

Listening Skills

Besides general platform skills, there are many quite specific ways of making effective contact with people. The last exercise was designed to help you find usable patterns in the communication of people who are especially effective and swipe them. I hope you also learned something about some of the general patterns in your own communication. This will give you the opportunity to add or subtract from your own behavior as you think necessary to make yourself even more effective.

Pacing is very important for a teacher. He or she must know what to pace, or watch for, in a child's behavior in order to establish rapport with that child. This task can be almost overwhelming. This is as difficult as watching the TV actor was: there is so much going on that it becomes hard to sort out. You have to "chunk down" your thinking to a level that is both useful and manageable to be able to pace.[1]

Besides this, though, there is leading. Teachers have to do more than match and pace their students. They also can lead the kids in more useful directions. It is important that a teacher be aware of how to send a message to a child, but it is just as important to help that child be able to receive a variety of different kinds of messages.

The importance of listening effectively is almost too obvious to mention. Except that most listening programs I have been exposed to don't really train you to do anything. Typical is the task of listening to someone talk and later having to answer questions about what he or she said. As I pointed out earlier, that is the least interesting portion of communication: the content. It is important to be able to do that task effectively, but a score on a listening test is not likely to add to your skill. It is more useful to know the patterns underlying what you do or do not hear. Then you can correct deficiencies and improve your skills.

Just as important as knowing what you hear and understand (or not) is knowing the same about the kids you teach. If you know what they hear and understand, you can pace them by using that kind of information. If you know the kind of information they do not hear or understand, you can lead them into understanding it. You simply need to know how to listen.

The most useful place to start is in hearing and identifying representational systems. This informtion is contained in the predicates of people's speech. Again, this means listening to the child's words in a way that tells you which part of his sensory experience—seeing, hearing, feeling, tasting, or smelling—he is using in his speech. This will force you to pay closer attention (listening) to exactly what children tell you. In addition, you will get higher quality information. You will know more about how the child thinks if you know more about to which portion of his experience he or she pays attention. The following exercise will help you develop your skills in this area.

Listening Experiment #1

Step 1

Choose a child who is having some sort of difficulty in class and who may appear to you to have trouble understanding, communicating, or behaving in some way. For this exercise, it really doesn't matter what the trouble is. Find a relatively private place in which you can spend some time with this child —ten or fifteen minutes.

Step 2

Ask this child open-ended questions, that is, ones that require more than a nod of the head for an answer. Use predicates that are unspecific regarding sensory functioning. In other words, do not guide his or her answers into a particular representational system. If you ask a child how he or she *feels* about school, he or she will probably answer you in the same representational system, *feeling* or kinesthetic. The question, "Do you *see* some problems in class?" asks for a *seeing* answer, one that is in the visual representational system.

The following are more examples of sentences that specifically guide the child to certain representational systems for his or her answer.

1. Are you getting the *hang* of this material?
2. How do you *feel* about class?

Sentences 1 and 2 ask for a feeling response from the child.

3. Do you *see* any problems in school?
4. Do you *appear* to be progressing satisfactorily?

Sentences 3 and 4 ask for a seeing response from the child.

5. Can you *tone* down your excitement a little?
6. Is this material *clear* to you?

Sentence 5 asks for a hearing response from the child, while sentence 6 can be either visual, auditory, or, to a lesser extent, kinesthetic. People can see, hear, or feel "clearly".

An *unspecified* way of asking questions might be the following:

Are you *understanding* the material well enough?
Are you *having* any special problems or difficulties in class?
If you *wanted* to *change* anything here, what might it be?
Is there anything special you'd *like help* with?

Here are some partial lists of specified and unspecified verbs. Look them over until you understand the idea. For a longer list, see tear-out page 7.

visual	auditory	kinesthetic	unspecified
see	hear	feel	know
observe	listen	hold	believe

view	tell	touch	understand
imagine	tone	grab	remember
look	speak		have

Step 3

Get the child to talk about his or her difficulty. As you converse, listen for the predicates he or she uses. Often, when a child, or anyone, is having a problem, their speech is limited to one representational system within the context of that problem.

Step 4

As you and this child talk, switch your own predicates to his or her representational system. Continue to discuss this problem in the same representational system as this child for about five to ten minutes. When you have finished this, answer the following questions:

1. What happens when you listen for predicates? Are they easy to pick out?
2. Did you find this child to be stuck in only one representational system?
3. What happens when you switch to this representational system? Do you seem to make better contact with this child? Does the child respond to you differently?
4. Is it hard for you to switch to this representational system and maintain it?

Listening Experiment #2

Find another child who is having some sort of difficulty. Repeat the steps above which were:

(1) ask open-ended questions, using unspecified verbs,
(2) get the child to talk about his or her difficulties in class,
(3) identify the representational system the child is primarily using, and
(4) match, or pace the child.

Step 5

When you feel you have established a good rapport with this child, using the same representational system, gently switch your speech to another representational system. The following illustrates how this can be done with a child who uses visual predicates:

"OK, I really do *see* better what is happening. But I'm wondering as you *look* over the situation just how you *feel* about it?"

With a child you're using auditory predicates with, perhaps:

"I really *hear* you now, but I'm wondering if you can *imagine* any way out of this problem."

Continue the discussion for a few more minutes, maintaining the representational system you switched to. Then stop and answer the following questions:

1. Was it easy or difficult for you to switch to a new representational system once you established rapport with the child?
2. What did the child do? Did he or she get lost or confused?
3. When you switched to a new representational system, did it seem to break the contact you had established? Did the child switch with you?

Listening Exercise #3

Choose yet another child having difficulty. Go through all the steps of experiments number 1 and number 2. This time, your goal is to lead the child into a new representational system. After you switch to a new representational system, listen closely and give the child a few moments to switch also. If he or she does, fine. If not, go back and make sure that you are pacing effectively in the child's original representational system. Then gently switch again. Continue this process until the child switches with you and seems to be able to describe experiences in both the old and the new representational system. If time permits, you might try to switch again so that you and the child can communicate in the three major representational systems: visual, auditory, and kinesthetic. Then answer the following questions:

1. Was it easy for you to get the child to switch? If not, were you able to *lead* the child after a few tries?
2. When the child switched representational systems, did it improve the contact between you?
3. Did you notice other changes, either in the child or yourself, when you switched? How about changes in breathing, posture, tone of voice, rate or rhythm of speech, and so forth?
4. Do your feelings about the discussion or the child change when you do this experiment?
5. Does this seem to expand your and the child's awareness of the difficulties you discussed? Do you find that you, and/or the child are better able to handle them?

These experiments are elementary NLP devices. They will teach you to listen for a particular portion of speech. This is a very useful level to start with for one particular reason: if you found a pattern in the way the students you worked with represent experience, and whether or not they are good students there is something you need to seriously consider. Perhaps you are only effectively teaching students who use the same representational system you do. If so, you are in luck. It only takes a bit of practice to be able to systematically switch systems and add to your flexibility as a teacher.

This is still only one way of listening; there are a variety of ways to hear language, beyond the meaning of the words. Our language has many internal structures and levels. Based on a branch of linguistics known as transformational grammar, Bandler and Grinder developed a tool called the Meta-Model. It is designed to help you quickly and easily understand how a person translates internal experience into language. Once mastered, it can be used to lead people in more useful directions of thought. Though not necessary for the purposes of this book, I suggest you pick up *The Structure of Magic,* Vol. I and II for a thorough explanation of the Meta-Model. For a brief synopsis of the Meta-Model, see Appendix II. It will increase your skill as a communicator immensely.

Besides the language someone uses, there is a whole range of patterns in speech that can help you and the children you work with to communicate more effectively. For example, when someone shifts their voice tone to a higher pitch than usual, it generally indicates internal visualization. On the other hand a shift to a lower tone often means a shift to feelings. A sing-song, rhythmic voice usually indicates auditory internal accessing. Listening for shifts in pitch, tempo, timbre, volume, and so forth in the speech children use can give you similar information about them. It will also give you more levels on which to pace your students.

Watching Skills

Did you ever hear of someone offering a course to improve your watching ability? I never did. Long ago, people realized that we just don't listen very well. But most assume that we see just fine. This is especially true in our highly visually oriented society. Personally, I don't think we see all that well. If we did, someone would have discovered the eye-movement patterns I described earlier a long time ago. No one did.

The eye-movement patterns are only one part of the story of our unawareness. There are many physical movements that are highly characteristic of a person's ongoing internal experiences. That's why people talk and write books about body language. But most of the work done in that area has been done at far too gross a level of analysis. Statements such as "if someone leans back when they talk to you, they don't like you" are too general. Sometimes ridiculous. Even if something like that were true in a particular case, what do you do about it? Go home and cry, I suppose. At any rate, body language can be very important. To make it useful, we should keep our observations as specific as possible. Eye movements are a good place to start.

Watching Experiment Number 1

Step 1

Notice how kids' eyes move when they talk or listen to you (see pp. 38, 39, 40). Tear out the chart in the back (tear-out page 1) to remind you of the patterns. Asking the questions on the tear-out will help you. You can do this with one child or a group. It doesn't matter. If you find a child that doesn't seem to fit the model, which is unlikely but possible, great! You have an opportunity to use your eyes to find out how he or she is organized. Everyone has some sort of internal organization. Find it. Most importantly, *do not stare,* just watch.

Step 2

When you feel fairly confident that you can recognize accessing cues, choose a particular child you feel comfortable with. Have a conversation with this child, and make yourself aware of the pattern of his or her eye movements. For example, if the child continually looks up just prior to speaking, he or she is probably accessing an internal, visual image and then talking about it in some way. Listen to your own speech. You may find that you are using the same representational system in your speech that this child accesses in his, or her, own. If this is a child you get along well with, it is possible that you are talking directly to his or her internal pictures.

Step 3

Now pick a child you do not get along with particularly well. Do the same as above. If you find yourself talking in a different representational system than the child accesses in, switch to the one the child is using. Then answer the following questions:

1. Is it easy to watch eye movements and pick out patterns? Does it make you dizzy?

2. Do you find either of these children to be stuck in one pattern?
3. What happens when you switch your speech to the representational system the child accesses in? Did you find some of the effects you got in the listening exercises?
4. Again, did you find the child you got along with better was organized more like you are than the one you don't get along with? Does this give you some more ideas about expanding your flexibility?

Eye movement accessing cues are valuable signals. But they are still only one of many things to watch for and use. The body can give you so many signals that it is almost unbelievable. Besides the eye movements, the next place to look is at breathing. Many people seem almost unable to think and breathe at the same time. It's something like the inability to walk and chew gum, only less funny. It is especially noticeable when people are stuck, confused, or unable to remember something. The trap is that, if you stop breathing, your brain won't care so much about remembering anything except how to stay alive. Try holding your breath for twenty to thirty seconds (out of shape, huh?), and then try to remember the capital of Montana or some equally vital bit of information. Or try and do a math problem in your head while holding your breath. Pretty tricky, eh? How do you spell relief?— B-R-E-A-T-H-E!

Watching Experiment Number 2

Step 1

Go find yet another child having some difficulty in class. If you've run out of kids with difficulties by now, go borrow one. Sit in relative privacy with this child and strike up a conversation about the difficulties he or she has been having. As the child begins to describe his or her experiences, watch his or her chest. Notice the breathing or lack of it. Notice at what points it hesitates or stops altogether, and listen for what the child is talking about at that moment.

Step 2

Teach this child to breathe properly. This may sound strange, but it is a very good idea. A full breath starts by filling up the abdomen, then the chest. Just as the chest becomes completely full, the clavicle, or collarbone, will rise slightly. Then both cavities will empty. The breath should be slow and smooth, without stops or interruptions. Try some yourself and find out if you feel more relieved. If you can't do it, find a yoga class, a Zen master, a Tai Chi instructor, or a hospital. When you have taught this child to breathe properly, and you are both doing so, resume the conversation about his or her difficulties. Continually remind the child to relax and breathe, and watch what happens. Then answer the following questions:

1. Are you more aware of how breathing blocks, as they are called, affect thinking in children or yourself?
2. Is this something you noticed before? Has anyone ever mentioned to you or taught you to breathe properly?
3. Did you notice immediate, or almost immediate, relaxation with the first few good breaths in the child or yourself?
4. Does this awaken or reawaken your awareness of the importance of the body to the mind?
5. Can you imagine how chronically tired or generally uncomfortable you would be if your breathing were constantly shallow or interrupted? Take a look around your classroom.

Eye movements and breathing patterns are the two easiest things to see in another person. They tell you a lot. In addition to those, there are certain kinds of muscle tensions that indicate emotions and discomfort. They aren't perfect indicators, but they aren't bad either. The study of body psychology is advancing all the time. The general public, however, still hasn't gotten much of the message. The following experiment will help you become aware of some of the most common and obvious muscular indicators of discomfort.

Watching Experiment Number 3

The following are common body cues to watch for:

raised or tight shoulders	anger, fear, or both
stiff or tight jaw	anger, fear, or both
wrinkled or strained forehead	anger, disgust, eye strain
slumped shoulders	sadness, fatigue
arms/shoulders held back	fear of contact or fear of "doing"
slumped appearance/chest caved in	hurt (emotional), fear

Even though you are at least intuitively aware of these, consciously watching for them can be quite helpful. There are many more, of course, but these six are enough for now.

Step 1

Familiarize yourself with the above list and any other similar indicators that you think you'd like to experiment with. Since all of these occur in all of our behaviors, choose one at a time to experiment with. Starting with, for example, raised and tightened shoulders, spend three or four days watching for this in your classes. Again, don't stare, just notice. If you stare at anyone, they are liable to hunch their shoulders. Don't cause it, just notice it. Spend three or four days on each of these body cues.

Step 2

When you think you can readily spot the occurrence of any of these, start paying attention to your own behavior. If you notice several children exhibiting the same or similar cues all at the same time, stop what you're doing for a moment. Check your own breathing, posture, and bodily tension. If you are tense, relax. If not, see if there is something going on that might be producing this response from the children. If so, change it. This is called flexibility of behavior.

Step 3

If you have noticed some children consistently responding in rigid patterns with their bodies, congratulations! If not, go back and look again. We all develop ways of holding or tensing our bodies at an early age. This is built into family life. It isn't good or bad, it just is, so start to notice how it affects the kids in your class.

Step 4

Now you have a chance to really help one of your kids to grow. Choose one of the children who is rigidly holding some part of his or her body. Teach that kid to relax the muscles he or she has been holding tensed. Then have him or her alternate between tensing and relaxing those muscles. This is one of those times when a gentle and loving touch is really appropriate. Ask how they feel as they tense or relax their muscles. The above interpretations (for example, anger or fear with tightened jaw muscles) may or may not be correct for this child. It doesn't matter. Find out what is.

Step 5

To really teach this child about his or her body and emotions, do the following: when he or she can relax and tense those chronically-held muscles at will, teach the child to breathe properly. Then experiment with the connection between breathing and tightened muscles. It is important for the child to become aware of them on the inside rather than hearing an explanation from the outside. Then ask the child if he or she has ever noticed that these muscles were tight before. If so, when? Then answer the following questions:

1. Was it easy for you to spot muscle tension in the kids?
2. Did you notice some of the children looking tense all over? Are they the ones who have the most trouble in class?

3. Did you notice that the more tension a child was holding, the worse his or her breathing was?
4. Were you able to help the child learn to feel more comfortable?
5. Can you imagine other, more general ways to teach the children bodily awareness?

The object of these experiments, both listening and watching, is not to drive you crazy trying to sort out visual and auditory input. It's to make you a better teacher. I know there are too many things to consciously watch and listen for. That's why we do these experiments. Practicing them will teach you to be proficient on an unconscious level. You will be able to do it automatically.

For those who say there is just too much to try and sort out, I say ridiculous! People constantly amaze me when they try to tell me all of the things they can't do. Consider a common activity: Driving an automobile. To perform this task, you have to do the following:

1. Watch the road ahead of you.
2. Watch two or three rear view mirrors as well as both sides.
3. Sort out the important or dangerous hazards and obstacles in at least four directions.
4. Read signs and signals.
5. Operate a steering wheel.
6. Operate two or three foot pedals.
7. Operate a variety of other devices and switches with hands and possibly feet—gear shifts, lights, horn, radio, and so forth.
8. Watch and/or listen to a variety of gauges and lights inside the car.
9. Guide this machine to the exact location you wish to go.

In addition to these, many of us can and do listen to the radio, carry on one or more conversations at various levels of complexity, light and smoke a cigarette, and drink a Coke—all at the same time. Not only that, but a lapse in any of the first seven of these could cost us our lives! I wonder if watching a child's eyes and breathing while carrying on a sensible conversation is really that difficult.

Interesting to me is that in medicine we have a process known as biofeedback. It is a clever outgrowth of some strange psychology experiments performed in 1969. Essentially, someone having muscle tension, headaches, heart trouble, or a variety of other stress-related ailments will come to a doctor's office. A technician will paste electrodes to certain muscle groups on the person's body. The ones listed above at the beginning of this exercise are the most typical. Each of these electrodes is then attached to an instrument(s) that looks something like a piece of stereo equipment. It comes equipped with a dial and headphones. One can watch the gauge and/or listen to the tone rise and fall as his or her muscles tense and relax. The machine gives the person visual and/or auditory feedback on his or her biological functions, such as muscle tension, hence the name biofeedback. Practicing on the machine helps people become aware of tension and stress and helps them to relax. In relatively rare cases, the machines can give feedback on such subtle body mechanisms as brain waves and body temperature. Again, I think this is the highest and most clever use of our technology—not to do boring work for us, but actually to make us better people.

What bothers me is something that I think is a greater comment on us as people. Even though tools like biofeedback are clever and effective, why the hell should we need them? Isn't it bizarre that we are so out of touch with our own bodies that we need machines to teach us what we're feeling? I think it is. I also think that a school teacher could be more proficient at biofeedback than any machine. It takes practice, and that's all. We could probably wipe out most stress-related disorders in a generation. We could also significantly advance the level of general health and education in this country.

Anchoring Yourself

I am sure you've found that with some kids these tasks are easy and with some they're hard. You have undoubtedly found some of the tasks require more subtle discrimination skills than others. You may also have noticed that *you* are more capable sometimes than at other times. Sometimes it can be because of the familiarity of a task, which is doubtful in this case. Other times, it can be your state of mind. We all have off days. We also have days, or at least times, when we are really *on*. Wouldn't it be great to be able to have a switch so that you could just turn yourself on when you need to? Remember anchoring? (See pp. 25, 26, 27 to refresh yourself, if necessary.)

There are certainly some states of mind you want to be able to get to in order to do your best as a teacher. The process of anchoring these is simple. You need only decide what states or experiences you want to be able to recreate in yourself.

Anchoring Yourself Experiment #1

Step 1

Sit in a quiet place where you will not be disturbed. Breathe comfortably and relax.

Step 2

Remember a time when you felt you had your class in the palm of your hand, one in which you and the children were enjoying yourselves and learning together effectively, a memory in which the energy level in the room seemed just perfect and everyone was comfortable.

Step 3

Close your eyes. Imagine, for about five minutes, that you are back in that same classroom experience again. You might start by visualizing the door to the classroom. As you imagine walking through the doorway, see the room. Listen to the sounds there. Become aware of the smells and tastes of that room. Pay especially close attention to your feelings. Get as close as you can to the actual feeling sensations you had at that time. You'll know when you get there.

Step 4

When you have the feelings the way you want them, anchor yourself. To do this, touch the tip of your thumb to the tip of your forefinger on your left hand. Use light but noticeable pressure. This is your general resource anchor for the classroom.

Step 5

Stand up, walk around, and take a few more deep breaths. Take a two or three minute break. Have a cookie. (It seems like a nice idea, but it's optional.)

Step 6

Sit down again and repeat steps 3, 4, and 5. It should only take a couple of minutes.

Step 7

Sit down again and "fire" your anchor by touching your thumb and forefinger in exactly the same way. Feel the feelings, then answer the following questions:

1. When you fired the anchor in step 7, did the feelings come back as before? Were they as intense? How about visual images? Sounds? Smells?
2. Wasn't this easy?
3. Are there other areas of your life besides teaching in which you would like to be able to access your internal resources? I sure hope so!!

Anchoring is almost unbelievably powerful. Sometimes, though, it takes a bit of practice. Further, there is no reason it has to be done with touch. I only chose that particular method because it seems an easy way to start. Besides, you have three more fingers and a whole other hand to continue with if you want to. That can give you a total of eight anchors to use at will. Other internal states to anchor include the following:

creativity	relaxation	curiosity
motivation	tolerance	humor
courage	patience	
excitement	perseverance	

The list of possibilities is almost limitless.

There are other convenient ways to set up anchors besides touch. Easiest for some people is to remember a particular visual image. An example might be the face of a particular person that produces a special feeling. That is how many people come to idolize someone. The internal image of that person's face is an anchor for a feeling of awe or reverence. Other people find sounds or words to be better anchors for them than either touch or imagery. These people will often have that one special song (as in "they're playing our song") to produce a passionate feeling or memory. How about words that produce a powerful feeling? George Carlin's "the seven words you can't say on television" immediately comes to mind. Actually, all words are just anchors to particular experiences. That's why we have them.

Anchoring Yourself Experiment #2

Step 1

Pick a time or subject in class that has been particularly troublesome or difficult for you. Decide, from the following list, which internal resources would make this difficult task easier and more enjoyable.

creativity	patience
motivation	humor
relaxation	perseverance

Step 2

For each of the above resources you choose, remember a time when you had that resource available: a time when you were extremely creative, motivated, patient, and so forth.

Step 3

Imagine yourself back in that situation, as you did in the last experience. See the room or place as you did then, hear those sounds again, recall those distinct smells and tastes.

Step 4

When the feelings are as close to those original feelings as possible, anchor yourself. You can use a touch. For example, touch the tip of your thumb to the tip of another finger. As an alternative, you may use a word or phrase. If you would like to try a sight-oriented anchor, go ahead. With that method, it may be easiest to look at some unusual object in the room. With practice you may try an internal visual image to anchor yourself with.

Step 5

Stand up, walk around, have a cookie, and so on.

Step 6

Sit down again and repeat steps 3, 4, and 5.

Step 7

Sit down again and fire your anchor. Feel the feelings.

Note: An anchor will either work or it won't. Be willing to try one, two, or three times. If it doesn't seem to work when you fire it, simply try another. That's why we test them.

Step 8

Once you have the effective resources you need at your command, imagine you are in that troublesome classroom situation. See the room, hear the sounds in the room, and so on. When you have the feelings that go with that difficult situation, fire your anchor(s). Hold it for about a minute, then answer the following questions:

1. How was it trying to anchor in different representational systems, that is sound, sight? Easy? Hard?
2. What happened when you imagined yourself in the difficult situation and fired your anchors? Did you feel strange or confused? Don't worry, those feelings are common.
3. When you think about that problem situation now, is it different somehow? Imagine you are in that difficult setting now. Are the feelings different?

This is a simplified version of a standard NLP technique called collapsing anchors. It is a way to (sort of) inject needed internal resources into a situation in which they are lacking. Once the changes happen on the inside, they will usually follow on the outside. This next experiment will help you insure this by adding a step known as future pacing.

Anchoring Yourself Experiment #3

Step 1

I firmly believe that any way you improve as a person will improve you as a teacher as well. Therefore, this time you have the choice of choosing an area of teaching or an area of your personal life that you would like to improve. It doesn't need to be a real problem. Rather, choose some area that you would like to handle better in some way. Perhaps you should choose something that you do adequately, but that you would like to do excellently!

Step 2

Imagine you are in this situation. Experience it as if you are really there. When you get there, anchor it. I know it may seem strange anchoring the limited situation you have chosen, but don't worry, do it anyway. This time, anchor by squeezing your knee with your hand.

Step 3

Stand up, walk around, eat something nonfattening. Go through the process again.

Step 4

Test your anchor by firing it. Remember to squeeze the spot with the same pressure. If the experience immediately comes back, fine. If not, go through the anchoring process some more until it does.

Step 5

Take another walking-around break. Breathe, drink something (whatever you want), and relax.

Step 6

Now decide what internal resources or experiences you would need in order to improve the experience you just anchored.

Step 7

When you have decided, remember a time when you had those resources.

Step 8

Imagine you are there again. When you have the feeling you want, anchor yourself. This time use the other hand, on the other knee.

Step 9

Take a break and repeat the anchoring process.

Step 10

Test this anchor as you did the others. Fire the anchor. Make sure you have this resourceful experience at your command.

Step 11

Now you have two anchors. On one knee, you have anchored a limiting experience of some sort that you want improved. On the other, you have the necessary resources to do the job. Both anchors work to bring out those experiences in you. Fire them *at exactly the same instant.* Hold them for thirty seconds. Then let the limited anchor go. Five seconds later, let the resource anchor go. This process is called collapsing anchors.

Step 12

Next, imagine yourself in the near future. In your mind, go through the next time you will be in that limited experience. It could be Monday morning at school or whatever is the next likely occurrence of it. When you are really there, fire the resource anchor again. This will add "juice" (technical term). This step, as discussed earlier, is called future pacing. Answer the following questions:

1. When you collapsed the anchors, what happened? Strange feelings? Pleasant feelings? New realizations?
2. When you imagine that *next time*, does it look (sound, feel, and so forth) better? Are you looking forward to it?

Anchoring is the most powerful and effective way of mobilizing your resources. It is also quick and easy. If you make it a habit, you'll thank yourself. But anchoring is too good to hoard. The children you teach deserve to have all their resources in class. School is supposed to make them better people also. Let's do it!

Anchoring Others

Many kindergarten teachers use anchoring. They just don't know it by that name. Remember when you were a little kid and your kindergarten teacher wanted the whole class to stop what they were doing and gather around? Did she play a few notes on the piano? Always the same notes, tempo, and volume? Didn't it work really well? It sure did for my kindergarten class when I was five. In fact, with the exception of paint splattering, my kindergarten teacher standing at the piano, patiently waiting is *all* I remember of that whole school year. Wouldn't it be great to have your students remember you as the one who taught them to be comfortable, interested, and productive in school?

Anchoring Others Experiment #1

Step 1

Pick a child who needs help in controlling his or her feelings: a child who is moody, overly active, nervous, frightened, or acts in any way that hinders him or her.

Step 2

Watch and listen to this child enough, so that it is easy for you to distinguish his or her comfortable times from uncomfortable ones. Even the most active kids have moments of relative calm. Be able to clearly tell the difference in this child. This is called calibration.

Step 3

Decide what kind of anchor you want to use: touch, words, etc. Some kids don't like to be touched at times (or at all). Do not be intrusive; you have lots of choices.

Step 4

When you notice the child in the state of mind you think is most appropriate, for example, calm, attentive, interested, comfortable, and so forth, anchor it. The same rules that applied to you apply here. If you are using a touch, and that is often the simplest way, make sure you know exactly where and with how much pressure you touch the child. Also, make it natural. Don't run down the aisle and dive on his or her arm. Just touch the child comfortably when you are already there.

Step 5

Repeat the last step six to eight times. This should be sufficient to establish the anchor.

Step 6

Test the anchor: when the child is in some neutral state, fire the anchor. See what changes occur. Then answer the following questions:

1. How did you feel setting up this anchor? What were your thoughts as you did so?
2. Did you wonder if your perceptions of this child's state of mind were accurate? With this in mind, did you really know what you were anchoring?
3. Did six to eight times seem like too many? Too few?
4. When you tested the anchor in step 6, what happened? Did you notice changes? Were they subtle? Dramatic? Did the child look different? Sound different?

This experiment constitutes the simplest method of anchoring. You simply wait until the person is in the state of mind that is most useful at the time. Then you anchor it. Once anchored, it becomes a tool at your disposal to help this child whenever needed. You should get in the habit of doing this. It will become totally automatic with practice.

Anchoring Others Experiment #2

Step 1

Choose three children to experiment with. Repeat the above experiments. This time, anchor each child in a different representational system, that is, touch, sound, and sight.

Note: anchoring with touch should be easy by now. For the child you are using sound with, pick a word or phrase you don't usually use. Take a few seconds to practice saying it with a particular voice tone. An example might be saying the words, "It's OK, relax," with a low, soft tone. For a visual anchor, choose a hand gesture that is natural, but that you seldom use. Add a particular posture and facial expression. Remember: with all three, it should be out of the ordinary (for you), natural, and identical each time.

Step 2

When you have established the anchors with the children, and tested them in a neutral situation, you will be ready to move on. For each of the children, wait until they are in the state you experience as a problem for them. Then fire the anchor you have established for their resource state and hold it. Wait a few seconds for the changes to appear.

Step 3

When the child has gone to the resource state you anchored, or some reasonable alternative to the one he or she was in before you fired the anchor, future pace. Simply say something to this effect: "Now, the next time you find yourself . . . (problem state) . . . you'll remember that you can . . . (resource state)." If the child was getting frustrated or stuck, and you fired an anchor for calmness, you might say: "From now on, whenever you feel uptight or frustrated, you'll remember the best thing to do is just calm down." As you say, "calm down," fire the anchor again.

Step 4

Sometimes this is enough to produce a real and lasting change in the child's experience and behavior. Often, however, it will take more than just once. Be willing to repeat steps 2 and 3 until you are satisfied that permanent progress has been made. That is called perseverance. If you need more of that, anchor it in yourself!

Questions:

1. Which representational system(s) was easiest for you to anchor in? In which do you need more practice?
2. Did you find it taking fewer tries to have the anchor established?
3. Are you finding your perceptual ability improving?
4. Did you find this method of anchoring and future pacing to be as easy and effective as it is?

You may have children that you feel would benefit from learning to anchor themselves. Really, all children can, provided that you pace and lead them through it effectively. You can even do it with a group or class. You have the choice of doing all the work yourself, having the child do all of it, or some combination. The following experiment will be a good start for you.

Anchoring Others Experiment #3

Step 1

Choose a child you think could immediately benefit from learning anchoring. Perhaps you have someone (or a roomful) who has real problems controlling his or her feelings and knows it.

Step 2

Find a time when this child seems to be at his or her very best. He or she is comfortable, relaxed, and attentive. Compliment the student on his or her present behavior and take the child aside somewhere. It will only take five minutes.

Step 3

Tell the child that you have discovered, or know, a way that people can feel this way whenever they want. Tell the child that it is easy and fun. Then ask if he or she would like to learn. With a setup like that, the answer will be yes.

Step 4

Show the child how to anchor with the thumb and fore-finger, just as you learned.

Note: Don't get theoretical or fancy in your explanation to the child. He or she doesn't really need to understand Pavlov to make it work. You might say something like the following: "This is like making a light switch for yourself, except with this switch, instead of a light going on, a feeling will." That's really explanation enough.

Step 5

Future pace by saying something like, "From now on, when-ever you feel this way at school, home, or wherever, just use your anchor (or light switch) and you'll be able to."

Step 6

Agree on a signal between the two of you: a gesture, word, or whatever. Use the signal to remind him or her to use the anchor when you think it's appropriate. Tell the child it is just a helpful reminder and that you are leaving the decision (re-sponsibility, choice) up to him or her.

Questions:

1. Was the child surprised or intrigued by your offer? Offers like that don't come along every day.
2. Did you find it very simple to teach anchoring to this child?
3. How well did it work? Was it as effective as doing the anchoring yourself?
4. Did this alter or improve your relationship with this child?
5. Did you notice the child using the anchor often? Did it seem to become a usual part of the child's behavior?

6. Were there other related or seemingly unrelated changes in the child? Improved self-confidence perhaps?

It should be apparent to you by now that you have many choices in using anchoring. You can anchor the child yourself or let the child do it. When you do it you have the choice of explaining it to the child, or keeping it to yourself. Also, there are almost limitless ways of establishing the anchor in any of the three primary representational systems. Further, you have the choice of waiting for the child to move into the state of mind you want anchored, or leading the child to that state. An anchor can be saved for a special time or collapsed with another anchor to produce a change. The most effective communicators can anchor entire audiences at once or different things in different members. With all of these possibilities to explore, you should be able to keep busy for a while longer, perfecting your skills. Have fun!

Guided Fantasy

In the last set of experiments, I instructed you to anchor states as they were occurring in the children. Utilizing what a child presents to you is most of what communicating with your students is about, but it isn't all. If we could only use what we already had, we would be extremely limited. But if we were meant to be that limited, we would not have been given an imagination. As long as we have it, we may as well use it to its utmost.

Most of us know that metaphor is one of the most powerful ways to communicate that man has ever devised; probably one of the oldest, as well. But powerful communication between people is much more than just the transfer of information. If that was all there was to it, things would get mighty dull. Besides, we can all transfer information towards another person. But making it meaningful and have impact on that other person is another story.

A good storyteller involves his listener. His voice becomes a symphony. His expressions and movements paint the most vivid of scenes. His words delve down to the deepest levels of feeling, leaving a taste of experience not soon to be forgotten.

All the while, this artisan of words watches the listener, knowing the effects of his words are truly felt. His presence is totally captivating.

The crux of the process is direction or, as a magician might say, misdirection. Remember my little classroom trips earlier in the book (see pp. 30, 31, 32)? These were nothing more than stories we call guided fantasies. They were designed to go in particular directions, however. I would tell the child what to see and hear in his or her mind. Usually the child would be feeling good and comfortable. In that case, I would simply tell him or her to pay attention to those good feelings while seeing and hearing what I had suggested. This would anchor good feelings to the sights and sounds of the classroom. I would also throw in lots of statements, such as, "And from now on, you will have these good feelings whenever. . . ." It is the way the stories are told that makes them effective.

Think about this: imagine playing tennis, football, jogging, and so forth; remember hearing one of your favorite jokes; or pretend you can smell the aroma of your local bakery. You will get back some of those original experiences. You may become excited, start to laugh, or get hungry (hopefully in that order). In fact, the experiments on anchoring yourself were designed to take you through your own guided fantasies and to bring back useful and pleasant experiences from your past.

There are far more choices than just past experiences, though. Again, that is why we have imaginations. You can use any experience from the past or the future and embellish it all you want. You can also borrow or steal an experience from some other person. Still you can add, subtract, or distort it ad infinitum. One of the most fun ways is to make them up entirely. Some people make up extremely expensive, highly technical guided fantasies. They call them funny names like *Star Wars* and *Raiders of the Lost Ark*. If they are clever enough, millions of people will pay their hard-earned dollars to experience these fantasies. Not only that, but they pay to experience them over and over. I remember seeing *Gone With the Wind* about the same time I took American History in high school. I remember more from that movie than I do from studying the same events in class, maybe even the whole year! I'll probably never forget Scarlet O'Hara or Rhett Butler. I'll probably never remember my history teacher. I looked at him or her far more than four hours, though.

Be all that as it may, the point is still that a good teacher will make a meaningful impact on students. He or she does this by involving them in some sort of experience. The following experiments are designed to sharpen your skills at creating meaningful experiences to produce specific results.

Fantasy Experiment #1

Step 1

Your first task is to write a guided fantasy and to use it for relaxation. Standard ones include (1) walking along a beach on a warm day (2) walking through the woods (3) sitting down in a large field of flowers, and so forth. You may choose any of those or your own favorite. Simply pick one.

Step 2

Sit down with a pencil and paper and make lists of the things you would see, hear, feel, taste, and smell in the setting you chose. If you chose the beach, your list would look something like this:

see	hear	feel	taste/smell
clouds, shapes	waves	warmth of	salt air
bright sun	birds	sun	humid odor of
horizon	wind in	hot sand	the sea
sea gulls	trees	breeze	
pale brown sand		across skin	
blue-green water			

Step 3

Now choose a student you think needs to be able to relax more.

Step 4

Take this child to a quiet, comfortable place. Have him or her sit or lie down, relax, breathe comfortably, and close his or her eyes.

Step 5

Start by saying something like, "Now let's imagine, or pretend, we are taking a trip to . . ." Then continue by describing the scene. Have your list ready to remind you. Begin with visual descriptions, then add sounds, then feelings, tastes, and smells. Talk slowly, in a calm, even voice. Describe this scene and the calm, relaxed feelings that go with it for no more than five to seven minutes. When the child appears to be as relaxed as needed, say, "And from now on, whenever you need to be relaxed, like you are now, you can simply remember this little trip."

Step 6

Tell the child: "It is time to come back to the room now, so take a deep breath, slowly open your eyes, and tell me how that was for you."

Step 7

Find out if this was comfortable and enjoyable for this child. Tell him or her that you do this sometimes yourself. Compare notes. Then answer the following questions:

1. Were you surprised at how effective this was?
2. Using your list, was it easy for you to make vivid descriptions?
3. Did you find yourself relaxing, or did this feel like work?
4. Did this seem to alter the way you and this child relate to one another?
5. How long did the relaxed effect last?
6. Would you be willing to do this on some sort of regular basis with this child? Perhaps once or twice a week for three or four weeks?

This technique is becoming popular among special education teachers. I have seen reports of semi-miraculous improvement in classes of "hyperactive" or "combative" children. This guided fantasy technique became a daily routine in some of these classes. The teachers had some extra training and really dedicated themselves to making it work. Apparently, the kids enjoyed this activity to the point that they actually looked forward to their little breaks from standard classroom routine. Also, they learned to cooperate with each other much better.

Fantasy Experiment #2

Step 1

This time pick a child who could use one of the resources we talked about earlier, i.e., motivation, creativity, perseverance, and so forth.

Step 2

Talk with this child about a time when he or she experienced this resource. Ask the child to remember a time when he or she felt this way and to describe it to you.

Note: Depending on the child's state of mind, this may or may not be easy. Take your time and be encouraging in a positive manner. Also, you don't have to find a memory that is *perfect*, just one that will come close to the feelings you want this child to have.

Step 3

Notice the changes in the child during the description of the experience. Then, tell the child you want to pretend that it is happening again.

Step 4

Have the child close his or her eyes and say something like, "Let's go back to that good time, now." Begin to feed back the child's description of that experience. This time, though, add to it. Make sure that you include at least sights, sounds, and feelings in your description. Do this for about five minutes. When you think the child is having the set of feelings you want, say something like, "From now on, whenever you need to feel this way, you will remember_____." Have the _____ be some very specific feature of this experience for the child.

For example, you may want the child to have feelings of excitement. The child might then describe an experience of going to an amusement park. You may describe back to him or her the sights, sounds, and feelings of an amusement park, based on a combination of his or her description and your own experience. At the end of the description, you might say, "And from now on, whenever you want to feel this way, you can just remember that roller coaster."

Step 5

The nice thing about doing it in this way is that the child now has an anchor for that feeling and so do you. In the above example of the roller coaster anchor, the child can remember the roller coaster whenever he or she thinks it is necessary. Or, if you felt at some time that it would be good for the child to have that feeling, you could simply ask, "Remember that roller coaster?" In remembering it, those feelings will come back to the child. Test the anchor to make sure that it works for both of you. Then answer the following questions:

1. Was it easy for the child to remember a useful experience? Did you have to suggest one?
2. From the child's description, were you able to get enough to start with?
3. Was it easy for you to embellish the story? Did you find yourself going through a similar experience to help fill in the blanks?
4. Did both you and the child enjoy this?
5. How well did the verbal anchor work for you?
6. Did you find that your relationship with this child improved?

The interesting thing about this sort of shared experience, between you and the child, is that it will make you more of a person in his or her eyes. Children often forget that teachers are people too. Letting them know of experiences you both have in common, such as roller coaster rides, is a good reminder for them. Another really nice thing is that these are semi-universal experiences. There are some things that just about everyone has seen, heard, and felt. Amusement parks are OK in some places, but more universal are certain TV programs that most kids watch, that first try at riding a bike, that trip to the zoo or museum that most children living in cities have had, and so forth. Most important is that the child has the experience that will be most useful on the *inside*. How he or she gets *to* the internal experience is less important.

The best thing about these somewhat universal experiences is that they allow you to work with a group of children with the same ease as an individual child. You can easily take the class through a fantasy of an amusement park, even if some of the children haven't been to one before. If your description is good enough, they'll get the feelings anyway. You can certainly use the same anchoring technique as in the above exercise with the whole class. It isn't any different than the kindergarten teacher's piano. If you thought about it for a few minutes you could probably think of several universal experiences for your repertoire.

Fantasy Experiment #3

Step 1

Choose a resource you would like your class to experience: curiosity, motivation, excitement, perseverance, enjoyment are all fine. Choose just one, though.

Step 2

Next, think of a situation that would naturally produce this feeling in everyone. Fantasize. The experience needn't be one that you or the children have ever had.

For example: to produce a feeling of curiosity, a trip to the bottom of the ocean in a submarine might be fun. Or perhaps a visit to a strange planet. Remember, it's a fantasy, so make it fun.

Step 3

Make another list of the visual, auditory, and kinesthetic (olfactory and gustatory, if appropriate) components of this experience.

Step 4

From your list, write out, or at least outline, the fantasy so that you are sure it will produce the feelings you want the kids to have.

Step 5

Take the entire class on this trip into fantasy. You can have them close their eyes and relax, to start with. From then on, it is all yours. It should last about ten to fifteen minutes for the best effect. Talk slowly and enjoy it! When you are satisfied that the children are experiencing the feelings you want them to, anchor them as you did in the last exercise.

Step 6

Have a brief discussion with the class afterwards. Get useful feedback. Then answer these questions:

1. Was it easy to think of an experience that would produce the specific feelings you wanted?
2. Did the class enjoy this?
3. Did you enjoy the creative process yourself?
4. Have you learned some useful things that will make you a better storyteller or communicator?
5. Do you have an appreciation of how moviemakers coordinate sight and sound to produce a feeling in an audience? And how difficult it is to produce the same feeling in everyone?

6. Do you think you will be more aware of your presentation of *all* classroom material from these experiments?

For years, teachers have been telling me that they are fed up with lengthy, theoretical discussions that lead nowhere. Constantly, they have asked me and others for how-tos, the real nuts and bolts of teaching and helping kids. Well, with the technology available now, the question is less "how to" and more "how many ways and where shall I start?" That is what this chapter has been about. It is structured to help you learn pacing, leading, anchoring, and future pacing. Your choices within each of these are as varied as your imagination.

NLP is not an abstract theory. It is the study of how things work. Once you know how they work, you have many more choices about making them happen. The techniques in this chapter were not invented. They were discovered, and they were discovered in the behavior of some of the most powerful communicators that have ever lived. NLP is about studying the most effective behavior you can find. But why stop there? Even the best you can find can probably be improved and/or combined with more of the best from somewhere else. It takes a bit of practice, but that's the fun!

We have the technology to solve almost any of the problems any teacher will ever encounter. But problem solving isn't all there is. That same technology can make us all better people as well. The responsibility that comes with technology is to use it wisely, but to use it. There are no valid excuses left for doing a bad job. Anything can be done badly. That just teaches us how to do it better.

I heard someone describing comedian/author/actor/producer/director Woody Allen on TV. They were talking about his renowned neuroses and lack of self-confidence. The most fascinating thing said was that when Allen is directing an actor, he takes total responsibility for the outcome of the scene. If the actor acts poorly, Allen apologizes for not having explained himself properly. He never complains about the actor, only his own poor direction that made the actor look bad. Then he explains what he wants again, and they do it until it's the best it can be. We should all have that neurosis.

Notes

Chapter 6

1. "Chunk down" is an NLP term for breaking down into smaller chunks.

CHAPTER 7

TO PARENTS

What did you want from your parents when you were in school? Can you remember? Probably, you wanted something more, something less, or something different from what you got. I seldom meet anyone who is totally satisfied with the way he or she was parented. I suppose some measure of imperfection is inevitable.

I believe that one of the trickiest parts of parenting is relating to kids about school. Arranging the respective roles of parents, children, and school involves a number of choices. Primary is deciding how school fits in, or does not fit in, to family life. Some parents think of school as an extension of home. But it really isn't, and kids are seldom able to think of it in that way.

More apt is the description I once heard from a juvenile-court judge. He said that children have two jobs in growing up. One is to play; the other is to go to school. It is an outgrowth of our play-versus-work ethic in this country. It's a real pity when we have to separate the two in our minds. Personally, I refuse to. But most kids seem to think of school as their *job.*

Think about your own job or jobs you have had in the past. A job can be drudgery, pain, misery, and exhaustion. It can also be challenging, exciting, and fun. Most often, it will provide bits of all of those. How about the relationships you've formed at work? Many people think of their boss as a mean

124

dictator. He or she could also be a caring and supportive guide or a combination of both. How about co-workers? Can't they be anything from a tremendous help to a massive hindrance, from good friends you enjoy to people you want to avoid?

Then there is the question of basic needs and wants. Besides getting paid, most people want other things from their job. Some primarily want to learn and to progress. Others want stimulation and excitement. Most want, and need, a sense of accomplishment. Others need to bolster or develop their confidence and self-esteem by doing a good job or by doing something new and creative. How many of us, I wonder, actually get all of our needs met at work? Just as important, how many really enjoy their work? Many people constantly complain to me that they hate what they do, but they don't believe they have a choice. Sounds an awful lot like school to me.

For kids, school can be all of those same things that work is for us. But kids have fewer choices about creating their experience. It is usually created for them. Children enter school, wanting to form good relationships with others. They want to learn, and they have a tremendously high level of curiosity. They also want to feel good about themselves, good about others, and just plain good. The extent to which a child develops and achieves healthy relationships, new learning, and good feelings is the extent to which school allows him or her to do so.

The name of the game is experience. The secret is to allow children to have experiences that are structured enough to guide them into useful learning, but unstructured enough to allow children's natural curiosity and creativity to flourish. Doing things for, or to, children seldom teaches them anything. Mostly, it makes them feel incapable or inadequate. What's just as bad is that they will think others feel they are inadequate. Bad idea!

In no area is this more true than in the area of developing self-discipline. I know few adults who feel that they can discipline and motivate themselves the way they would like to. Most do so out of routine and habit. This robs them of a feeling of accomplishment. Usually what they experience is the boredom that comes from acting like a robot: switch on, switch off. It can come from too much discipline from the *outside*. If all you do is follow orders, why bother to motivate or even think for yourself? And, what kind of self-esteem will you develop by just doing what others tell you to do (think, feel)?

All of these things are true for most of us. Some people are more comfortable with more structure, some with less. Eventually, however, we need to develop our own structure.

Most of us need to have what we perceive is a safe environment to do so. This is equally true for children when they are in school and at home. For most people, home is a safe refuge from the world. It should represent some stability, physically and emotionally. If children have love, respect, and a reasonable amount of freedom at home, they will generally develop a substantial level of self-worth to take to school with them. Hopefully, the school will foster this. Sometimes it won't. If the school doesn't foster these feelings, a particularly harmful pattern can develop. The following is an example of this pattern. A child feels good at home and is doing well. Then some difficulty develops in school. The child's self-esteem suffers a blow. Too often, when the parents hear about trouble in school, they immediately *react*. They punish or criticize the child further: the child's safe refuge isn't so safe anymore. Self-esteem suffers at home as well as at school. The cycle builds on itself, then builds lousy anchors for the child.

Parents fall into this trap for a number of reasons. Many are concerned about school, rightfully so, but tend to jump in too fast, trying to make everything OK. It doesn't have to be OK all the time. If it was, kids wouldn't learn to take care of themselves. Some parents automatically assume that the school must know what it's doing. They forget that the *school* doesn't know anything. It's the staff and teachers that know. And they are quite human. Sometimes they know a whole lot of stuff that just isn't so.

Another kind of parent is the one who takes problems in school personally. So many times I've heard anguished parents bitterly ask, "How could my child do this to me?" It is very seldom that a child is doing a school problem *to* anyone.

There are exceptions, but they are far rarer than the complaints from parents would indicate. A little less paranoia and a little more logic goes a long way.

Understanding schools and teachers really isn't that much different from understanding kids and parents. Teachers have the same needs from their job that people in general have. To start with, though, teachers are very poorly paid. Second, they are poorly educated to perform their functions. Third, they don't get much respect. Everyone knows of the massive problems of education, but few will recognize an individual teacher who does WELL. While the job of a teacher is certainly challenging, the rewards are often quite meager. That's a generalization I *am* willing to make.

As a result, teachers, no matter how well-meaning they are, can fall into several traps. The first is disappointment, discouragement, or both early in their careers. I have seen many first- and second-year teachers in despair over the difference between what they expected and what they have found in their profession. Those who don't or can't make the adjustments they need, stand a real risk of falling into the second trap: burnout. The symptoms include apathy on the job and/or in other areas, poor health, seething anger or massive depression, a jaded attitude towards students, and a host of other noxious symptoms to which we don't want kids exposed. But the teacher can't be blamed any more than the social worker, doctor, nurse, policeman, and so forth. Both of these traps represent teachers' ways of rebelling against being stuck in the system, just as the children do. It's a natural response. It is also the reason we have so many good people leaving the profession.

Teachers as a group are catching on to what is happening to them, but so far most of the approaches are remedial. In other words, "When you realize you have burned out for a while, take these steps to recover." That's a far cry from preventing it in the first place, but, one thing at a time. There are ways that parents can help, or at least avoid aggravating, these situations when they run into them: they all boil down to effective communication skills.

First, recognize the teacher(s) as a human being(s). Second, listen to them, just as you should your children. Don't jump in too quickly. I know lots of parents who have told me that allowing teachers to get stuff off their chests can help troubled situations tremendously. I've personally found this to be true repeatedly. Like everyone else, teachers need someone to spout off to. Let's be a little tolerant and a little sympathetic. It's worth it.

Third, and most important, share your experience of your child with teachers. That doesn't mean your pet theories on child development. If you know something that works or will not work with your child, share it. Give an example of a time that it has worked (or not), and make sure the teacher understands. Like everyone else, teachers are usually willing to take advice or try something new if it makes sense to them. Fourth, if you think of specific instances in which the teacher might be able to try something with your child, tell him or her.

When talking with teachers, remember a couple of things. Teachers, kids, and you have similar needs as people. Both you and the teacher really have the same ultimate goal: your child's successful education. Sometimes that goal gets obscured by systemic problems or human weakness. It's OK, that's why we have each other.

At this point you may be saying to yourself, "Gee, these steps seem like pacing, leading, anchoring, and future pacing, with a common worthwhile framework. But how will this help teachers who are discouraged or burned out?" People get discouraged and/or burned out because they have lost sight of their purpose or because they have lost hope. Their needs are no longer being met. Anything someone, especially someone from outside the system, can do to reverse those tendencies will help immensely. *That* will help your children.

It is also an appropriate use of the communication skills presented in this book. Better (more) and clearer communication between parents and teachers is always helpful. Don't forget that the same holds true for parents and children. There is no reason in the world not to help your children with the techniques you've learned here. There sure are plenty of good reasons to do so, though. We have a lot of new technology. It is our responsibility as intelligent people to use it wisely. That means, use it.

For example, you can easily do some of the experiments in the preceding chapter with your own children. Find out what happens. If you impress yourself or learn something important, tell a teacher, or a school board, if you're brave. This is called being a good consumer. If you had an infection and went to the doctor, you'd expect him to use the best treatment available. You pay him to do his homework and keep up with the latest developments. The same with lawyers, mechanics, and anyone else who delivers a service. Expect it from your educational system, and you're more likely to get it. Let them know that you know what is available to them. Let them know you expect them to use what is there for them. If you don't tell them, they won't know. The squeaky wheel gets the grease. Go get it!

CHAPTER 8
DIRECTIONS

What needs to happen next? One of our next steps in education will be to make a major change in its focus. Rather than teaching kids what to learn, we will first teach them how to learn. This is the kind of revolution in thinking that is necessary for advancement of the art and science of education—now. It parallels the technological advancement being made in a variety of fields, such as computer science and communication theory. With computer programs now available to the general public and school systems, we'd be foolish to wait around bemoaning the problems we face. We'd be wise to face them with our best tools.

This also (fortunately) parallels advances in thinking in the field of medicine. More and more, doctors and the general public are looking towards viable means of prevention rather than just alleviation of illness. Healthy nutrition, exercise, a *lifestyle* of health, and so on are becoming paramount in many people's thinking. Holistic medicine is making slow but sure strides. Health consciousness is becoming an epidemic. I hope it gets everybody.

How about holistic education? We used to call our most well-rounded and capable people "Renaissance" men or women. But now, we're so worried about "the basics" that we often lose sight of just how much a human being is capable of accomplishing. This is progress?

We are far too concerned with specialization. Teachers get all kinds of specialized training. This leads to separatist thinking. What a loss. We should be teaching teachers and children about connections and "synergies" (the ways in which things fit and work together). If we don't, it will be our loss.

We should also be teaching teachers about systems and organizations. Our failure to do so is like teaching a scuba diver all about the bottom of the ocean, but forgetting to provide him with the equipment to breathe under water. It's a painful thing to forget. Too many of our teachers are sinking, when they need to be swimming. We need them to stay afloat.

Teachers ought to be taught that all systems and organizations have at least two goals. First, their stated purpose. The purpose of education is to help develop the minds and bodies of the current generation of children. Its system and organization must deliver that needed service. But all systems and organizations automatically have another need, one that is seldom stated out loud: survival. This goal has become their prime objective, often to the detriment, if not exclusion, of service delivery.

People working in such systems usually complain bitterly or leave the system. Others burn out. Giving up is not the best use of human ingenuity.

People in the system *are* the system. It may appear to have a life of its own, but that is deceptive and can lead to surrender. If you understand the channels, directions, and processes of communication in the system, you can discover some really useful and fascinating things about how it operates. Information is the lifeblood of social systems. Understanding and influencing the flow of that information creates the ability to influence and control the direction of the system as a whole.

I have worked in hospitals, prisons, and social service agencies for years, as well as consulting in schools. Certain things have been true of all of these settings. First, the people at the top, administrators, wardens, and principals, didn't actually run the show. These leaders surrounded themselves with administrative staffs who did direct things. These staffs weren't always official, either. Sometimes they were just trusted allies, quite often a secretary or two, who had been on the job longer than anyone else, knew where everything was kept, and how anything could be done. Those were the people I got to know first.

Second, there always seemed to be someone at the actual service-delivery level who knew the important information. Again, it didn't matter what the title of that person was: guard, orderly, teacher, nurse, or whatever. For example, a friend of mine used to do consulting in mental hospitals. He insisted that it was far more important to talk with the staff members who worked directly with the patients than to talk with the physician in charge. He reasoned that the doctor could tell you lots of historical and theoretical information about the patient. That's OK, but the staff members could tell you things like, "Don't look cross-eyed at that patient in the corner, or he'll bite you." For some reason, my friend always felt that that sort of advice was real good to have.

People, in organizations, who surround themselves with allies fare far better than those who isolate themselves. Peers can really form solid support groups. They are more likely to effect change than isolated individuals. Sometimes, there really is safety in numbers.

What is the best way to apply these principles to education? First, understand how these naturally occurring phenomena are already in operation. For the sake of survival, and the sacrifice of progress, a lot of people have jumped on the back-to-basics bandwagon. The thinking is that education has gotten too big for its britches, with all its special programs, and has gone downhill. This is partly true, but it is not the whole story. Equally relevant is the reason why so many programs have failed: because they were thrown together just to qualify for federal grants or to satisfy special interests. Because a lot of people have developed ineffective, hodge-podge programs in the name of progress hardly means progress should be abandoned. It simply needs a viable form in which to develop.

Sure, education needs to redeem itself. But simplistic approaches will only limit success to a few areas—that isn't likely to impress anyone. In fact, it will probably go unnoticed as do other small successes. People in this country are impressed by the dramatic. They want to see clear, direct results. NLP technology is powerful enough to provide the drama necessary for this process. It has already done so in the field of psychotherapy. Life-long phobias are being cured in minutes. The same with other major problems people go to therapists for. NLP has revolutionized that profession and will do more in the next few years. In business, this same NLP technology is being used in personnel, employee relations, negotiations, advertising, public relations, and more. Major corporations are regularly using some NLP technology and coming back for more. They have something called a ledger that helps them make the decision. The next field will be education.

Teachers can make this happen. They know their training is inadequate, but their dedication isn't. Just about every teacher I've ever met who has been exposed to NLP has been really turned on. Most are hesitant to take on the responsibility of spreading it around. They feel their responsibility begins and ends in the classroom.

Teachers should teach *up* the "ladder" of their system as well as down, to the children. I know teachers who have pushed for particular programs within their school systems and gotten them through. They have, generally, more credibility with the powers that be than outsiders have. School administrators are less threatened by teachers within their schools than by outside experts. They are more impressed by united efforts of teachers and parents, working through the proper channels, than they are by "renegades" from inside, or outside, the system. I like the renegades better, but school administrators don't seem to share my view.

In this book, we have touched on many of the various troubles in education. Families in trouble can cause children to have trouble in school. Poor funding, outmoded approaches, and bad teaching can certainly cause all kinds of problems. Poor health will certainly undo much of the good even the best schools can provide—that includes a poor diet. All of these things are relevant to the overall problems and are important to consider.

This one volume aims at only one major facet: technology. We have what we need—*now*—to be able to teach children exquisitely well. *There are no learning disabilities.* There are only teaching disabilities. They can be alleviated, in most areas quickly and painlessly, by using the new knowledge.

Teachers and parents alike often feel anxious, frustrated, angry, bored, discouraged, and afraid when they run into a problem or group of problems involving school. This can cause confusion. But confusion isn't bad. In fact, it can lead to curiosity. Curiosity can motivate people to look around and to listen for something new and unusual. A curious and motivated person is certainly someone to be reckoned with. These feelings can lead to real creativity and growth. Maybe even a new sense of hope . . .

APPENDIX

APPENDIX I

NOTE: The following is from a friend/student of mine named Judy Kopfler, M.Ed., who is an educational consultant. She was a teacher for nine years in a variety of settings and is quite creative. She found this fantasy in a book. It was written by a prominent neuro-linguistic programmer. She changed and adapted it to her own style, using her creativity. She added her own NLP skills of pacing, leading, anchoring, and future pacing to make a good tool into a great one. Here it is as she presented it to me.

Preface to J.O. Stevens' *Motorcycle Fantasy*—as used by Judy Kopfler, M.Ed.

I have used this guided fantasy with children of all ages in the classroom and with teachers in teacher workshops. Children and adults are amazed at their travels.

From experience, I have found it extremely helpful for children classified as emotionally disturbed or behavior-disordered, learning disabled, hyperactive and with kids who are tense.

The uses are many, and they have all resulted in positive learning. The child/student gains a better understanding, awareness of himself, and is better able to conscientiously control his behavior in an academic and nonacademic environment.

Here are some tips for taking the guided fantasy. Take the trip yourself first, with the help of a friend. After you read the guided fantasy, I will list ways to modify it for children who may not want to go for a motorcycle ride. I find that one idea creates many more and that, with our creative abilities, we can do anything. Relax and pause frequently so that your students have sufficient time to experience this.

Note: Discuss the fantasy only with those who volunteer to do so. Those who don't will learn on their own. Kids love it, and you will see a positive change right before your eyes.

MOTORCYCLE FANTASY

As a teacher and now a teacher/therapist, I would like to thank John O. Stevens[1] for this idea. I have found this can be used with children, teachers, and adults.

To teachers. "Anything you can do to increase communication in your class will reduce your need to impose order by authority. The class will become more a place for listening and learning, and less a place for fighting and antagonism."[2]

Prepare your students for a brief fantasy experience. Speak softly and pause between sentences so they have sufficient time to visualize your instructions. Here goes—

Imagine that you are a motorcycle. Notice what kind you are and what make. You are being ridden now: Notice who your rider is. How do you get along with each other? Have a dialogue with your rider. Finish the dialogue. Become aware of how fast you are going. Where are you? What kind of condition are you in? Notice all of your various parts: is everything working smoothly? Any badly worn parts about to cause trouble? Where are you now? How do you feel as a motorcycle? Your left handlebar has a brake grip for the front wheel; your right handlebar has the acceleration grip. Let the front-wheel brake grip on the left talk with the accelerator on the right. What is each saying and feeling? You are being stopped now. Where did you stop and how? How do you feel after your ride?

After I finish I find it best to ask: who went on the ride? I then ask: who would like to discuss their trip? (Have faith, there will be a volunteer: this fantasy has an amazing effect and it's contagious.) Allow as many as want to discuss their travels to do so. Focus on how they get along with their rider, who their rider is, and how fast they are going. (Please don't overquestion the kids—work only with what they want to volunteer.)

Their description of themselves as bikes and how well they are working will often give you new insights into their unconscious perceptions of themselves. Also, kids who are hyperactive (or, as I prefer to describe them, fast processors of information) travel at one hundred miles per hour or well over that. Anchoring is very effective for students who travel rapidly. I have been able to physically slow down such children by touching their left fist (the brake grip) as I speak to them slowly and softly. I point out that they can set their own speed, slowing down when they are speeding and speeding up when they are tired. Touching the left hand while talking to them is the anchor. I have seen six-year-olds and sixteen-year-olds gain greater control of their behavior merely by squeezing their own left hand. The change occurs within thirty minutes. When they appear to be gearing up, if I pass by them and merely touch their left hand, they immediately begin to slow down.

Note: Taking the ride is of utmost importance. If the student cannot relate to a bike, he or she won't go for the ride. Ask your class, "Who likes motorcycles?" If the response is low, consider using this fantasy in other ways. Try alternative vehicles, such as a ten-speed bike, a jet, a rocket, a car, a go-cart, a horse, even a boat. This fantasy can be modified and molded to fit your specific classroom needs. Use your imagination and your students'.

The following are responses from students and teachers who went for a ride. Kids, at the outset, usually think I'm weird.

I tell them just to humor me and go along: "It's a way of getting out of class without skipping and without a pass!" (That has been rather successful!) Once they become the bike with a rider, they react: smiling or frowning. Some take their best friend, their parents, or me with them. Some go to California, to Florida, to New York. Some travel down country roads, others in the city. Some race in the superdome. One teacher took her most difficult student out on a ride in the country, dropped him off, and headed back to school much to her amazement! (She was shocked, understood her student better, and became much more effective with him.)

All know how fast they are going and what kind of condition they are in. Some kids' bikes are falling apart and end up stopping by crashing into, or through, a wall. I was rather surprised at the kids with that response. I had bought their well-disguised cover of being cool and collected.

Most kids are smiling, calm, and happy when the fantasy ends. They open their eyes and ask to go back to where they were. I encourage them to go back for that ride when they feel discomfort or tension in the classroom or elsewhere. I also ask those who need repairs to their bikes to take care of themselves. To those who crash, I recommend that there are other ways of stopping that wouldn't hurt so much.

The list is endless, the trip is never the same, and the positive changes in your children are more than worth the risk.

Notes

Appendix I

1. John O. Stevens, *Awareness* (Moab, UT: Real People Press, 1971).
2. John O. Stevens, *Awareness* (Moab, UT: Real People Press, 1971).

APPENDIX II

THE META-MODEL
by
Robert Dilts

The meta-model was developed by John Grinder and Richard Bandler to identify classes of natural language patterns as a means to help increase the flow of information between human beings. The basic premise is that words (surface structure) are meaningful only in that they anchor in an individual some sensory representation (deep structure). During the codification of sensory experience into words (as an individual speaks) and the process of decoding (as a second individual listens and transforms the auditory stimulus into his/her own sensory representation) important information can be lost or distorted. Deletions and distortions of experience may also occur within an individual as he/she codes sensory experiences.

The meta-model provides an identification of linguistic patterns which could become problematic in the course of communication and a series of responses through which two individuals may insure more complete communication. Attention to non-verbal gestures and behavior and to context will also greatly enhance the unambiguous transference of information.

I. *Gathering Information*
  A. Deletions
    1. *Simple Deletion:* when some object, person or event (noun phrases or noun arguments) has been left out of the surface structure.
       e.g., I'm really uncomfortable.
       Response: Uncomfortable about what specifically?
    2. *Lack of Referential Index:* when an object or person (noun) that is being referred to is unspecific.
       e.g., a) They never believe me. Response: Who specifically never believes you?
             b) That doesn't matter. Response: What specifically doesn't matter?
    3. *Comparatives Deletion:* when a referent is deleted during a comparison (i.e., good-better-best; more-less; most-least).
       e.g., It's *better* not to force the issue.
       Response: Better for whom? Compared to what?
  B. *Unspecified Verbs:* verbs which are not entirely explicit where sometimes the action needs to be made more specific.
     e.g., He really frustrates me.
     Response: Frustrates you how specifically?
  C. *Nominalizations:* when an ongoing process is represented as a static entity in a way which may distort its meaning.
     e.g., I can't stand her insensitivity.
     Response: Her sensing what about whom? and how specifically?

II. *Limitations to an Individual's Model*
  A. *Presuppositions:* when something is implicitly assumed in the other person's communication which may, if taken for granted, cause limitations to a person's choices about the experience.
     e.g., If you knew how much I suffered, you wouldn't act this way.

There are three presuppositions in this statement: 1) I suffer 2) you act this way and 3) you don't know.

Response: 1) How specifically are you suffering? 2) How specifically am I reacting? 3) How do you know that I don't know?

NOTE: There are a large number of different types of presuppositions that can be identified. For a listing see *The Structure of Magic* by Richard Bandler and John Grinder.

  B. *Modal Operators of Possibility and Necessity:* statements identifying rules about or limits to an individual's behavior (i.e., possibility=can/can't, it's possible/impossible, will/won't, may/may not; necessity= should/shouldn't, must/must not, have to, etc.).

    e.g., 1) possibility: I *can't* relax. Response: What stops you?

        2) necessity: I *shouldn't* let anyone know what I feel about that. Response: What would happen if you did?

  C. *Complex Equivalence:* when two experiences or events come to stand for each other but may not necessarily be synonymous.

    e.g., She's always yelling at me . . . She hates me.

    Response: Does her yelling at you always mean that she hates you? Have you ever yelled at anyone that you didn't hate?

III. *Semantic Ill-Formedness*

  A. *Cause-Effect:* when an individual makes a causal linkage between their experience or response to some outside stimulus that is not necessarily directly connected, or where the connection is not clear.

    e.g., This lecture makes me bored.

    Response: How specifically does it *make* you bored?

  B. *Mind-Reading:* when an individual claims to know what another individual is thinking without having received any specific communication from the second individual.

e.g., Henry never considers my feelings.

Response: How do you know that Henry never considers your feelings?

C. *Lost Performative:* Statements and judgments that an individual considers to be true about the world which may be generalizations based on the individual's own experience. (Lost performatives are characterized by words like: good, bad, crazy, sick, right, wrong, true, false, etc.)

e.g., It's bad to be inconsistent about what you think.

Response: Bad for whom? How do you know that it is bad to be inconsistent?

D. *Universal Quantifiers:* Words which generalize a few experiences to be a whole class of experience (characterized by words like: all, every, always, never, etc.).

e.g., She never listens to me.

Response: She *never* listens to you? How do you know that she *never* listens to you?

APPENDIX III

Behavioral Engineering and the Computer
by
Robert Dilts

Behavioral Engineering designs and produces software for the computer and other interactive media, such as arcade games and video systems, that make *people* more effective and productive. This is accomplished by identifying desired behavioral outcomes and skills and then using the principles and technology of neuro-linguistic programming (NLP) to make an explicit, step-by-step model of the thought processes or mental "programs" that produce that behavior. This mental strategy is then incorporated into an interactive computer or video program, so that when a person plays with or uses the program, the thinking strategy becomes systematically and unconsciously ingrained in the user.

As an educational tool, the computer surpasses other media in that it engages all three of the primary senses simultaneously. School books engage one representational system: visual. Videotapes engage two: visual and auditory. Through its interaction with the user, the computer engages not only visual and auditory, but kinesthetic as well. This accounts for its popularity on the market.

The computer can evaluate the user's response immediately and give the appropriate feedback *while* the user is engaged in the activity of learning. This is something that a book or videotape will never be able to do.

Perhaps the most important feature of the computer is its infinite amount of patience: it gears itself to the pace of the student.

Anyone working with a computer learns a great deal unconsciously while using a program or playing a video game. Programs are designed to utilize and enhance the motivational framework provided by the computer and video environment to help people learn unconsciously and be more productive while enjoying themselves.

For example, the popular Spelling Strategy program (currently being marketed by Apple Computer through their SDS program) leads the user's eye movements and uses color graphics and computer animation to develop visualization. The mental strategy used by almost all successful spellers. The program produces immediate, observable results and has even turned children who were previously thought to be learning disabled into effective spellers.

Programs that install thinking strategies for creative writing, typing, reading, second language acquisition, creativity, and decision making (which innovatively uses the computer keyboard to get unconscious feedback from the user) employ the same principle.

We are committed to integrating the latest computer and video technology with the behavioral technology of neuro-linguistic programming to increase and accelerate human productivity, potential, communication, and evolution on a personal, organizational, and international scale. The Industrial Revolution marked the beginning of man's efforts to develop and refine machines to make them better and more effective. Through these efforts, we now have machines that can help make human beings more effective.

For further information on specific computer programs contact:

NeuroLink International
www.NLPU.com

PHOTOCOPY PAGES

Visual accessing cues for a "normally organized" right-handed person.

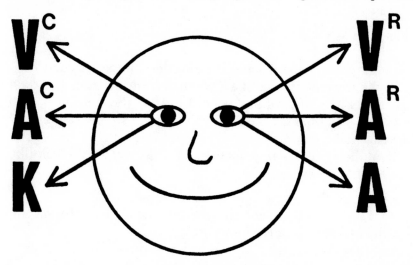

V^C Visual constructed images. V^r Visual remembered (eidetic) images.

(Eyes defocused and unmoving also indicates visual accessing.)

A^c Auditory constructed sounds or words.

A^r Auditory remembered sounds or words.

K Kinesthetic feelings (also smell and taste).

A Auditory sounds or words.

Tear out page 1

Questions (Note: Forget about the answers, watch the eye movements.)

To elicit visual remembered information and accessing (V^R):

1. What color is your favorite toy (dog, cat, car, hot-air balloon, etc.)?

2. What does your favorite TV star look like? (Small and green?)

3. How many knobs does your TV set (Pac Man, computer, stove, etc.) have?

4. Make a picture in your head of your living room (clubhouse, girlfriend, etc.).

To elicit visual-constructed information and accessing (V^C):

1. What would it look like if you had a purple ice cream cone covered with mustard and peanut butter? (Scrumptious, eh?)

2. Can you imagine a pink elephant with yellow stripes and orange polka dots?

3. Make a picture in your head of what you would look like standing on your head.

To elicit auditory information and accessing (A):

1. What does your favorite record sound like? Musical instrument, bicycle horn, breaking glass?

2. What sounds do you hear when someone plays an electronic game? (Pinball, tennis, etc.)

3. What does your own voice sound like to you?

4. Listen inside your head to the sound of your own voice (or anyone else's; preferably someone who does not evoke an emotional reaction.)

To elicit kinesthetic information and accessing (K):

1. How do you feel right after a big meal? Athletic event, long walk?

2. Do you remember how you felt inside the last time you were really excited? Cold, warm, happy, scared?

3. What does it feel like when you touch something rough, like sandpaper? Smooth like glass, gooey like melted chocolate?

4. Pay attention to how you feel inside your body right now.

Questions that are unspecified regarding sensory functioning:

1. What are you thinking about?

2. How do you know when you are learning something?

3. How do you know when you believe something?

4. What are you aware of?

SPELLING STRATEGY [1]

1. Prepare a list of words or use spelling words from the child's current text.

2. Using the eye-movement-pattern tear-out page, or the skills you have developed in determining accessing cues, find the direction of the child's gaze while he or she is accessing visual-remembered material.

3. Explain to the child that it is easiest to remember what something looks like when his or her eyes are pointed in that direction.

4. Ask the child for his or her favorite color. Explain that it will be more fun to learn to spell if he or she remembers the words in that color.

5. Show the child the first word in the list. Have the child pretend to take a snapshot in his/her mind's eye.

6. Have the child look up and to the left, or wherever you have determined is the best direction, and *see* that picture of the word in his/her favorite color.

7. Ask the child, while s/he looks at that picture, to read the letters to you *backwards*.

Note: Spelling the word backwards insures a purely visual strategy, since it is virtually impossible to sound out a word backwards. For this reason, you may find that children and adults find it easier to spell backwards than forwards.

8. When the child spells the word correctly backwards, ask him or her to spell it forwards.

Note: Errors will occur. Go slowly enough to insure that the child has enough time to get the picture and reproduce it in the proper color. If you notice glances in other directions, usually down and to the child's left, be aware

[1]Adapted from SPELLING STRATEGY by Robert Dilts.

that the strategy is being contaminated. If this happens, gently interrupt the child. You only want the child to go through the proper strategy.

9. Future pace by telling the child, "from now on, whenever you want to spell this word, you will simply remember this picture in your head and spell the word correctly."

10. For each word in the list, repeat steps 5 through 9.

Here are a few tips that will enhance the speed, ease, and effectiveness of the spelling strategy. First, make sure that the child is comfortable at all times. Watch for muscle tension, breath holding, slumped posture, or fatigue. This is not a race. If the child gets tired, stop. If his or her muscles get tense, help the child relax. If necessary remind him or her to breathe.

Take as much time as necessary to explain each step. The child needn't understand the underlying neurological principles involved, just what to do. If he or she does not understand the strategy, your explanation must have been faulty.

Break longer words down into three-letter chunks. This seems to be the chunk size that is easiest to handle. An alternative is to isolate a part of the word that is particularly troublesome for *this* child. For example, "relieve" sometimes causes difficulty because of the *i* and *e* that people often reverse. You may want to isolate *iev* from the rest of the word if it helps. You may need to experiment with each word for each child. With a little practice they'll do the rest.

Some people visualize better than others. If a child has difficulty making an internal picture, there are many things you can do. Ask him or her to imagine turning up the brightness of the picture (just like on a TV set). Find a comfortable level of brightness for the child. Then do the same with the distance of the internal picture. Have the child move it closer and further until it is comfortable and easy to see. Repeat this with the size, clarity, and even the color. Only the child can know what is best. Take the time now. It will pay off later.

Remind the child that with a little practice, this will become automatic. It is easier than riding a bike, tying shoes, or playing games or sports. It is also exactly what good spellers almost always do.

MATH STRATEGY[1]

Note: This strategy is essentially the same as the spelling strategy. All of the tips to enhance the spelling strategy apply here as well. This strategy is for visual memorization. It is ideal for multiplication tables. Using this format, many children have been able to memorize tables through tens or higher in as little as two days. It is also effective for formulas, constants, and anything else the child should have memorized.

1. Prepare a list of formulas or problems you wish the child to know. You can use the child's current text as a source.

2. Using the eye-movement-pattern tear-out page, or the skills you have developed in determining accessing cues, find the direction of the child's gaze while he or she is accessing visually remembered information.

3. Explain to the child that it is easiest to remember what something looks like when his or her eyes are pointed in that direction.

4. Ask the child for his or her favorite color. Explain that it will be more fun to learn math if he or she learns equations in that color.

5. Show the child the first formula or equation (e.g., $4 \times 5 = 20$, $20 \div 5 = 4$, $2 + 16 = 18$, $18 - 16 = 2$, and so forth). Have the child pretend to take a snapshot in his or her mind's eye.

6. Have the child look in the direction you determined in step 3 and *see* that picture of the equation in his or her favorite color.

7. Ask the child, while he or she looks at the picture, to read the equation *backwards.*

8. After the child reads the equation backwards, ask him or her to do so forwards.

9. Future pace by telling the child, "From now on, whenever you want to remember that equation, you will simply remember this picture in your head and remember it correctly."

10. For each equation or formula, repeat steps 5 through 9.

---

[1]Adapted from MATH STRATEGY by Robert Dilts.

MOTORCYCLE FANTASY*

Teacher: Emphasize the italicized words—they are anchors that will be useful from now on. As was discussed in Appendix I, the left hand will be the anchor for slowing down, and the right hand the anchor for speeding up. Where you see . . . pause and allow the children to do or experience what you have just said. Speak slowly and clearly. Once you have done this fantasy, you can repeat it and embellish it as much as you like. The point is the anchors.

Imagine that you are a motorcycle. Notice what kind you are and what make. You are being ridden now. Notice who your rider is . . . How do you get along with each other? . . . Have a dialogue with your rider. . . . Finish the dialogue and become aware of how fast you are going. . . . Notice where you are. . . . What kind of condition are you, the motorcycle, in? Notice all of your various parts. Is everything working smoothly? Any badly worn parts about to cause trouble? . . . Where are you now? . . . Notice how you feel being a motorcycle. Your *left hand* lebar has a *brake grip* for the front wheel . . . and your *right hand* lebar has the *acceleration grip* . . . . Carry on a dialogue or conversation between the front wheel *brake grip on the left* and the *accelerator on the right* . . . . Notice carefully what each is saying and feeling. . . . You are being stopped now. Where did you stop and how? How do you feel after your ride?

*John O. Stevens, *Awareness* (Moab, Utah: Real People Press, 1971). It is reprinted, with slight changes, with permission of the author and publisher.

COMPUTER FANTASY

Teacher: Emphasize the italicized words. They are anchors that will be useful from now on. When you see . . . pause and give the children time to experience what you have just presented to them. Speak slowly and clearly. This fantasy can be done in the classroom or, preferably, outside—depending on your surroundings. Following the fantasy, have a class discussion about when up time and down time would be useful in class or elsewhere. This fantasy can be repeated and embellished as much as you like. The point, again, is the anchors. Begin with the children standing up.

Pretend you are a very special computer. You are on wheels so that you can move around. This computer takes in data from the outside world through sight, sound, touch, taste, and smell. When it's taking in *outside* information it is in *up-time.*

This computer also processes data on the inside. It makes pictures, hears sounds, talks to itself, has feelings, tastes, and smells inside. It remembers everything. When it is doing these things *on the inside* it is in *down-time.*

Begin by going into up-time. Walk around and take in data from the outside. Look around. What do you see? . . . Now, listen. What do you hear? . . . Touch a few different things. How do they feel? . . . Do you smell or taste anything? . . .

Stop where you are. Close your eyes and go into down-time. Pay attention to the inside. What pictures do you see inside? . . . What do you hear inside? . . . Are you saying anything to yourself silently on the inside? . . . How about smells or tastes? . . .

Spend another minute in *down-time,* aware only of the *inside.* . . .

Now open your eyes, go back into *up-time,* and walk around a bit more. Be aware of what is around you on the *outside.* . . . Stop. Close your eyes again and go back *inside to down-time.* . . . What is happening *on the inside* now? . . . From now on, when I say *down-time,* you'll know to go *inside* . . .

Now open your eyes and come back into *up-time*. From now on, when I say *up-time*, you'll know to *pay attention to the outside*.

How was it being a computer? Fun?

SAFARI FANTASY

Teacher: Emphasize the italicized words. Each one specifies sensory functioning. When you *see* . . . pause and give the children time to experience what you have presented. Speak slowly and clearly. The point of this fantasy is for children to comfortably move from experiencing one sensory mode to another. Following the fantasy, discuss the importance of using all of the senses to fully experience, enjoy, and learn from an event.

Close your eyes. Sit back, relax, and take a deep breath. Let's pretend we are going on a safari through the African jungle. We start at the edge of the jungle where we *see* a path into the trees . . . We're walking in now, *looking* down the path, *feeling* the soft brush under our feet . . . We can *see* lots of strange plant life, animals, shapes, and colors. . . . As we *look* around, we begin to notice the special *sounds* of the jungle . . . We hear the screeches of monkeys in the trees above our heads, the roar of a lion in the distance, the buzzing of insects, . . . and more sounds that we don't understand . . . While we *hear* these unusual *noises,* we notice the *warmth* of the jungle air . . . and we can *feel* the dampness. It makes us feel *hot* and *heavy* . . .

All of a sudden, we *hear* something in the distance. . . . It almost *sounds* like *thunder,* but it doesn't stop . . . We begin to *walk* faster through the *dense* brush toward the *echoing sound* . . . As we get closer, we *hear* water *rushing.* We realize the *sound* we *hear* is a giant waterfall. We become even more *excited* and *anxious* as we *hurry* on our way. . . . We *hear* ourselves *trampling* through the brush. Then we *break* through the trees into a large *clear*ing, and we *see* it: It's the *biggest* waterfall we have ever *seen* . . .

We gather in the clearing to just *sit* down, *rest, watch,* and *listen* to this spectacular sight . . . We think to ourselves how lucky we are to have *eyes, ears,* and *feelings* to *appreciate* the *beauty* around us . . . and we can remember to use all of our

161

senses—sight, sound, touch, taste, and smell—to enjoy and learn as time goes on. . . . Now slowly come back into the classroom. . . .

Did you enjoy your safari? Let's talk about it.

Tear-out page 7

The following is a list of common and useful verbs categorized into representational systems. They will be helpful when you are listening to children's speech to determine which system(s) they are consciously representing their experiences in. They will also help you to switch to representational systems you don't normally use. The list of unspecified verbs will help you become more aware of choices that *don't* lead children into any particular representational system. Feel free to add to this list.

VISUAL	AUDITORY	KINES-THETIC	UNSPECI-FIED
see	listen	bite	seem
view	hear	burst	be
observe	overhear	bend	aware
witness	sound	bind	have
sight	quiet	break	think
spot	order	fall	believe
look	ask	catch	allow
glimpse	beg	fight	become
glance	ring	go	be able
peer	chime	grasp	have to
peek	yell	grab	must
peep	scream	hold	want
survey	sing	hit	shall
eye	speak	climb	know
examine	talk	run	do
inspect	shout	struggle	make
gaze	whisper	throw	understand
stare	groan	walk	create
glare	moan	jump	contemplate
pale	whine	push	ponder
find	buzz	feel	desire
read	call	grip	appreciate
show	click	handle	sense

BIBLIOGRAPHY

Bach, Richard. *Illusions: The Adventures of a Reluctant Messiah.* New York: Delacorte Press/Eleanore Friede, 1977.

Bandler, Richard and John Grinder. *Frogs into Princes.* Moab, UT: Real People Press, 1979.

Bateson, Gregory. *Mind and Nature: A Necessary Unity.* New York: E.P. Dutton, 1979.

Dilts, Robert B., et al. *Neuro-Linguistic Programming I.* Cupertino: Meta Publications, 1979.

Dilts, Robert B. "Math Strategy." A Behavioral Engineering computer program, 1981.

Dilts, Robert B. "Spelling Strategy." A Behavioral Engineering computer program, 1981.

Goodman, Paul. *Growing Up Absurd.* New York: Vintage Books, a division of Random House, 1956.

Laing, R.D. *The Politics of Experience & The Bird of Paradise.* London: Penguin Books, 1967.

Morris, Desmond. *The Human Zoo.* New York: McGraw-Hill Book Co., 1969.

Stevens, John O. *Awareness.* Moab: UT: Real People Press, 1971.

META-CATION

VOLUME II

New Improved Formulas For Thinking About Thinking

by
Sid Jacobson

Meta Publications
P.O. Box 565
Cupertino, California 95014

Library of Congress Card Number 83-60320
I.S.B.N. 0-916990-17-6

CONTENTS

ACKNOWLEDGEMENTS

The author would like to thank the following people and sources without who's help this work would have been more difficult and less productive.

How Real Is Real? by Paul Watzlawick, copyright © 1976 by Random House, used by permission of the publisher.

Dilts, Robert, "Applications of NLP in Health," in *Applications of Neuro-Linguistic Programming*, copyright © 1983 by Meta Publications, Cupertino, Ca. I would also like to thank Robert for allowing me to repeat his outline of the Meta-Model here, as it appeared in Meta-Cation, and for apt and timely guidance in describing his work in the field of health.

Liv Ullman, quoted in "Liv Ullman: Making Choices," by Leonie Caldecott, copyright © July, 1985 by *New Age Journal*, used by permission of the publisher.

Drucker, Peter. *Adventures Of A Bystander*. New York, Harper & Row, 1979, used by permission of the publisher.

States of Consciousness, by Charles Tart, New York, Dutton, copyright © 1975 by Charles T. Tart, currently in print with Psychological Process, Box 371, El Cerrito, Ca. 94530. Used by permission of Charles T. Tart.

Miller, G., E. Galanter, and K. Pribram, *Plans and the Structure of Behavior*, copyright © 1960 by Henry Holt & Co., used by permission of Patricia Galanter.

The Structure of Magic, Volume I, By Richard Bandler and John Grinder, copyright © 1975 by Science and Behavior Books, Inc., Palo Alto, Ca.

Therapeutic Metaphors, by David Gordon, copyright © 1978 by Meta Publications, Cupertino, Ca.

Kaypro™ for making such wonderful computers.

Goetz, Michael. *Adventure*. Michael Goetz, 1982. (This version of this computer game is NOT in the public domain, though it is available from some of the distributors of public domain software.)

Steve Frieman for timely suggestions on the appendices for this series.

Ed Meyer for allowing me to use a personal experience of his for illustration as well as constant support, thought provocation, and friendship.

John Grinder for the many ideas used throughout this series which were originally his.

Richard Bandler, teacher, friend, publisher, source of countless ideas and other relevant ravings.

My many students and friends for continually teaching me to teach them as well as I can.

CHAPTER 1

MORE (Not So)
RANDOM THOUGHTS

When I wrote Meta-Cation a few years ago, I had several intentions. First and foremost, I wanted to provide people with a readable introduction to Neuro-Linguistic Programming. Too many people had complained to me that the books written up to that time were incomprehensible to normal humans. In varying degrees, they were right. Second, I wanted to get educators interested. NLP could change the world in a generation if we could get it into the schools where it belongs. Third, though it isn't too easy to admit, I wanted to thumb my proboscis at the educational/psychological establishment that I felt had missed the point with too many people for too long, myself included.

Looking over the latest releases from publishers of this kind of work has sickened me further. Psychologists are entrenching themselves more deeply in the "learning disability" debate. But instead of admitting that it is a lousy idea, they are doing what they always do: counting everything. Instead of looking for creative new ways to teach *everyone*, they are, it seems to me, worse than five years ago, further defining their myriad disability classification schemes. This is of course what academics do best. They redefine when they should discard. They say, "The populations must be different," when they should say, "Hey, maybe we were looking at the whole thing from the wrong perspective."

I am reminded of the official position given by the American Psychoanalytic Association years ago toward the treatment of phobias. Behavior modification therapists were regularly treating phobias, with pretty good success in a matter of weeks. And they weren't treating anything but the fear itself. They ignored root causes in childhood, or wherever, and simply cured the patient. Psychoanalysts, however, had a long tradition of less than mediocre success with treating phobics. It often took years of painful, complex, expensive, and time consuming analysis "on the couch." They could not, therefore, swallow the success of these upstarts. Their official response was that, since this new treatment couldn't possibly be truly effective, all of those cured people must really have been suffering from some other ailment. This is a classic example of a "self-sealing argument."[1]

You would think that the people who are the self-proclaimed experts on ego defenses would recognize their own. I don't know if they still think that way. As far as phobias go, it really doesn't matter. I know people who routinely rid others of long-standing ones in a few short minutes. I used to myself. Unfortunately it isn't very difficult, complicated, painful, or mystical. So it will probably take a long time to catch on.

When we are making decisions about what to believe, I guess personal experience is all we ultimately have. That sounds too esoteric, but it keeps me on track most of the time. I know I have had powerful experiences that have shaped my thinking. A few of them have been from books. I wanted my first book to provide special experiences for some of the people who read it. It has. I have gotten the word back from a number of people, mostly schoolteachers, who were deeply affected by Meta-Cation. A few said it gave them specific things to do in certain situations. Most, though, said that in addition to the numerous tips they got a renewed sense of their own worth as teachers. They gained hope that things could be better.

Teachers have suffered from the educational system at least as much as anyone else. Maybe more. For one thing, they know their training in school was grossly inadequate. They also know that if they are really going to learn how to teach, they are most likely going to have to teach themselves. This is the painful realization many people come to when they first graduate from college or even professional school. I have met thousands of psychotherapists all over the country. Universally they thought their graduate school training to be, at best, mediocre. Usually they don't feel *that* good about it. Fortunately there are lots of training programs they can go to where they can, at least, see someone else being truly competent. Whether they can learn from the training is another issue.

Education doesn't seem to have a parallel system. Sure, there are lots of workshops, seminars, and training programs. But it doesn't work the same way. In a therapy training program you get to watch and directly experience real work being done. In an education workshop you don't often have a classroom full of kids to watch demonstrations with. Even if you did, a brief example with a live group still isn't the same as going in every Monday wondering how the week will turn out. There is only one way to get that learning.

Even though most of my true learning came "in the trenches" I know that there have been books that helped me along the way. Most often they didn't tell me exactly what to do when. More often they made me think in new ways. Then I could devise my own ways of proceeding through whatever I was proceeding through. Training has provided me with those same kinds of mind-altering aids. It also gave me just enough experiment and practice to know how much more I needed. The rest was up to me. I know that in NLP we can give the same thing to teachers. The problem is to avoid scaring them off while doing it. Or worse, insulting their intelligence.

I find teachers in general to be an interesting group of people. In nearly all respects, the responses to Meta-Cation were predictable. I expected to raise a lot of eyebrows, and did. Also, I expected many teachers to tell me they loved what I did but wanted much more. I tell them there are about 20 other books on the subject, training institutes all over this country and Canada, and what they need more than anything is this new point of view and some practice. They generally respond that they would love the reading, training, and practice and, "By the way, does the training cost anything? Where am I supposed to get the money and time ...?"

As I said, these responses were predictable (read boring). I got some that were interesting though. I did not know if teachers would appreciate my barbed sense of humor and my disgust at some of their clan. One friend of mine, who does workshops for teachers, said I should watch out. She was hesitant to recommend the book because of its mildly acidic tone. I told her that with all the complaints teachers get I thought they could take what I had to say. I also thought they would agree with most of it. Anyway, I stand by my opinions, regardless of the response. A number of teachers surprised me though. They told me they agreed with what I had to say, but, "No other teachers I know besides me could take the criticism." In other words it was all right with them but since they were so unusual ... This got even more interesting after I'd heard it several dozen times. It made me wonder if there aren't an awful lot of resilient folks out there.

Another response was predictable, but still interesting. Many of the teachers, who will try anything despite their circumstances, came to me wanting much needed advice. They wondered if I had any tricks up my sleeve for doing a good job, bucking the system, and staying out of harm's way — all at the same time. It turns out there are a lot of teachers out there who fit this description. It is a hell of a juggling act and unless you enjoy politics, which I don't, I wouldn't suggest it. The problem is that unless you can "play the system" like a pro, you have to go underground. It can be all at once selfless, difficult, and unsafe. It means doing a truly splendid job in secret. The risk is that you'll be discovered and disciplined, whatever that means. In the rare instance in which you have understanding superiors, e.g. a good principal, you may come out OK. Otherwise ... Most of my friends in this situation bide their time, quit, and go into private consulting. I did the same thing when I was a therapist, so I guess I copped out with the rest of them.

These issues get me to think back on the teachers I had

throughout school. I don't remember many of them. I tend to recall the best and the worst and I suppose that's natural. I also think if I had a few more like the best I would have enjoyed and profited more from my formal education. I even, while remembering them fondly, wonder what they must have gone through at the time. As it now stands, though, most of my work is in spite of what I learned in school rather than the result of it. What a shame. Though it is sometimes devious fun to make a living based on the inadequacies of my past lousy teachers, I know there are easier, more enjoyable ways. I also fear that I'll hurt the good ones. I doubt it though. They probably know who they are.

Part of my nature is to respond to others. I don't ignore life well. I also generally look for what I see around me that doesn't make sense. Then I try and fix it, while staying out of trouble as much as possible. I occasionally envy those robot-like people who can just ignore the chaotic destructiveness around them. They have trained themselves well. They have learned to be blind, deaf, and dumb (in more ways than one). Some of them did it to learn to control the pain. Good hypnotists teach the same procedures to people in *physical* pain. It works just as well. So, those whose fear and pain was getting the best of them, I can sometimes forgive. When people's feelings get out of hand, and they have no other way to cope, turning them off can be a healthy response. But those who shut down their humanness out of laziness I have no use for at all.

I have less use for those who teach laziness to children, their own or other peoples'. We don't need another generation of robots. Psychological laziness is a terrible epidemic. One of the co-developers of NLP argues that much of his work is a response to that epidemic. It's a worthwhile response. Maybe we'll get lucky and there will be some sort of social backlash and people in general will become logical, creative, and decent. If teachers knew what to do with young minds we could do it.

I often respond to my own hopes and dreams with tremendous skepticism. I'd like to think it tempers my judgment but I know it can also temper my enthusiasm. It's a constant battle. On a good day I can produce a tremendous amount of good work. A good day usually starts with an internal reminder that there are no excuses. Then my motivation strategies kick in and I'm off. I think that is what is meant by personal responsibility. I've been working on ways to isolate it and sneak it into the food chain.

Every communication theory I have run into attacks the notion of personal responsibility in one way or another. Most do it pretty well. NLP says the meaning of your communication is the response you get. Period. You have to decide whether that response is worth having or not. If it isn't, change what *you're* doing and get a different one. This way of thinking about it takes away the excuses you use for other people's misunderstanding. It also places it back firmly where it belongs: on your shoulders. Or, more precisely, in your mouth. No more, as one of my friends says, "donating responsibility." If you need to draw a picture to get the (whichever) fool to understand you, do it. If you don't, you get to be the fool.

I still laugh out loud when I hear people talk about listening skills being so important. Not because they aren't, mind you, just that they are only the tip of the iceberg. How about the reverse: skills necessary to get people to listen to you in the first place? What of the ones to organize information into the right sizes and shapes? Those are kind of useful, too. Certainly people listen badly, but they do so much more even worse. Let's not let our inadequacies become unbalanced. If we do we'll have even more to be skeptical about.

Skepticism can be turned around on itself in an interesting way. My friend Robert Dilts loves to teach people about counter-examples. It is a really deceptively simple though unbelievably powerful concept. Rather than disagreeing with someone directly, Robert will usually try to get that person to come up with an instance in their experience that flies in the face of their own argument. These generally take one of two different forms, but they boil down to something like, "Has there ever been a time when what you are saying was *not* true?" If you phrase the question just right you can really find

out what assumptions lie hidden beneath the surface of someone's point of view. Assumptions, as we all know, can be the
underlying source of many disagreements.

He gives the example of talking with a doctor who was about
to put Robert's mother on a potentially toxic hormone treatment for her "terminal" cancer. Robert and his family were
uncertain about the necessity of this treatment, though the
doctor insisted it was necessary. In trying to clarify the available options, Robert asked the doctor a brilliant question. He
wanted to know how the doctor would know when it was time
to *stop* the treatment. The question was so unusual that the
doctor was not sure what he meant. Robert repeated the question once or twice. The doctor then responded with, "Well,
when it stops working."[2]

With that rather unpleasant presupposition now clearly
stated, it was obvious that even the doctor who was insisting
on the treatment had little faith in it. Robert's continued questioning and clarification helped the medical staff, and his
family, make informed and intelligent decisions under some
very difficult circumstances. Mostly his unique contribution
was in clarifying everyone's thinking about health and disease. His mother improved rapidly. Three years later she is still
in remission. They decided against the hormone treatment.

One of the stumbling blocks with doctors, therapists,
teachers, and all professionals is that they get caught in their
own routines. This doesn't mean they are bad people. It is very
easy to just "do what you do." Unfortunately, in this world of
unique individuals, "what you do" may have nothing to do
with "what they need." Our great successes often convince us
that we have found the true secret to whatever we are doing.
That is a very limiting, and obviously in some cases needless,
way to think. Careful thought and good questions can always
help.

When I was in training one of my instructors gave us a rule to
work by. The stretch rule goes: Once you absolutely know how
to do a job in a particular way, you are no longer allowed to do it
that way.[3] You can always fall back on it later if you need to.

This forces you to keep developing your talents and prevents complacency.

The problem with most professionals, including teachers, is that they haven't been given the equipment, either in skills or strategies of approach, to be able to apply this notion. In fact they often don't know what to do to begin with. We have the technology for teachers to be able to make that quantum leap now. NLP training can build in flexibility. This is a skill whose time has come. It is also an interesting way to give people the tools and the responsibility for their own training. People find it much more rewarding when they can be successful and secure at the same time that they are experimenting. Many of my students complain that they have *too many* choices about what to do in working with people. It's a problem I would like to share with everyone. NLP offers that, but it is a lot of new learning. Oddly, I find myself wanting to apologize to teachers for asking them to learn something new, again.

That is a strange feeling aside from the paradox. The implications are frightening. These must be the same feelings people have when they talk about competency tests for their childrens' teachers. No one wants to make teachers' jobs harder or less secure. Everyone knows it's a demanding job. They just want what's best for the kids.

By the same token, no one I know of has ever rebelled more against tests of this sort than the teachers of America. I know about all the political issues, the problems about who will make up and grade the tests, how they will be used, etc. I just think it would be great if teachers would take the whole idea as a rewarding challenge. One they could learn, and grow from, much less get paid better for. I think it is the concept of testing itself that is the real issue. I wonder what educational system gave us these headaches. I also wonder how these underlying attitudes toward test-taking come across to our children, consciously and unconsciously.

The heart of teaching is modeling. A teacher is a model for students, for better or worse. Most of us realize this in one way or another. It is amazing to me that our educational system has spent so little time teaching teachers to be models. More amazing is that they have not studied the modeling process itself. Most of that has been left up to social psychologists. And they have not studied it on enough different levels to make a dent in what is potentially there. NLPers seem to be the first to take the idea really seriously. Now business and industry, the psychotherapies, the military, and others are buying it from us. It is as if it were "ours" in a sense. How silly.

I recently read an interview of a great chemist who was complaining about the competition among researchers. On the one hand I agreed with him that it has brought about lots of the negatives of competition such as cheating, stealing, false promises, and second-rate (hurry up before someone else discovers this) work. On the other hand, lots of important breakthroughs have been the result of people from divergent fields jumping in to rummage around in the theoretical territories of others. That is the history of NLP. I'd sure love to have a band of energetic teachers get together and learn this stuff. If they worked at it they could do a lot better with it than I ever could. They would also undoubtedly see applications in their field that I never would.

One of my dreams is for that band of teachers to decide what an educated person really is. Then they could build useful models of how to get to be one. I would love to have them figure out how to get first graders to think about health and disease like Robert and his mother do. They could teach it along with spelling. In fact, my understanding is that some of the same thought processes are at the core of good spelling and good health. Of course, when you talk about teaching people to use their brains lots of previously divergent ideas get connected.

My personal bias is that what we need to do with children, before anything else, is teach them to think and learn. That means we'll have to learn first. It turns out, though, that we now know enough of the basics to begin the process. Admittedly we are still in our own kindergarten, but we know enough to make a real difference already. Besides, I remember kindergarten as a lot of fun. I am really looking forward to going through this new education we are embarking on. It has to be more productive and enjoyable than the first one I went through. And the way technology is advancing, much more interesting.

Throughout this second volume you will have continued opportunities to think differently. You will get to find out that you have been pretty dumb in some ways and real smart in others. Take it all if you can. You will find use for it somewhere, sometime. Feel free to experiment in your own ways. Volume III is an entire book of experiments for you. But you don't need to wait. You need to learn from your own experience. The only way to have any is to make it. You may enjoy it more if you trust your instincts along with what you see, hear, and feel. Trust all maps only as far as they take you to where you want to go. From there, you're on your own.

Notes

Chapter 1

1. See *How Real Is Real?* by Paul Watzlawick, New York, Random House, 1976, p. 50 -note.
2. Dilts, Robert, "Applications of NLP in Health," in *Applications of Neuro-Linguistic Programming*, Meta Publications, Cupertino, Ca., 1983, p. 13.
3. This was suggested by John Grinder.

CHAPTER 2

SHOOTING TARGETS, NOT FEET

Before we begin, I'd like to tell you a story. Several years ago I was watching an old episode of Columbo, with Peter Falk on The Late Show. I usually enjoyed this show because I am one of those people who loves mysteries. It is only for the simple reason that I am always dumbfounded by the people who figure out the puzzle. I never know until the famous scene in the drawing room, what the hell happened. You know, that's where the brilliant detective is going into excruciating details about the motives, means, and actions of the butler, the maiden aunt, assorted wormy relatives, and whoever else has been lurking about. And he cracks the case on the spot as if he were opening a Coke bottle. Then I feel like a jerk. I should have known all along, what's the matter with me, how could I miss such an obvious clue, etc., etc....

This was one of those episodes. It opens in this scientific think tank and research center. Everybody in the place is a brilliant and famous scientist. Major breakthroughs are achieved regularly. The action begins with an old scientist arguing with the director of the place, in private, regarding the director's son. The old scientist is telling the director, himself a scientist of great repute, that he knows the son's recent work really belonged to one of their colleagues who had recently died. He knows the son found the proverbial missing notebook. That the son does not really deserve the unnamed prize he is to collect in Stockholm. The son is truly a theory thief and he is going to blow the whistle, even if it costs him his position. We scientists have our integrity and all that, you know. The director/father says he can't have that. The old scientist storms out. The father watches him through the dark, sneaks out, gets in his car and runs the old guy down. End of whistle-blower. End of impending public truthfulness, and shame, for father and son. The father protects the son.

At this point, the director/father has a problem. It seems dead bodies aren't a usual occurrence here, and he needs to make it look logical. He takes the body inside the victim's own house, knocks the living room around a bit, takes a few things. His plan is to try to make it look as if the man surprised a burglar and got beaten to death for his trouble. He is fairly good at this sort of track covering, though one wonders where he got the practice.

At any rate, next we have police milling about doing various detective activities. "Take this down to the lab boys" and all that. In wanders the wily, but disheveled as usual, Lieutenant Columbo. Several of the boys say "Hi Lieutenant" and look at him shaking their heads in a fashion to which Columbo watchers have become accustomed. He asks the typical questions and noses about. He comes to an ashtray. In the ashtray is a single burned match. Columbo picks it up, looks at it as if he had never seen anything like it before. A seemingly irrelevant question or two to the other officers, a look as though he is daydreaming, and his typical absent-minded exit, muttering to himself.

Soon comes the inevitable scene between the wily Lieutenant and the think tank director/father/dastardly deed doer. It's all small talk. "A terrible tragedy...How long have you known the deceased...Anything more you can tell us..." Obvious stuff. They have a couple of cigars, Columbo acts suitably baffled and confused, the perpetrator gets irritated, nothing more. Yet, for seasoned Columbo watchers, it's apparent that Columbo now knows who did it. Also, like most seasoned viewers, I have no idea how he figured it out. I know I'll feel dumb later, but that's to be expected.

It is nearing the end of the show. Columbo has continued to hound the murderer unmercifully. It's what he does best, a real master. He has also discovered the son's pilferage of the deceased genius's notes that caused all the ruckus to begin with. The son, his girl friend, murderous father, various scientists and other laboratory research types, are in the laboratory, conveniently gathered. In burst the boys in blue, led by Lieutenant Columbo. Warrant held high, the wily detective arrests the *son* for the murder. The sticky-fingered young quasi-genius is dragged off, dazed and confused, lost in a sea of uniforms and lab coats. Now Columbo is beginning to get on *my* nerves and I haven't even killed anyone.

Everyone else has gone down to headquarters for the usual processing. Columbo and the real murderer are the only ones left. I wonder for a brief moment why Columbo is loitering around here when all the action has gone "downtown." My curiosity is soon answered. Dejected, Columbo's true quarry confesses to save his son from the murder rap. Now I am less irritated. The detective again has my awe and deepest respect.

Columbo tells the man he knew the father would protect the son. He knew the father protected the son from the embarrassing publicity of the filched discoveries, so he would follow suit again. "The father protects the son," he says knowingly. He also admits the blackmailed confession may not have been his most elegant move, but it was effective.

"But how did you know?" are the familiar, mandatory words from the mouth of the foiled felon. "It was supposed to look like a burglar did it," he offers somewhat sheepishly. "Yeah," I utter in agreement, as if I am as much a part of the scene as he is, and therefore equally entitled to an explanation. I put down my popcorn. The brilliant detective deserves my utmost attention.

Columbo sits down on some steps in the hallway. His newly bagged prey joins him. They light up a couple more cigars. I realize Columbo will have to spend several minutes milking this one for all it's worth. This *is* television after all. "I suspected you 10 minutes after I met you," he says triumphantly. He mentions that first cigar they shared in the man's office when they met. He holds up the match he just used to light their cigars. We notice that the match is burned almost all the way to the bottom. A true finger-scorcher. I remember my father's cigars and wonder if I can somehow use this crucial information to my best advantage in the future — but set aside the thought as the detective continues. "Only a cigar burns a match all the way down like that," he explains, as if the scientist should be appropriately impressed with Columbo's rather formidable powers of observation. It turns out that neither the victim, son, other personnel, nor anyone else involved smokes cigars. Columbo goes into excruciating detail about who smokes what, and how they ignite their various vices. He says he found a match burned just like the one he is holding in the ashtray at the scene of the crime. The muddled murderer looks at Columbo like he is a raving lunatic. He points out that smoking is absolutely irrelevant and Columbo is clouding the issue along with the hallway. Besides, why isn't he out combing the countryside, looking for a burglar with a bloody blunt instrument or something? I am still in agreement with the reasoning of the bad guy — truly an unenviable position.

Columbo looks him dead in the eye. Now it's coming. He says, "I never believed it was a burglary from the start. I couldn't give a hoot in hell about a burglary." All of this is said with truly uncommon emphasis for the detective. All humility has faded now, as he prepares to lower the boom. He says in his most deadly earnest tone, "No sir, I never was looking for a *burglar*. I was looking for a *cigar smoker!*"

I find the structure of the detective's approach somehow familiar, though I have yet to catch my first red-faced murderer. Interesting is the fact that, as in most of his cases, he spent his time looking for something that seemed irrelevant to everyone else. He starts in the same place though: the scene of the crime. He has the same data, so to speak, as the other officers. But he looks at it differently.

He goes first to the one thing that seems out of place. As I said in Volume I, we notice differences. That is the way our sensory apparatus is arranged. Knowing that it is a difference, and then focusing on that, is what sends him in the direction he goes. Columbo always finds the difference that makes a difference.[1]

His next step is to ask himself some questions. You can bet his questions are always different from anyone else's. His telltale faraway look tells us the wheels are turning. At some point he has to ask himself a question that goes something like: "How is it possible that this piece of evidence got to this place at this time?" In other words how *could* it fit and still make sense? This is a key question. It is as if he is following a map that all of a sudden no longer works. There is something in the road that doesn't belong here according to the map. Everyone else *ignores* the obstacle. If it hadn't been for the Lieutenant they would probably have thrown it (the match) out. The wily detective throws out the map. In essence he must have said to himself, "The burglary map led us in the wrong direction. Let's pull out the murder map and see where it leads."

Once he has asked himself these questions, and come to his new conclusions, he can begin the task at hand. He has to gather new information, because he is on a new path. He asks everyone about their smoking habits. He also checks to see which one of these unlucky people will join him in a fateful cigar. This makes sense only in the context of a murder, not a burglary. Since no one else knows it's a murder and not a burglary, they think Columbo is a little out of context. Some people get drugs for that, but since he is the Lieutenant ... well, never mind. Now he has gathered the relevant information about who he is dealing with, by process of elimination. He has also carefully watched everyone's responses to him, as he always does. His outlandish behavior always serves him well. Characteristically, his adversaries seldom see the humor in their respective predicaments.

Once the cigar charade is finished, he knows who his man is. Next he digs up the motive. That's obviously the easy part for him. He knows what he is looking for and he knows where to look. He discovers the old "lost notebook" of many a mystery. Routine.

Now he has to set up the conditions of his experiment to put his current conclusions to the test. He has not only isolated the motive, but he has at the same time found a crucial pattern in the behavior of his target. "The father protects the son." He also has a model for how to get the father to tip his hand. He simply has to threaten the son, just as the murder victim had done. In addition, he has the perfect excuse: the son really had the lost notebook, so the finger of guilt ought logically to point in his direction anyway. Columbo simply plays his cards, and waits for his sucker to fold. Then, like all good TV heroes, he has to gloat just a little. We wouldn't feel complete otherwise.

Teachers haven't been effectively taught what is worth looking for. Sure they get a lot of courses that are supposed to tell them what and how to think in a variety of situations. But the constraints they are put under very effectively undo any good that might have been gained. The rare course that attempts to instill flexibility of thinking and action is usually squashed under waves of useless theory, guidelines, and rules.

Teachers' constraints come in the form of the context they walk into and the maps they are given. Lesson plans, tests, reports, and the like tend to guide the thinking of teachers as well as students. Like all of us, they notice things that seem *way* out of place. Perfect test scores, really low ones. Some will notice really great behavior sometimes, gross misbehavior others. But they haven't been taught what to look for besides these obvious violations of the norms. Or what to ask, do, or think. Mostly they don't take the systematic approach they need when they want something to be different. Worst of all, they seldom know what they have when they have it. Teachers, like most psychologists, researchers, or policemen, are out looking for burglars. If only they would notice the oddly burned match and seek out the cigar smoker. He is right there in front of them.

One of the best ways to teach people to think in these alternative frameworks is to get them to be specific. That means in their thinking, their questions, and their goals. The old saying goes, "If you don't know what you're looking for, it will be hard to find it." Even if you do, you might not recognize it.

In NLP we talk a lot about outcomes. A clearly stated one gives you a clear target to shoot for. Though most of us don't need to get a confession out of a murderer, we certainly do like to get certain responses out of the people we deal with. That is what teaching is all about. Getting responses. The ones teachers go for, though, are usually fairly rigidly prescribed. No wonder so many kids get labeled as disabled. They just haven't given the prescribed responses. That is not to say some responses aren't worthwhile in general, just that you are not likely to get them from everyone in the same fashion at the same time. That's life.

NLPers have spent a great deal of time to come up with conditions that define a "well-formed" outcome. Essentially this means one that is so specific that there is no room left for misunderstanding or misinterpretation. Though I probably just stated the impossible, let's look at this idea a little closer.

When we talk about outcomes, we are talking about careful planning. This is something every schoolteacher knows is important. But we are not just talking about planning what you will do. We are also talking about being sure you know exactly what results you want, and how you will recognize them. Also, what you will do if the results don't match your expectations. And, that the result is worthwhile.

We have pretty good guidelines for this. Also, they are the kind you can do in your own head. That way you measure yourself against your own goals, not someone else's. The first of these guidelines is that an outcome be stated in the positive. This means that you will shoot for what you want, rather than what you don't want.

We all know that when you tell a child, or anyone, what not to do, you are less likely to get compliance than if you give specific instructions about what to do. The same goes for your own thinking. If you mutter to yourself that you are going to get that kid to stop ... Well, you will do better if you mutter to yourself that you intend to get him or her to behave in a certain way, rather than stop "mis"-behaving. It is not possible to not behave. So pick the behaviors you think are worthwhile and try to get people to give you those.

Some examples might be to get a child to get a certain number of words correct on a spelling test. Or to get two children to cooperate with one another long enough to finish some task. Perhaps you want someone to sit quietly and work on a particular project for a minimum amount of time that you have chosen. These are all stated in the positive. We could have stated them differently. We could have said we want that first child to stop doing so poorly on his spelling tests. We could have commented on our two uncooperatives by hoping they would quit their misbehavior. Our last child could easily have been told to stop squirming in his chair, quit getting distracted, etc.

This may seem like a silly distinction. To some people it may seem that to not do one thing automatically means do another. But *which* other? Try this for a moment: Do your best to *not* think of a pink and blue elephant at all as you read this sentence. How did you do? To "not" think of something, you first have to access a thought of that very something in your mind, to know what not to do. It is a true double bind. The only way to "not" think of something is to actively think of something else instead. Period. Why not just give them the something else in the first place?

Our language includes negation for convenience of speech, not thought. Negation in speech tells people what you want them to not do. They then have the task of figuring out the alternatives that will be acceptable to you. If you simply tell them that the first time, you provide them the thought, literally. They will be forced to access a thought or image about what you have asked them to do, as opposed to what you wish them to not do. People are more likely to do what is in their heads than what is not. Using negation in your language forces into the heads of your listeners exactly what you don't want to be there. Changing your language will directly change people's thinking. That will help you to guide their behavior. When you begin to actively plan your own behavior, this whole idea will make even more sense.

Speaking of your own behavior, this is the second area of our conditions for well-formed outcomes. An outcome must be related to what the person involved can do. This is as opposed to what you hope for from others. When Johnny comes up and tells you to get Jimmy to stop whatever obnoxious thing Jimmy is doing, how often do you hear yourself saying, "Don't you worry about Jimmy, you just take care of yourself." We always expect this of children, so how about ourselves? In other words, if you want that child to sit still longer, you first have to decide what *you* can do to get him or her to be able to do that.

Rather than only telling Jimmy what he needs to do differently, begin with yourself. *How* you tell Jimmy what you want can obviously be just as important as *what* you tell him. Though everyone knows this, it is something that has to be repeated and practiced. When you make it a part of your thinking, you will find that you take much more responsibility for your own actions. Consequently, you will get more accomplished. The meaning of your communication is the response you get. Period. If you don't like what you get, the only way to get something else is to change your communication.

Which brings us to our third rule. To know if you got what you wanted, you first have to know what it looks and sounds like. This is where we focus on specific behavior. For example, you can easily recognize 11 correctly spelled words. You will know by the clock if you had 20 minutes of cooperation or attention to a single task. Those are different than looking for a "new attitude." People used to march kids into my office to get one of those on a regular basis. I would routinely search through my desk drawers intently. Then I would turn to the exasperated adult and apologize for being fresh out. It usually made my point.

Behavior is something that can be specified. A person does one thing or they do another. If you use your head you can always come up with what you want in very clear terms. That way you'll know when you get it. Also, when you communicate to your students, in the same clear terms, they will know when they are doing what you expect. Many teachers get very angry at a kid who constantly asks: "Am I doing this the way you want?" Sometimes the kid is trying to drive the teacher to an early retirement. More often than not, though, he or she really doesn't know. Ultimately that understanding has to be the teacher's responsibility. If everyone knows the measure of success for any task well ahead of time, there will be far fewer misunderstandings later. This is another one of those points that everyone knows, but few act on. When people are under pressure, this is especially true.

The next rule has to do with when and where specific behavior is expected. Most of the things teachers work on with children are deceptively obvious with respect to time and place. Clearly, you take the spelling test when it is given. You get wild and crazy at recess or when you have a "substitute," not when you are taking a math test. You keep your eyes on your own paper whenever the child next to you knows the right answer, and so forth. But there are instances when this is an important consideration that would not normally be apparent. Time and place are vital considerations when you are helping someone to make major changes in the *structure* of their thinking or behavior. This is yet another way of saying that the context of any behavior is just as crucial as the behavior itself.

I know that seems a little out of context itself. Let's try an example. A good one is learning spelling. In Volume I the Spelling Strategy was included in the back of the book. It is a method for getting kids to make, literally, visual images of the words they are to spell. When they are asked the word, they move their eyes to the position in which they best see internal images, then read the word from their own picture. *All* good spellers do it that way, necessarily, since words aren't always spelled the way they sound. This same strategy is good for visual memorization tasks such as multiplication tables, names and dates, and so forth. It is absolutely lousy for some other things. Learning to sing is one of them. That is a task in which, while learning, hearing your own external voice is crucial — especially for the poor music teacher who has to listen to a room full of untrained voices. His job is to get the ears trained along with the throats. The Spelling Strategy is also lousy for some abstract reasoning tasks. In those it is necessary to manipulate and alter internal images, rather than hold them constant. Creativity requires some very different internal mental structures than memorization and repetition. I am sure you can think of lots of other obvious examples. We'll explore these things throughout this volume and the next.

We often talk about "ecology" in NLP. What we mean is similar to the biological term. Here, though, we are referring to both behavioral choices and individual circumstances. The best way to say it is: Give children useful ideas and information, but make sure you don't create new problems while solving old ones. The similarity to conservation is obvious. Don't build a dam to save water in one place, while drying up another place in the process.

A clear and timely example is in the recently renewed interest in "assertiveness training." Lots of people are teaching kids to speak up and stand up for themselves. This is, of course, a great idea. But it has its limits. It must be stressed that there are times when it is not wise or safe to do so. There are situations in which adults will not tolerate direct disobedience, no matter how righteous. Anyone who has done this work with people knows that if you tell a group of kids (or adults for that matter) to say everything that is on their minds to their parents, some of them will tell you it isn't safe. They may be right. It is necessary to teach where and when, as well as how, to be assertive. Getting along with peers often involves different skills than getting along with parents. There have been a number of horror stories about people, trained to say what they feel, showing up bruised and battered to the next assertiveness class. This is also one of those things that "everybody" knows except those other people....

An ecological understanding for a child will always include the bigger picture that surrounds his or her words and actions. The same goes for you. Obviously ecological considerations are closely related to putting things where and when they belong.

The last but definitely not least important rule is that each outcome you seek has several possible paths. This is flexibility. If you have only one choice, you have no choice at all. Two choices, quite often, is little more than a dilemma. Three is the start of something more practical.

Another story is in order. Several years ago a colleague and I were invited by a college basketball coach to help one of his stars. This newly acquired freshman had been one of the greatest high school basketball players in the country. Real pro material with a great future in sight. He began his first college season, however, in a terrible slump. The new star was benched. The coach said to us, "This kid is the finest athlete I have ever seen in 25 years of coaching. He has it all. But at the moment he is a complete spastic." We got the point.

When asked what he had tried so far he replied, "I've tried *everything* to get through to help him. He is not only the best athlete I've ever worked with, he is by far the smartest kid on the team, so I can't understand it. First I tried being a father to him. Then I was a big brother. Then I was a buddy. Last I tried being an asshole. Nothing worked. See? I've tried *everything*."

When we sat down with the despondent player we asked about his relationship with the coach. He said he had lost a great deal of respect for his once greatly admired coach. We asked him why. He said he felt that the coach treated him like an object instead of a person. He felt like he was just someone to try techniques on, without any real concern behind them. He thought the coach was more interested in his own ego than in the welfare of his players as individuals. That the coach just did things by the numbers. We asked how he had gotten that impression. He said, "It's obvious, first coach acted like a father, then a big brother, then a buddy, and then an asshole, now he's just about given up."

Now we *really* got the point. The coach's idea of "everything" and ours were a little bit different. Whenever I used to hear someone say, "I've tried everything" I would get this faraway, slightly devious look on my face. Then I would say something like, "How about tearing off your clothes and running naked through a shopping mall?" Not a graceful response perhaps, but people were less likely to use that ridiculous phrase around me after they'd heard that. There is no such thing as having tried everything.

So we have six main rules for developing a well-formed

outcome. I suggest you think about them in several areas of your life. They are just plain good planning skills. To summarize:

1. *State what you want in the positive.* Notice negation words in describing your outcomes such as "stop," "don't," "won't," "not," and "shouldn't," and restate your outcome sensibly.
2. *Relate the outcome to what you have to do,* not others. You can control yourself and therefore influence people based on *your* behavior and communication.
3. Be able to *verify, with specific behavior,* what will constitute success or failure to meet your goal. If a child's specific behavior is involved, make sure you *both* know what measurements are involved.
4. Make sure the *outcome* or behavior *occurs where* it belongs *and when it will be useful.* The *context* in which it happens is as important as the behavior itself.
5. Make sure that the new result maintains *only useful and safe by-products.* Then it is truly *ecological.*
6. Be aware of *several possible alternative ways* of getting the outcome you want. In other words, you have *multiple paths* for getting to your target.

A brief note about our basketball player. A little work got him out of his slump by the next morning. Using the principles outlined here for developing a well-formed outcome, and treating him with the respect he deserved, was most of what he needed. He knew exactly how he wanted to *feel* when he stepped out on the court. This feeling would be reflected in his performance. He knew it was ultimately *up to him,* and not the coach. He *knew how he would play* if he got out of the slump. And he *knew when and where* he needed to do it. In addition, he had to do so *within a new kind of relationship* with his coach. This was the *ecological* consideration. And we gave him *several methods* for helping himself. He did the real work once we showed him how. Why wouldn't he?

Notes

Chapter 2

1. "The difference that makes a difference" was a phrase often used by Gregory Bateson, one of the greatest anthropologists of our time. The founders of NLP were his colleagues. Study of his work is invaluable.

CHAPTER 3

NOW SEE HEAR ...

One of my interests is Eastern philosophy, culture, and martial arts. I used to enjoy watching Kung Fu, with David Carradine, and I must admit I still enjoy the reruns. What I always liked more than the fighting, though, were the dialogues between the young disciple Caine and his blind master, Po. Particularly telling for me was a well known scene in which the young Caine was looking dejected and confused. The master sensed something wrong and asked him about it. After some resistance the young student, with much embarrassment, confessed his worry. He said he did not know how the master could manage to live without the use of his eyes. He was overwhelmed by the sense of pain and loss he felt, in sympathy for his beloved teacher.

The old master embarked on one of his legendary demonstrations. He asked Caine several questions, forcing the young boy to use his own perceptions. He asked if he could hear the water rushing in a nearby stream. Caine admitted he did not. He asked if he could hear his own heartbeat. The student could not. He asked if he had noticed the grasshopper at his feet (which resulted in his nickname "Grasshopper"). Of course, the boy hadn't.

After several demonstrations by the great teacher, all of his unique abilities to perceive the world, the youngster was astonished as well as embarrassed. He asked, "But master, how is it possible that, lacking eyes, you see so much?" The wise old master replied, "How is it that, even with your eyes, you do not?"

The answer, of course, is the same reason the rest of us don't. Life hasn't trained us, and we have been far too lazy. Meta-Cation had a number of exercises in it designed to help sharpen your perceptiveness. That is because I firmly believe that sensory acuity skills are a prerequisite for doing useful work of any kind, involving learning or changing, with other people. Until your senses are at least partly trained, you can't effectively do much of anything except blunder around. There has been enough blundering by all of us and I don't wish to perpetuate it.

As I said in the last chapter, it does little good to do magnificent work with people if you don't know what effects it had. You can't know that if you don't know where to look. Even if you do know, but can't clearly perceive, you're in the same leaky boat. As you have probably detected, children are experts at sabotaging life preservers. That's my rather kind way of saying that if you haven't done the basic exercises in Meta-Cation, I suggest you do. They'll help you keep afloat.

Another thing that will help you to direct your attention is the way you think about what you are doing. If you look at your job as one in which you change people, it will help. By change, I am including all learning and growth, of course. If you think of it that way, maybe you won't think of it as difficult. The curse of our culture, as I have mentioned before, is in teaching generations of us that change has to be hard and painful. As long as you believe it, it's true. Thinking like a change agent, out to do good for people, can help free you from the curse. It will also make you automatically point your senses in the right directions.

I am reminded of the story of the famous drunk crawling around in the gutter late one night. Two passers-by notice his condition, as well as his position. One of them bravely asks him what he is doing and he gurgles in reply, "Looking for my wallet." Since they join in the search for a moment, but see no sign of a wallet, they ask where he lost it. He blubbers, "Around the corner in that alley." Incredulously the onlookers ask why he is looking here rather than in the alley. His, to himself logical, reply: "Because the light is so much better here ... "

It does little good to sharpen your senses if you don't know where to find what you are looking for. One of the great truths of life is that we generally look only where the light is best. As I have said ad nauseum, most people have never been taught *what* to notice in others. If they knew *where* to look it would become more obvious to them. That is the reason for all the sensory acuity exercises in Meta-Cation. Once you begin to notice the things that tell you what a person is experiencing internally, you start to see and hear it everywhere. Many students of NLP complain during their training, much to the gratification of their instructors, that the world becomes temporarily intolerable. They are overwhelmed with the constant signals and messages people barrage them with. They often complain and ask if we can "turn it down" for them. We apologize and mention "genies extracted from bottles" and other such fare ... Gradually, though, they learn to filter out the useless information and hone in on the really crucial things that people communicate.

Years ago a wise, somewhat wacky, old man implored: "Lose your mind, and come to your senses."[1] What he meant was to stop paying so much attention to your thoughts and interpretations about life, and just experience it for a change. He was keenly aware of the differences between content and form. He was also right about lending more credence to your senses than your thoughts, for some things. Often though, especially in the case of those who help other people to learn and change, we need to do a combination. It is that balance that is so important. Another brilliant man, like the one above a father of the human potential movement, told us that people's needs make sense only in terms of hierarchies.[2] You have to meet the basic ones first, before you go on to more advanced ones. It does little good to discuss the plight of man and human potential with a person who hasn't slept or eaten. He isn't likely to provide stimulating conversation. He also isn't likely to be very friendly.

Your perceptions need to follow these patterns as well. There really are orders in the world. This may sound strange, but it isn't. The order in which we use our senses and our interpretations of them will often determine their worth. For example, if you go to a doctor because you are ill, the doctor will notice several things first. She or he will make notes, at least mentally, about your general appearance, whether you appear well nourished, well rested, strong or weak, and so forth. This is good practice. Then the doctor will investigate specific complaints. The same needs to be common practice for teachers. To say that a child who is not well rested, properly nourished, adequately clothed, and the like will not learn as well as one who is, is almost too obvious to mention.

However, there is a lot more that you can tell by observing someone purely on the level of physiological functioning. As was mentioned in Meta-Cation so many times, if a child is not comfortable and at ease, he will also not likely learn what you present (with certain exceptions). It is easy enough to notice posture, breathing, muscle tension, and other useful indicators of present functioning. Once you have practiced really seeing and listening for these things, you can stop doing so consciously. You'll notice them automatically. A child holding his breath will be as obvious to you as if he or she were waving the proverbial red flag. The same goes for all the other indicators.

Once you become as adept at noticing these physiological signals as you need, the next step is to notice changes in consciousness. This was heavily implied, but not as clearly stated in Vol. I. I think if you got through that, and are reading this book, you are ready to go to this deeper level of analysis. The state of consciousness a person is in will determine sensory functioning, internal processing, and later recall. Those are pretty important things. In fact, they are the real basis of teaching and learning. The best lesson plan in the world is useless to a child not letting the information in to begin with. In addition, no amount of clever dialogue will help you if the child is scrambling everything inside his or her head. And clear input and accurate storage is useless if the information is locked away forever, beyond the child's capability of retrieval.

Again, these remarks may seem trivially obvious, but I have yet to meet a teacher that has ever been trained to use these concepts to anyone's advantage.

The most interesting thing about states, for me, is in what order they occur. People go through patterns in their states of consciousness just as they do in their thinking and behavior. In fact, these are all the same phenomena. If you remember the eye movement patterns from Meta-Cation, you will understand this more clearly. Entire books, most notably NLP, Vol. I, have been dedicated to perceiving, largely through eye movements, the order that people go through in accessing information from their own brains. A good argument can be made for the idea that each one of these movements coincides with a shift in consciousness.

Essentially, perceiving the states, and patterns of states, people go through gives you the ammunition you need to help them make changes. Or learn. If you can perceive the states and patterns that work best for a child, in a given situation, you can use them whenever that situation arises. By the same token, you can help change patterns that don't work where they are needed. This is a little heavy for now, so relax, we'll come back to ideas about states of consciousness and sequences later.

A central idea here is that it is what the child gets that counts, not what you do. You will only know what a child is getting if you have the perceptiveness to detect any changes. Essentially this means noticing first things first. In NLP we call that calibration. Just as you would calibrate a laboratory instrument by setting it to some basic value, you can notice certain basic responses or conditions of the children you are working with. It is like tuning a guitar. Once you have all the strings tuned to each other, you will notice if one of them goes out of tune, by comparison, later. If a child has really changed, you will know by comparing the child at that time to how they were at the beginning. It is just like those before and after pictures you see in magazines. But in this case you will be able to see, and have control over, both of the pictures.

I think I have sufficiently stressed the importance of paying attention to physiological indicators a child is showing you. That is the first thing I think you should calibrate to. Second, it is good to notice what state of consciousness the child is in. Again we will come back to more "how to's" later, but this is the second thing you need to notice. The next thing to look for are things that seem to affect the child's state or physiology. If you remember anchors, you know part of what I am talking about.[3] Then notice recurring sequences of behavior or other changes the child goes through. Once you have determined these things accurately, using your senses and good judgment, you can decide what changes you want to make. Then, after you have made the changes, you will have clear measures of their success. Let's look at this in list form:

1. Physiology
2. State(s) of consciousness
3. Things that affect physiology and states
4. Sequences of states and behaviors
5. The effectiveness of these, needed changes
6. What effect your input produces

That is what I mean by order. Obviously, also, if you have calibrated well enough to your students, you will know what kinds of behavior on your part helps or hinders their learning. This way you get to adjust yourself and be the flexible teacher you want to be. Matching your abilities to your students' needs will make you and them more effective. And that will make your job a lot more fun.

One recent evening I gave an introductory workshop on NLP to a small group of people. During an exercise, one of the participants mentioned that she has a "float studio." Since I had had some limited experience I explained some of the value and principles behind this to the people in the room.

The concept is based on sensory deprivation experiments done in the '60s in psychology labs. A float studio is a place with a sensory deprivation tank in it. You go and use the tank, usually for an hour, for a small fee. The tank itself is actually a wooden box about eight feet long, four feet wide, and four feet high. It has a door that somewhat resembles a hatch allowing you to get in and out freely. There is no latch on the door, but usually a large black rubber strip around the edge to prevent any light getting into the tank. From the outside, it resembles a large shipping crate, with a small door.

Inside the tank is about eight to ten inches of water. The water has been supersaturated with epsom salt, making it incredibly buoyant. Also the water is constantly filtered and continually heated so that it maintains an exact temperature of 92.5 to 93 degrees. This is the normal temperature of the outside surface of the skin on the human body. The air inside the tank is also filtered and heated in the same way, to the same temperature. The tank is completely lined with plastic, making it air- and watertight. So, from the inside, the tank somewhat resembles a completely enclosed, entirely darkened, high-tech bathtub.

The studio is usually in the back room of a store or somewhere equally peaceful and private. You will discuss the procedure with someone in the front, pay your fee, and be led into the studio. Then you are on your own. At this point you will undress and take a shower in the adjoining bathroom. This is important to keep the water completely clean for others, in addition to the filtering mechanism. Then if you have any cuts, for example a shaving nick, you would dab on a bit of petroleum jelly and cover it with a bandage. You want to avoid getting supersaturated salt water in an open sore, for obvious reasons. Next, with or without a bathing suit, which is up to you, you walk into the room with the tank. The room is also darkened to about the level of a movie theater at the beginning of a show. Then you open the door, climb in the tank, and close the door behind you. At this point you undoubtedly notice the resemblance the tank has to a coffin — then you remember that to get back out all you have to do is open the door. It just lifts open.

The first thing you notice when you get into the tank is the buoyancy of the water. It is a bit difficult to sit up because it feels almost as if the water wants to lift you out of it. You also generally notice the not unpleasant saltwater smell of the humid air. Then you slowly allow yourself to lie back and relax. As you do, the incredible dark catches your attention. You look around, as you would in a darkened theater, for any light to grab hold of, just to get your bearings. There isn't any, and you knew there wouldn't be, but the reaction is automatic. Then as you finish the slight splashing your movement has caused, you hear the quiet. It strikes you that you are in absolute dark and absolute silence.

Your feelings are the only place to focus your awareness. Naturally, you experiment. One of your first will be to feel where the water line is on your body. You are aware that you are floating absolutely flat at the surface of the water. No part of your body sinks, not arms, legs, feet, torso, or head. In that sense it is a little strange — not like floating on any water you have been in before. Then you realize that you don't feel "wet" on your body, or "dry." Searching your experience you come to the conclusion that, normally, your sense of moisture on your skin comes from the water being cooler or warmer than it was when you were dry. But in here there is *no* sensation of temperature at all. The air, the water, and your skin are all exactly the same. As you gently move your arms and hands up and down to feel the water clinging, you find that even that seems almost imperceptible. It is nearly impossible to tell where the water meets the air. This is something you did not anticipate and you find yourself fascinated at how hidden the obvious seems to be.

Next you graduate from attending to the feelings on the surface of your body to those inside. There is nothing to physically do but relax. So you try to see how relaxed you can get. It is almost a challenge. Immediately you begin to notice slight muscle tensions, especially in your chest and stomach. Maybe you realize that these are the muscles you would normally use to help keep you afloat if you were in a pool. So you slowly relax them. They aren't needed here. Then the tension at the back of your neck and shoulders becomes apparent. You slowly notice it more and more deeply and closely. Each individual muscle has its own characteristic feel. You may notice similar sensations in your hands and wrists, lower back, calves, and feet.

Slowly they relax, but maybe not quite as much as you would like. Mentally you chide yourself for not being able to do absolutely nothing, and just relax. Then you remember that giving yourself a bad time will only make it worse.

As you decide to let your body take care of itself you then become aware of the faintest sensation of light over your head. You focus your eyes and notice it is coming from the door to the tank. Mentally you try to imagine any light getting through that carefully fitted door, with the crack completely covered with a black rubber mat. You remember the dark room the tank is in. How can this be? Maybe you remember hearing that the human eye is extremely sensitive, and that when it is adapted to total darkness, the pupil opens as widely as possible to let in *any* light that is available, no matter how small. Curious. You notice that as you look you can actually see a faint corona of light all the way around what must be the door. It seems to become brighter and clearer as you watch — just like gradually seeing more clearly in a theater as you get used to the darkness while walking down the aisle.

Fascinated by your ability to see the light, you decide to close your eyes and experience as much total darkness as possible. You have probably noticed your internal dialog chattering away as you explore all these new marvels. Trying to shut it off is difficult, but you try your best. Then you notice something. A distant rumbling of some sort. You wonder if it is thunder outside. But, no, it doesn't quite sound like thunder and there is some rhythm to it. It is definitely coming from outside. Your hearing seems to reach out for the sound — to identify it. As you listen more closely, it almost sounds like cars going past. How could you hear cars? Then you realize that sound conducts through water as any wave or vibration would. You realize that you are feeling, in your ears, the sound of the tires going by on the street out front. The vibrations carry through the ground and are transmitted through the water to your ears. Deprived of any other stimuli, they have become immensely sensitive, just like your eyes. You marvel at your own sensory acuity. You wonder if you will be able to maintain some of it later.

Next you notice sounds that are closer. You can feel your facial movements as you move your eyes and head to see the light and hear whatever sounds are there. You notice a strange, almost squeaking noise, as you open and close your eyes. Exaggerating the movement it is immediately apparent that you can hear the sound of your skin moving and stretching on your face. It is almost unbelievable at first. But it is undeniable. A little trial and error confirms it. You can actually hear yourself blink.

Directing your hearing away from this and holding still, so as not to distract yourself, you begin to listen for any other sounds your body is making. An occasional rumbling from your stomach is apparent. It sounds oddly muffled through the water. Then you realize a faint, rhythmic, pulsation coming from near your ears. You try to pinpoint the exact location but you can't. You realize it is coming from everywhere, but is easiest to hear around the area of your ears. It is your own *heartbeat*. As you listen it becomes stronger, clearer, louder. The feeling is intense, emotional, complete. You feel as if you have really just met your body in a way you never thought possible. Your head swims with awareness, oneness, satisfaction, wonder ...

There is a faint but clear knock on the outside of the box. It is gentle, respectful, but final. It is time to get out. You wonder if it has really been an hour. Time has become a foreign consideration. You feel yourself beginning to stir inside — like waking up when you don't want to. Then you remind yourself not to struggle. Stay relaxed, slow, calm. Maybe you are a bit disappointed at your inability to physically relax certain areas of your body. You notice the tension at the back of your neck is now a dull pain. It reminds you how long it has been since you really relaxed. You wish you had relaxed as much as you intended, instead of playing with your senses. You are torn between congratulating yourself for your increased awareness and complaining, internally, about the way you missed the opportunity to let all of your muscles *really* let go. Then you try to sit up.

Your final surprise is that you can't, at least not yet. Your entire body feels like lead. You can barely lift your arms and head. The super-buoyant water throws you back, almost comically. So you rest a moment on your elbows, gathering the strength to move. Very slowly you sit up again. You turn to lean against the side of the tank, getting ready to stand and get out. As you climb out you feel weak, almost out of control. Even gravity seems to conspire against you. Your motions are very fluid, but not well coordinated. The slightly cooler air is startling, nearly assaultive. You talk yourself, logically, out of feeling a chill. This room seems almost as bright as daylight, though you know it is really pretty dark.

You go to get your clothes. Sitting down to put on socks never seemed such a chore until now. You can hear other people talking, moving, breathing as you walk into the office in front. The light is almost too painful to stand, but your eyes adapt quickly. Sounds are bouncing around you like you were in a swarm of insects. You expect people to move slowly to match your internal clock. Then you realize they are trying, having been there themselves. You also know they can only guess at your state. You sit down and share your experience. Sheepishly you ask if you are crazy to have thought you could see and hear what you have. They assure you you aren't, at least not for that. Slowly, you get up to leave. You want the world to conform to your sensitivity, but know it won't. For the rest of the day you hold on to as much as you can of your experience. And remind yourself how it *can* be.

Notes

Chapter 3

1. Fritz Perls, the father of Gestalt Therapy, was noted for this and other aphorisms. He also was noted for knowing how to make a point.
2. Abraham Maslow.
3. See *Meta-Cation*, Chapter 2 and Appendix III in this volume.

CHAPTER 4

DISCOVERING DISCOVERY

One of my other passions, besides those I have mentioned, is reading or hearing the thoughts of people I admire. I get several magazines primarily for the interviews. One of these is *New Age Journal.* A recent issue contained an interview with a woman I have admired for years. Liv Ullman, in my opinion, is the greatest living actress. What I did not know is that she is also a great humanitarian. Since 1980 she has been UNICEF"s official Ambassador of Goodwill, the first woman to hold such a position. She is deeply committed to children and their needs, whether those needs are food, or food for thought. In the interview she described an example of brilliant teaching. Her words say it better than I could:

> My daughter told me when she was ten or so that her teacher had done something marvelous: she said they were going to have a lesson about awareness of the world. This was in a school in Norway. Everybody was to bring some wonderful cakes and things from home, and in the intermission all the goodies were collected by the teacher. And she said, "The biggest part of the group, you are the Third World." Then to the smaller group, "You are the Iron Curtain countries." Then to the smallest group, "You are Europe and the United States."
>
> Then the smallest group — to which my daughter did

not belong — got most of the cakes. Then to the Iron Curtain countries, somewhat less was given, a lot less. Then to this big group where Linn was sitting, two or three cakes were given — or not even that. And they were furious! They said, "But we are the biggest group — how come we get so much less than them?" And the teacher just said, "If you belong, remember where you belong. This is how it is." Linn that day didn't really understand. The children bad-mouthed the teacher, thought she was crazy. It only dawned on them weeks later what had happened. And it's with Linn still as a part of her conscience.[1]

The essence of teaching anyone something new, is in providing them with a new experience. This experience must create in them new ways of thinking. This means changing their consciousness. We all do it all the time. To do it systematically, inescapably, humanely, and intelligently like the example above, is rare indeed. A lesson like that is worth ten thousand math problems. I would gladly trade every spelling word in the language for this kind of appreciation of the world.

To think that this sort of creativity is beyond the reach of most teachers is false. It flies in the face of its own existence. It is possible to think this way whenever you teach children. It is also possible to structure everything you do in this fashion. I know because I have had to learn to teach NLP that way. It wasn't easy and I have a confession to make. I am much more kind and traditional in print than I am in person. My students suffer a good bit. A lot of their beliefs get utterly shattered. They go through many different emotions. Some of those, ones they like and ones they don't like, get dredged to the surface when they least expect it. Something like life.

The idea of teaching directly through people's sensory experience is not new. Montessori was doing it, fairly well, at the turn of the century. Learning by discovery was, likewise, invented prior to last week. But these are ideas that are still only theoretical possibilities to most teachers. They can usually discuss the premises and concepts fairly decently. When it comes to putting them into practice, though, no dice. I some-times hear comments like, "Well the lesson plan didn't call for anything special at this point so ..." More often, and more sickening, I am told, "My principal would never allow any-thing as out of the ordinary as ... (whatever)." Whether these things are true is irrelevant. It is how you think about what you are doing that will guide you. If you really understand how to create worthwhile learning experiences for children, you will do it automatically, within the bounds of relative safety and propriety.

Again, the most important concept in discovery involves timing and the order in which you present information. I'll give you an example. Most professional training programs use a similar format, whether it is teacher training, management skills training, or anything else. Generally an instructor will present some new concept or skill. Next that skill will be justi-fied, either by research data, logic, or anecdote. Often this will be followed by a demonstration. Then, if the training is at all worthwhile, there will be some sort of experiential exercise, using the new concept. This can be anything from a discussion to a role playing practice session. I have no quarrel with this kind of presentation. It is adequate for most things and has been successfully used for years. However, it can be made better simply by changing the order of events.

I like to rely on discovery prior to explanation. I will begin by giving instructions to the participants. They will have an exer-cise to do. And it won't be a "role play" with them pretending to do anything. They will have a specific, overtly stated purpose in doing whatever I have asked them, and they will simply be themselves. The stated purpose may or may not have anything to do with what I am really getting them to learn, however. The experiment, and it is usually designed and explained as one, will take them through some strange and unusual experience. That is the major component of the word ,experiment: experience.

After they have done their assigned tasks, I will ask them to tell me what they learned. Invariably they will have disco-vered at least some portion of what I intended. Each person

will have done so according to their abilities and past experiences, of course. Only then will I begin to discuss with them
what I think they should know on an intellectual level. That,
however, is only provided that I think they learned enough. If
not, it is my responsibility to design another experiment,
demonstration, or whatever, to get them to the experiential
level they need. Explanation always comes after experience. I
may then demonstrate some aspect I think is important. From
this basis, the next experiment is begun, beginning the process
over again. So the order goes:

1. Experiment - discovery
2. Information gathering regarding their experience
3. Explanation, discussion, and possibly demonstration,
   based on discovery
4. Next experiment

If you remember the building rapport — leading — attending
— building more (BLAB) model from Meta-Cation Vol. I (pages
82-84) this may seem somewhat familiar. Essentially, the steps
can be thought of as the same. First establish rapport. Then
present the new information (i.e. lead), in this case the experiment. Next attend to your students and perceive their
responses to the experience. Then build further on it with
explanations, demonstrations, anchoring, future-pacing, and
the other useful tools you already know and use diligently (that
was only a suggestion).

The first step of establishing sufficient rapport has to be
stressed again. I could not pull off the things I do with my
training groups if I did not spend a lot of time and energy
nurturing mutual trust and respect. Learning by discovery can
be *very* frustrating. There are many times when students in
this approach can be totally unsure of what they are getting.
They can be confused, irritated, and even frightened. Within a
safe and respectful environment, though, all of this is acceptable, and can even be helpful.

One of my instructors was commenting on this set of phenomena once. He can be absolutely insufferable at times. He
can force people to learn painful lessons, whether they want to

or not. Some of the worst sometimes involve having to put up with him. When questioned about it, his reply was, "If you can put up with me, you can put up with anyone." The more involved explanation included the concepts of anchoring, states of consciousness, and memory. Essentially he said that most of us go through communication skills training in soft, warm, safe, loving environments. That is all right except for one thing. If you are a therapist, teacher, doctor or nurse, or other professional who has to deal with people in pain or other stressful situations, a strange set of circumstances can develop. You learn wonderful skills and practice them well, in that soft, warm, safe, loving environment. Then you are confronted with a person with whom you really need those skills. But if he is yelling and screaming, confused, scared, etc. and you are not in your soft, warm, safe, loving environment, you may not remember your skills.

We have all had the humbling experience of looking back on a badly handled situation, knowing exactly what we should have done, and wondering why we didn't. If you remember anchoring and state dependent learning, the reason should be obvious.[2] We think, experience, and remember differently under stress than we do in a soft, warm, safe, loving environment. Life will not necessarily conform to the setting of our training. If you are a teacher it is wise to take that into account.

With that said, I am not advocating that all learning be undertaken with a great measure of fear and pain. I am saying that certain learnings involve specific emotional content as well as information. One without the other is not the whole lesson. This will make much more sense to you after you go through some of the exercises in Volume III.

It is enough to know, for now, that when we teach, we alter reality. Again this may seem too dramatic, but it isn't. We all have internal maps of the world. These constantly change in response to our experience, if we have any sense. People who rigidly hang on to outmoded maps usually experience the world as a pretty hostile place. For them it is. This is because they see and hear each challenge to their map as a challenge to their personal integrity. People who can't separate their internal view of the world from their external sensory experience are in big trouble. This is the structure of hallucinations. The map and the territory are two different things. The world is full of people who keep trying to change the world so that their ridiculous and out-of-date maps of it will still work. Why so many of them seem to go into politics or administration is beyond the scope of this book.

Thinking about reality and its structure in people's thinking will help you to organize information. If you know how someone structures their internal reality, their map, you'll know what to do with the territory, your information, so that they'll take it. That was a mouthful. Suffice it to say that children will teach you how to teach them if you pay attention. Then you can structure experiences in which they'll naturally expand their maps to more closely match the world. Isn't that a pretty good definition of education?

Most of the teaching I have observed, or been assaulted with, is of a style that simply provides a new piece of reality. Whether I or anyone else takes it, or even understands it, seems to be determined by random chance. Or coercion. I am one of those people who needs to have both halves (in other words the whole thing) of my brain appreciated. I need the pieces of the puzzle presented to me in a logical order, and I need to see the whole puzzle before I'll change my internal map. Many other people are the same. Real discovery provides this. When someone discovers a worthwhile new reality in the right time and place, they'll take it.

Coercing students into a new reality is only one way of approaching the problem. That is what I find traditional education to be. "Learn, believe, memorize, and regurgitate this, or else." It works fine with compliant students. Often it short-changes their growth, however, because when they get older they will look back on their education more as "feeding" than learning. Original thought may be difficult if they don't get the opportunity to experience and practice it in school. This is a complaint I hear from many adults. They were "A" students. Now they are "C-" adults. This is especially true in the area of creative and fresh approaches. Life can be exceedingly dull without some change in it.

Teachers who are creative models for their students will do infinitely more for them than teachers who simply "present the material." The act of directing learning is in itself great teaching. That sounds self-evident but what I mean is that if you do a really creative job of guiding your students into new realities, they will learn to go there themselves later on. A creative teacher can model creativity for students. One way to begin this process is to understand how to set up useful learning experiences to begin with.

Some years ago John Grinder set down some terrific rules for designing exercises and learning experiences. I am deeply indebted to him for these ideas and hope to do them justice here. I suggest that you treat these as minimum guidelines for good learning experiences.

1. Make each experience you set up *possible.* It is not useful to embarrass kids with impossible tasks for any reason. There are better ways to get them to shoot for excellence.
2. *Gear each experience for success.* Kids should be able to do something right that you can compliment them on during each task.
3. Make sure that *each person involved* in the task *learns something.* This is aimed mostly at tasks that involve kids working together. You might include yourself in this as well (though that is only one of my never-ending list of suggestions).
4. Openly state something that you expect them to learn or find in each task. This is your *overt purpose* in having them do it.
5. Save at least one hidden thing you also expect them to learn. This is the *covert learning* I mentioned earlier that should be built into all teaching. This is the part you want them to discover for themselves.
6. Make sure that each task *stretch*es the students' abilities at least a little. Make it a challenge.
7. Make the learning lead to some new learning that will come later. This is called *heuristic* learning. The essence

of the idea is that answers are most useful when they lead to new, better, and more interesting questions.

Again, these are guidelines to help you outline experiences you design for kids to help them learn and think differently. Using all of the other techniques you have learned, the ones in Meta-Cation and the ones in Volume III, will help you do even more. Remember that you always begin by making sure you have established good rapport before you begin an experience with your kids. Beyond that your individual style, creativity, and perseverance will serve you in good stead.

I'd like to close this chapter on experiential learning with another example that I think displays a brilliant use of these concepts. See if you can find all seven of the principles outlined above, as well as a variety of others, in this work.

I have a good friend named Ed Meyer who has been working with children, in a variety of settings, for many years. Both of his parents were outstanding career schoolteachers and I think they influenced his ability to understand kids greatly. This is a story he told me several years ago that I have never forgotten. I have shared it with many people who work with children and it always seems to spark their understanding as well as their creativity. A number of them have shared it with others.

At the time of the particular set of events in this true story, Ed was the director of a string of halfway houses for problem children. The kids were all about 10 years old. One of the houses had four relatively new arrivals who were causing quite a stir. The staff was at their collective wits' end. They told Ed these kids were hopeless and would never learn to cooperate with anyone, least of all each other. Ed is one of those people you *never* say *never* or *hopeless* to. It just makes him weird.

He gathered up camping equipment for five people. A nice big tent for himself and two smaller ones. Each of these small ones was perfect for two kids to share. He gathered lanterns, food, a couple of good books for himself, and other necessary wilderness gear. Then he walked into the house, gathered up the four misfits, and announced to everyone, "We're going camping for the weekend, we'll be back Monday morning." He was followed out the door by four slightly crazed children and a lot of blank stares from staff members. He told me that he thought he also heard some strange mumblings about his sanity ...

They drove out to the woods and found a good spot. Ed got out of the van, unloaded the equipment, and stacked it neatly at the edge of the clearing. He turned to the kids and told them they were now two groups of two and assigned them to their respective teammates accordingly. He said he would show them how to do anything they needed to know. He was an expert at camping and would be a total resource for them. He also suggested that if they would cooperate with one another, they would have more fun.

They immediately became four wild 10-year-olds, on a weekend pass from the home, literally. Ed said, "Suit yourselves." He began the task of pitching his tent, gathering kindling and a few logs for the next day's breakfast, and generally preparing himself for a *very* comfortable evening. The kids laughed at his boring behavior. He made a few more suggestions about cooperation and teamwork, but reiterated that it was totally up to them how they wanted to handle things. He told them he really wanted them to learn about camping and enjoying the great outdoors.

At dusk the mosquitos were just beginning to get active. Ed's tent, including mosquito netting, lantern, good book, etc. was all set up. The kid's equipment was still where he had neatly left it. The kids were climbing trees, chasing each other with sticks, putting worms down each others backs, and so forth. Dark was approaching, so being a good camping guide, Ed made his suggestions a few more times. The kids responded as they had earlier. They told him not to worry about them, they knew how to take care of themselves.

Ed said, "OK kids, good night!" They watched a little bit startled as he climbed into his tent, closed it up nearly airtight, curled up with his good book, and had a very pleasant and quiet evening. He said he couldn't help but overhear their immediate reversion back to their precivilized customs and rituals. They continued to roughhouse until late that night.

When they got up the next morning it was about 8:00 a.m. Ed swears it was the smell of fresh brewed coffee, bacon and eggs, that aroused them. He knew this because he had called them several times to come if they wanted breakfast, but got no response. He also didn't think they slept too well since all four of them were huddled under one partially unfolded tent. None of them was very well covered, all were scratching numerous mosquito bites, and complaining about the cold, the dampness, each other, and life in general. They stumbled over to his nice campfire.

Unfortunately for them, as they did so Ed was pouring the last bit of hot coffee over the fire to "prevent the possibility of forest fire." He then took a big stretch and remarked about the wonderful night's sleep one gets under the stars. As he scraped the remains of his breakfast into the ashes he was of course stirring to prevent their rekindling he mentioned what a great book he had read last evening, and that he hoped they had just as terrific a night as he did. Before they could interrupt him he broke into an animated walk, with them tailing after him ...

"Nothing like a brisk morning walk through the woods," he bellowed. He announced that this was the nature walk he had planned for them. He diligently lectured them on the splendors of nature: the flowers, trees, birds, etc. He kept them as busy as possible until mid-afternoon. There was no time for naps and, indeed, not much for rest. They were so tired, they were ready to drop. They were hungry because they were only able to eat what they could manage during his "planned activities." It was enough to survive, but didn't even remotely match the breakfast he had dumped into the fire.

By late afternoon they were interrupting him frequently to rest, get water, have something to eat, etc. When they got back to the camp site, Ed commented on what an excellent spot it was to set up tents and have a fun weekend. He also made a comment or two about the high regard he had for good camping equipment, mosquito netting, a nice fire, the wonders of nature.

It was nearing dusk again as he pulled out another good

book to curl up with. This time, before he could get to his tent, he was barraged with questions. The kids asked him everything anyone could ever want to know about pitching a tent and avoiding insects. He used the opportunity to show them how to do everything in efficient two-person teams. He showed them how to gather kindling, what size logs to use for the next morning's fire, etc. He mentioned to them that he didn't want to interfere with their fun, so he would let them cook their own breakfast in the morning. He would be up nice and early if they had any questions.

The rest of the weekend was remarkably smooth. When they marched back into the house Monday morning, they were two teams of boys, with their humble wilderness guide. They efficiently carried their neatly arranged equipment to its proper storage area. They unloaded the van in an orderly manner, and went quickly to their rooms. They emerged moments later with their books, ready for school. The four of them bounded off to school as if nothing out of the ordinary had taken place.

The dumbfounded staff looked on. They asked Ed what he had done to cause this miraculous transformation. "Why, we went camping, of course. I told you we'd be back Monday morning in time for school. Well, here we are."

Notes

Chapter 4

1. Liv Ullman, quoted in "Liv Ullman: Making Choices," by Leonie Caldecott, *New Age Journal*, July, 1985, p. 30.
2. See *Meta-Cation*, Vol. I p. 29-30, and the note on p. 33, for an explanation of state-dependent learning related to anchoring.

CHAPTER 5

NLP TODAY

We have all known people who seem to be excellent at just about anything they do. They are great athletes, students, business people, and friends. Those activities are very different from each other but these people seem to be good at all of them. It often appears to us that they are just stronger, smarter, more clever or insightful, or just "gifted." But the gifts came, at least in part, from within. And I am convinced that we can all give ourselves the same ones.

If you pay attention, you find that these individuals have some important things in common. The first one is usually awareness. This means they know how to pay attention to what is going on around them. They also have an inner awareness. Seldom are they the numbed robots I talked about earlier. Awareness is free. We can all have it and use it. Using it well takes a bit of practice and training, but it is well worth the effort.

The second thing these people generally have plenty of is flexibility of behavior. That comes from flexibility in thinking. They are not afraid to let their thoughts wander in seemingly ridiculous directions. They are open to new ideas and willing to entertain just about any possibility. This doesn't mean they act on all of them, just that they consider them. Mistakes don't terrify them so they seem more willing to experiment with the unusual than the rest of us.

The third thing they seem to possess is a combination of motivation and perseverance. It seems to stem from having strong beliefs to begin with. Not rigid ones, necessarily, but strong ones. I think this means they don't give up too easily. I recently saw a quote from the acknowledged dean of management consultants, Peter Drucker, that went: "Whenever anything is being accomplished, it is being done, I have learned, by a monomaniac with a mission."[1] Successful people seem very willing to make lots of mistakes that they can learn from. I suppose that's a form of practice. They are anxious to carry out the plans they have organized and they seem to logically figure out the steps they need to take to get them accomplished. I would not be the first to point out how doing things, making mistakes, and learning from them, over and over, is crucial for success.

The fourth and possibly most important thing these people have is trust in their own experience. That doesn't mean that they never listen to others, just that they relate what people give them to what they already know or can verify. It's what I said earlier about ultimately deciding what to believe based on our own experience. We must trust our own eyes, ears, and feelings. Some people call this "following instincts," but I think we all know those instincts were learned. We're not born knowing how to make decisions. Some people never learn. Successful people usually learn early and well and they keep learning.

It's a little funny that I mentioned each of these characteristics as something that people "have." Then I went on to talk about what they "do." Ultimately I think that's the point. I believe we are all just as capable as each other, in most ways. Sure some people aren't tall enough to play professional basketball, but that's not what I mean. If we used the tools that I just talked about, we could be good at just about anything. It's sad, but often when I talk to people about strategies for success or achievement, I run into the same arguments (excuses). The list includes the following (but knows no bounds):

1. "Well, you don't really believe that WE could be as good as

THEM, do you?"

2. "Don't they have some special success gene or something? Isn't that what made them make better choices than the rest of us?"

3. "Don't they have some different sort of metabolism that makes them stay motivated and think more clearly than the rest of us?"

4. "Didn't they learn their flexibility, self-trust, awareness, and perseverance (take your pick):

    A. In the womb
    B. In the first few months of life
    C. In better schools
    D. From healthier families
    E. As a result of better psychosocial developmental cycles
    F. From lots of unconditional positive regard
    G. In (the proverbial) better environment
    H. Through magic
    I. All or some combination of the above"

5. "Aren't they JUST DIFFERENT?"

People can always find wonderful excuses for self-limitation and mediocrity, can't they? Even if the above reasons for success are based on good scientific reasoning, they are still irrelevant. For every problem you can think of there are many examples of people who have overcome it. Everyone has to overcome some imperfections. Some more than others. As I said earlier, many responses from people are predictable and boring. It would be nice never to hear any of the above list for the rest of my life. My current skepticism tells me to remain prepared to be polite, explain graciously, be "open" ... and maybe I'll get lucky. Hopefully, because you are reading this book, you know that you can learn, or teach, anything you need to. Teach your kids the same thing.

Neuro-Linguistic Programming began as the study of excellence itself. Certain extremely talented people were closely observed. Systematically, their language, nonverbal behavior, and overall approaches to their work were analyzed. As patterns began to emerge, these were categorized and studied in more detail. Soon a workable model of their behavior was formed. One that could be taught to others.

The state of NLP technology now is staggeringly thorough compared to its beginnings 10 years ago. Knowing how things generally work out, though, 10 years from now it will undoubtedly look childishly archaic. The most important thing to remember, though, is that NLP is not a theory or concept. It is a *model* based purely on observation and experience. As such it is constantly being changed as more experience is being gathered. Anything that doesn't work is pitched.

That is the nice thing about not having a theory to try to prove. It makes letting go of ideas, concepts, or techniques easy, if they prove useless or outdated. It also tends to make later refinements easier and more natural. The model truly gets simpler each year, rather than more cumbersome as theories tend to be. That isn't to say that we don't find a lot more information as time goes on. It's just that it gets better organized.

We are not so naive as to believe that any of the information is really "true," however. Ultimate truths don't fit into model building. Models are used only to guide people's thoughts and actions to worthwhile results. In that sense they are only maps, not the territory itself. The map is never the territory. Again, that is what allows us to refine the model. We are just updating our map based on new exploration of the territory.

NLP itself is human modeling, i.e. making models of and about humans, their thoughts and actions. The ultimate goal of NLP has always been to provide the design tools we need to make the best possible models of what people do that works. At this point we can pretty well create a model of how someone achieves something as long as we have access to that someone. It doesn't matter whether the something is worth modeling or not, the design tools are the same. In other words, it's just as easy to figure out how someone fails as how they succeed.

The original model that Bandler and Grinder developed, based on their early studies, is called the Meta-Model. This means, literally, model of a model. In this case the language someone uses is considered to be a model of their internal experience. This makes obvious sense and is why I spend so much time emphasizing the importance of *how* things are said, as well as *what* things. The Meta-Model is a model of the model: language. In actuality it is a system of questions, sometimes called challenges. Remember the Columbo story? If you know which questions to ask, you'll get where you need to go. The basic idea behind the Meta-Model was originally to discover how those special people they studied always seemed to be able to gather the right information. The Meta-Model is also used, now, to lead people in better directions. But the point is that the right questions are always a good place to start.

When we begin the process of helping someone change something, there are several things we want to know. One of these is their state of consciousness at the moment they are experiencing difficulty. We call this the *present state*. We don't call it the problem, block, or other such code word because we don't think about it that way. Again, we think about *outcomes*. It's another nice piece of the NLP model. Rather than making judgments about results, we just decide whether that result is worth having or not. If it is we try to get it again. If not, we try to get one that is, in this case a more useful state of consciousness. We call that one the *desired state*. The point here is that a person's state of consciousness will determine their experience and their behavior. It doesn't matter what they are doing at the time. They are in *some* state of consciousness. It either helps them or it doesn't.

So, in building a model of what someone is doing, worthwhile or not, we start with where they are and decide where they need to go. Present state, desired state. Remember, a state of consciousness is not a static entity. It can sure seem like one when you're stuck in it, but it isn't. It is an active process and can be easily altered to better fit the desired results. That's what is meant by the term altered state of consciousness, a state that is different from some other state. There are lots of different ones. Perhaps you know some people who demonstrated this state-altering phenomenon in the distant past known as the '60s ... I know some people who are still pretty altered to this day.

Another key idea here is that states don't just happen. They usually come in response to something else. That something else could be something on the outside or something internal. In general it is some combination. Since you know about anchors, from Meta-Cation, you know what I'm talking about. Also, since you know about anchors, it may be obvious to you that states aren't that difficult to control.

Most interesting is that often there is a series, or sequence, of events leading up to a particular state. We call this sequence either a strategy or a chain, depending on the form it takes. It is the build-up to an event that people are sometimes aware they go through just before IT happens. It doesn't matter what IT is. You can think of this as a higher level of analysis than states of consciousness themselves. Sequences of states. In addition, if you look at the ways these sequences occur in someone, often you will find interesting patterns. That is an even higher level of analysis.

The reason I bring up the ideas of different levels of analysis is that it helps me to organize this information for you. It also helps me organize it for me. Once you arrange information into levels and types, you always have another way of thinking about anything you do. Again, remember our wily detective friend. Thinking about murders and cigar smokers was more effective than thinking about burglaries and blunt instruments. They are different types of thinking, based on different types of information. Recognizing and using the pattern of the father protecting the son is a higher level of analysis than looking for more clues on the trail of the stolen notebook. This is the kind of thinking and analysis that all teachers could readily learn to use, if only *someone* would teach them logical types and levels.[2]

Well, since no one else has, I guess it's up to me. I think most of us recognize intuitively that there are different "levels" of experience, but we haven't spent the time to figure out what that really means. I break these down quite simply into a convenient set that helps guide my thinking, especially when I get stuck. Remember, this isn't "true," just very convenient and useful. I have a list of the *levels of internal experience*. In other words the things we can experience on the inside. It looks like this:

Beliefs
Contexts
Sequences
States
Sensory Modalities
Submodalities

I know this doesn't make sense to you yet, but it will. The list is organized from the general, at the top, to the specific, at the bottom. Or from large chunks to small ones, a la NLP. A brief description of each will get you started. By the end of Volume III this will be second nature to you.

Beliefs

The first level, beliefs, we are all familiar with. Once you are familiar with the other levels, you'll even know something about how they actually work inside our minds. But in this level we are including our generalizations, attitudes, opinions, etc. Or, to be blunt, our delusions.

Our beliefs actually resemble more systems of thinking, rather than conclusions based on actual information gathered through our senses. Many people, for that reason, refer to "belief systems" rather than attitudes, opinions, or even just beliefs. Those systems are mostly made up of experiences and decisions, often randomly stuck together with the vaguest of logic. Conventional sensibility rarely enters into most of the opinions formed by these decisions. Years ago Freud coined the term the "psychopathology of everyday life," the ridiculous, inexplicable behaviors we perform but can't explain. That isn't to say there is NO logic involved in any of this behavior, just not the conventional sort.

This is also the level of superstition. We are all superstitious in the sense that we act in these inexplicable ways, without common sense. Superstitions and delusions are really pretty much the same: ideas, based on some form of experience, usually forgotten, at least unavailable consciously, but as real to us and influential on our behavior as any agreed-upon reality. Or to quote the great philosopher George Carlin, "You know, we're all pretty weird."

What is frightening to most people when they deal with this level of experience, is that lack of apparent logic. Most of us think of ourselves as pretty sensible. When we behave without apparent reasonableness, we get edgy. What we should or shouldn't do is often decided based on our generalizations about life and existence. That's why our existential crises seem so overwhelming. Our behavior and experience of ourselves can be totally altered by one of these crises.[3]

Most of us get caught in the trap of trying to change our beliefs by using our best logic. We attempt to talk ourselves into feeling a certain way or believing a certain thing with our most leak-proof arguments. We forget that that isn't what created the "wrong thinking" to begin with. Therefore, very rarely will it have the desired effect. Understanding, in nauseating detail, every possible explanation for why we believe something usually solidifies it rather than making it change. If you don't agree, try as many different ways as you can think of to forget that stupid song you heard on the radio that you can't stand, but it keeps going in your mind all day, even though you know where you heard it, know it's irrelevant, would thoroughly enjoy crippling the person who wrote it, etc., etc., ... When you have finished that, and regained your ability to think rationally, consider the enjoyment you would get from strangling the person who told you that all you have to do is understand and clarify your attitudes — then all your problems (even your acne) will clear up. So much for rationality.

Contexts

This is the level of ideas, thoughts, and feelings about particular subjects and topics. It is a step more specific than the level of beliefs in general. It also includes actual sensory experience of contexts. For example, instead of talking about things in general that you should or should not do, here we are talking about whether you should or should not do a specific thing in a specific time and place. At some point when I described the rules for well-formed outcomes I mentioned that it was not enough to know what behavior you were shooting for, but also where and when it should occur: the context.

To put it in a positive light, some people believe they are going to succeed in life. That is a general belief (the kind you get from certain personal growth seminars, but don't worry, you can get well from it). To put this in some reasonable context, you may be able to get them to be specific enough to say, "I am going to succeed in my business, here in this town, by the end of next year." Better still is to get them to define what they mean by success, perhaps by putting a dollar amount of sales on paper. Now we have:

the context of business
specifically their business
in a stated environment
within a known time frame

They may be nuts, or even worse obnoxious about it, but at least they put the belief into a context we can all experience. Businesses have known activities and products, towns have boundaries, calendars give a measure of time. That way when they fail you have a clear basis for ridiculing them unmercifully, like they did to you.[4]

Sequences

One chunk size more specific than contexts is the level of sequences. As I said, most of us logically know that we don't just arrive at particular thoughts or feelings (states). We go through some series of steps to get there. Let's say for example that we were talking with our self-proclaimed, about-to-be-successful-in-the-next-year, obnoxious friend. We ask this person about what he or she has been doing and they describe their latest near-miss. In the very next breath they describe how good they are feeling about their new about-to-be accomplishments and how they are so relieved that they have finally made it. We would undoubtedly wonder, to ourselves, that there are several steps one would normally go through to get from the feeling of failure to the feeling of success. And how come they managed to skip them. This is to say nothing of wondering, possibly aloud, how they intend in the real world to go from failure to success without doing a few things in between.

Most of us have had the experience of going from one experience to a vastly different one. We also seem to know that there are usually several different feelings and thoughts that help us make the transition. Too quick a jump can be disorienting. People who move too fluidly from one to the other are often viewed strangely by the rest of us. We think they went to a bizarre seminar or something. Those who continually behave this way are often sent to a place with locked doors, bad food, and lots of strangers asking about childhood traumas.

The order in which we go through these steps on the inside will often determine the quality, as well as the quantity, of many of our experiences and abilities. If the sequences work smoothly to get us from one experience to a more useful one they are worthwhile having. If they don't, they can cause us grief. Since I will devote an entire chapter to this idea, we'll go on for now.

States

We have already talked about states a little, and we'll also spend a whole chapter on them later, but I'll be more explicit about this level of analysis now. In NLP we have a useful notation to indicate a particular state of consciousness. It is called the 4-tuple. This term only means that it's a single unit, made up of four parts.[5] These are:

V - Visual

A - Auditory
K - Kinesthetic
O-G - Olfactory-Gustatory

These are, of course, each of the five senses, as we discussed earlier. As a reminder, visual refers to our internal pictures, auditory to internal sounds, kinesthetic to feelings, olfactory-gustatory to smells and tastes respectively. A particular 4-tuple, or state of consciousness, is simply the sum of each of these four parts at a given time. Remember this is only a *description* of our *experience* of a state of consciousness. For anything we would use the concept for, this is more than sufficient. It doesn't include any verifiable *physiological* data because that isn't important for us. If you hooked people up to machines used for such purposes, though, each different 4-tuple would register differently. When you have trained your senses, internally and externally, you will be able to distinguish between states easily. Your own and other people's. Machines are fun but eyes and ears work too.

What is important is that we understand what states are, in terms we can easily use. That way when we go to alter them later, we will know what we are talking about in verifiable *sensory* terms. We can't always know when we have changed physiologically. We can know when we have changed something in our experience. That is at the heart of everything all of us do in teaching and changing people.

When one part of a 4-tuple, and therefore a state, has changed, it will have a ripple effect on the other parts. That is how we go from one state to another. A 4-tuple can be one step in a sequence. Again, we usually judge the value of the sequence by the usefulness of going from the first to the last state. If the last is better than the first, it was worth going through. If we have a well-formed outcome the first state might be the *present state* and the last the *desired state*. If we are really efficient about it, all the states in between would have some useful function, as well.

Sometimes what we're after isn't necessarily just going from a state we don't like to a more tolerable one. As in some of our previous examples we just want to be able to get to a particular state whenever we need to. Another way of saying that might be, "to be able to get to a particular state from any other state" (which seems to be more than some airlines can manage).

Then there is the task of maintaining a state as long as you want it. For some things, a brief moment is all you need. An example is that instantaneous response you have to avoid a car accident. Your state actually changes in that moment that you react. But when you need to write a chapter in a book, let's say, you may need a certain state for hours at a time. Some people have trouble maintaining their attention on one thing for more than a few moments. We call them names like childish, hyperactive, scattered, lunched, teenagers, etc. What is literally happening is that they are changing their states of consciousness so quickly, and with such fluidity, that those around them can't keep up. Robin Williams makes a fortune doing that on stage in front of lots of adults. It is just that he does it in a good context, i.e. when and where people pay for it.

In sum, there are times when we want to get from one state we don't like to one we do. Other times when we want to achieve a state just long enough to perform a specific task. Times when we highly value the ability to maintain a state for extended periods. There are states most of us would like to avoid (it's hard to resist mentioning certain parts of the East Coast). Finally, there are times when it is worthwhile to be able to fluidly go through a variety of states, quickly, at will. Understanding this level of analysis is very helpful in controlling thinking and behavior.

Sensory Modes

Each of the sensory modes, i.e. each portion of the 4-tuple, can be thought of as an independent part. Often, we are only aware of our internal visualizations to the exclusion of all else. The same can be true of each of the other senses. It is obvious how changing our awareness from one sense to another alters our total experience. That is a part of what we really mean when we talk about expanding (heightening, increasing, etc.)

our awareness. We often do so one sense at a time.

Undoubtedly you remember how much time was spent on this level in Meta-Cation. Representational systems are sensory modes. The kind of language, i.e. which representational systems a person uses in their speech at a given time, tells you which sensory mode he or she is consciously aware of. Accessing cues, for example the eye-movement patterns, tell you how the information is organized and retrieved from the unconscious. This kind of thinking is probably second nature to you by now but for review, see Meta-Cation, pages 88-101.

Submodalities

Different people in NLP, as in everything else, tend to have their favorite levels of analysis. Some people concentrate on one, or a few, to the exclusion of others. I like to keep them all in mind as much as possible when designing a worthwhile package for people. But I do have my favorite: the submodality level. In a sense it is the most powerful — not most important or best — just most powerful. A simple change at the submodality level can instantly change every other level, simultaneously and *permanently*.

The submodality level, in logic terms, is called the *form of content* level. So we are talking about a smaller chunk than each individual sensory mode. Within each sensory mode, there are a number of characteristics that make up the form of the content within that mode. That is why they are called *sub*modalities. For example, one of the submodalities of the visual sensory mode is brightness. Another is size. Another is color. You can change the brightness or size of a picture without changing the content. An 8" x 10" color glossy photograph looks different from a wallet-size black and white. But they could still be the same picture. That is what we mean by changing the *form* of the content, while leaving the content itself unchanged. The form or quality of the image will certainly govern the effect it has on us when we look at it. This goes for internal pictures often more dramatically than external ones.

We can also change auditory and kinesthetic submodalities. The different tones of voice people use certainly affect us. Changing them can affect us for the better or worse. This is just as true of our internal voices. The most interesting thing about submodalities, for me, is that changing a submodality in one sense, changes other ones in other senses. In other words, changing that wallet-size black and white to an 8″ x 10″ color glossy will change the way I *feel* when I look at the picture. This is what makes this such a powerful tool and level of analysis. Since I will also be spending an entire chapter on submodalities, I'll leave you in suspense for now.

The preceding has been some of what is in my head when I think about NLP. It helps me understand it and explain it to others. But it isn't the only way of thinking about it. It isn't "right," it's just my map. I find it useful. Perhaps others in NLP would quarrel with certain parts or descriptions. They may experience the territory differently. That's OK, maybe they'll help me to think more clearly and expand my understanding.

Also, I am aware that I am talking about things without giving you much experience here. This is the "what," not the "how," of the NLP model. "How" will come later and especially in the next volume. In the meantime I think it's important to have a framework to think in while you read more detailed information. Frameworks help me and seem to help most other people. I wish the pure discovery method I described earlier were as applicable in book form. You know, experiment first — explain later. I don't think it is. So the discovery will come in a different order, in smaller, more devious, chunks.

Small and devious chunks reminds me of some fun I had recently. A few weeks ago I had friends over for a barbecue. One of my friends just moved to this country from England and hasn't spent much time around computers. He asked me to show him mine. Well, to be honest, he asked me to show him some games. I pulled out a classic, public domain, game called Adventure. This was given to me by a friend and I had not really played it yet, though I had looked over the rather meager instructions.

We booted it up and began to play. There are no graphics in the game at all. In other words, it is a question and answer type of interaction with the computer, and you handle your own pictures inside your head. Most of your choices are east, west, north, south, up or down. You can go in or out if there is something obvious to do that with, like a building, door, or cave. You can also pick up objects the computer tells you are nearby. You never know what you will do with them, and some of them you don't quite recognize. The rest of your choices you have to guess at as you go through the game and encounter different situations. Your instructions must be simple enough for the computer to understand you. It will tell you if it doesn't. It will also tell you if you, or it, can't do what you asked it to do. It will also ridicule you severely at every opportunity. For my friend and I, at least, it told us how we got stupidly killed, repeatedly. Getting killed, by the way, is not winning.

There is a building in some woods where you begin. The object is to get some treasure away from some unfriendly pirates. As you move in the allowed directions, you find a forest, a road, a valley, a river bed, a mountainside, a series of tunnels and caves inside the mountain, and an incredibly complicated maze filled with nasty dwarfs. I say they're nasty because they throw knives at you and make other unkind gestures. As you encounter each new place, you guess at how to handle whatever creatures, objects, and directions you find, based on your logic. At the same time, you try to build a mental map of the tunnels and mazes so you can get around. I read something about the game somewhere and it said that if you're smart you leave a trail of unneeded items you have picked up, to mark your path. Unfortunately until you have enough experience, you can't tell what you'll need and what you won't. So you tend to keep everything with you. Also, since you don't know how big each place is, you don't know how frequently to drop markers. At one point we got stuck in the maze, with nothing left, and our only exit blocked by an angry dwarf with a big sharp knife. We didn't win.

The most interesting sequence happened in that same stupid maze (I know mazes aren't smart or dumb, just the people who get trapped in them, but give me a break — I lost, remember?) All we had was a lamp we could turn on or off at our leisure. It was very handy when the computer told us we were in a pitch dark tunnel and if we tried to move we would likely fall into a bottomless pit. If our lamp was on, we were safe (my friend tried to jump the pit once when we didn't have the lamp — a truly dumb move). Dwarves threatened us constantly. When we would try to kill the dwarf (any dwarf — there seemed to be a never-ending supply on hand) the computer would ask, "With your bare hands?" We said no, of course, being prudent dwarf killers. Each time it just said in response, "OK." We thought that was a strange, slightly suggestive, response. Suggestive of what we weren't quite sure. Once when we said yes to the "bare hands" question, we got killed, so we were pretty sure that wasn't a good idea.

At one point we were getting stuck repeatedly in the maze. There was always a dwarf blocking our path. We could kill each one but every dead dwarf just produced another live one, complete with big knife. Since we couldn't move, we were forced to construct an experiment. Through trial and error we found that we could kill the dwarf with our bare hands, *provided we turned off the lamp!* I won't confess how long it took us to figure that one out. We didn't expect patterns like that in the game, and were quite impressed with the programmer. We also found out that, at this point in the maze, this combination of bare hands and unlit lamp was the only way to save our hides.

After a few hours of this, we had had enough for the night. We had only seen the pirate with his treasure once. We "heard" him several times, sneaking behind us. The machine said so. But we couldn't seem to find him when we moved. We fully realized that this game would take practice and time to get good at. The more we played the more we would develop our internal map of the mazes and other playing arenas. And we would find out how to use each thing we picked up. We are both still wondering just how good we could get ...

Notes

Chapter 5

1. Drucker, Peter. *Adventures Of A Bystander*, New york, Harper & Row, 1979, p. 255.
2. This concept of logical types and levels was originated by Bertrand Russell. It is the basis of "sets and subsets" in modern math.
3. By the way, you don't get to have an existential crisis unless you have read the right literature, followed the right procedures for such disasters, and seen a social worker. Otherwise, you're just a little nuts and confused like the rest of us.
4. It is remotely possible that I get all the obnoxious ones who tell me what all my problems are and if only I went to ... (whatever) ... I would be so much more "prosperous, fulfilled, balanced ..."
5. Four lines of code from computer jargon. The term "two-pull" meant two pulls on a lever, signaling a new line of code in early computers. Ain't technology clever?

CHAPTER 6

PARTS IS PARTS

I am a real movie buff. That doesn't mean I am particularly skilled or knowledgeable, just that I pay attention and I know what I like. As I get older I notice more of the filmmaker's art in each movie I see. Undoubtedly that has a lot to do with my training, but I think I am drawn to looking for it by a fascination that's hard to explain. Part of it is that I want to know how a director, writers, cinematographers, actors, and crew get me to feel the things I do when I go to the movies or watch them on TV.

I think a good director, with good writing behind him (or her) can make me feel just about anything. I have taken to watching videotapes of the great directors for just that reason. I want to know how and why I am so easily controlled. One of my favorite directors, who does much of his own writing as well, is Woody Allen. I know some people can't stand him. He brings out the extremes of feeling in people. I recently got the opportunity to look at one of his classics again: *Manhattan.* It was on a station with E.G. Marshall introducing the film, letting us know why it looked like it didn't fit on the TV screen. Woody filmed it in whatever is the widest possible lens. The movie looked very broad, and didn't fill the screen from top to bottom. Also, it was in black and white. The overall look of the movie, in addition to the story, was very powerful. This was especially apparent when the scene was of the entire skyline of Manhattan. It fit so perfectly that it felt like the city was made just for him to film it.

I was particularly interested in his camera angles. The way he picked them so that you see the interactions between people from different characters' points of view makes you really feel like you're a part of what's going on. He is a master of the close-up during intensely human moments. When he is being pragmatic and final, at the end of the film, he pulls back to that broad view of the entire skyline. He placed the camera at just the right distance. Also notable is his use and choices of music — conducting what you hear as imaginatively as what you see. His musicianship comes through even through his directing. The whining clarinet from Gershwin's *Rhapsody in Blue* at the beginning of the movie is brilliant. You can almost hear the people whining with it. And they are not even on the screen yet. He has me from the start. I love having my experience be created so skillfully.

One of the most interesting experiences I have ever had in a movie came a couple of years ago when *Wargames* first came out. I got completely caught up in this movie. The sound of the teenagers' voices, juxtaposed against the sound of the artificial voice of the computer, got me cold. The camera angle shifts, from the face of the computer whiz kid to the "face" of the computer, made me a part of the emotions as well. The choices of words were so believable that, coupled with the camera angles, I was — literally — into the conversation. I found myself saying the words out loud just as the kid did. I felt like I was him. About the third time he and I said the same words in perfect unison, I startled myself. Our tones and inflections matched so perfectly that I was struck dumb. I looked, a little embarrassed, to the people I was with just in time to see their jaws drop and their eyes open real wide....

Dialog is interesting all by itself. Lately I've also taken to watching foreign films. If the subtitles are well done enough, and easy to read, I can sometimes get just as involved in the movie as if it were in English. I recently realized that I memorize the overall look of the film in the first few minutes. After reading the words, it's as if I already know what the scene should look like. My internal images match the pictures well enough so that I am not interrupted or surprised. It makes watching the movie as fluid as if it really were in English. That is, provided that it's a good movie.

If it isn't well written and directed, it's immediately obvious to me. I find I jump from the words to the pictures and nothing ever seems to quite fit. I'll generally do one of three things at that point. If I think the dialog is stupid, but the acting is good, I'll just watch the people for a little while. Often I find that I can skip the dialog for several minutes and still seem to understand the flow of the movie. That is a tribute to the acting. I can sometimes enjoy it by itself. Of course I don't know if the movie is badly written, badly subtitled, or both. Sometimes if I wait long enough the words and action will begin to fit for me. On the other hand, if I think the acting is bad, I can ignore that. Then I just read the story and make my own internal images. The only problem I run into is if there is music as well as dialog. Then I sometimes get distracted because the music usually matches their scenes better than mine. My third choice, if I am watching at home, is to turn the damn thing off altogether and do something else.

Some movies don't work as well on a small screen: science fiction, especially with lots of special effects. Sometimes the massive panoramic views look so miniature that they don't fit into what my brain has in mind. Also after listening to, and feeling, some of the incredible sound systems theaters have now, the translation to a 2-inch speaker is kind of a drag. Motion seems different when it is scaled down, as well. Riding on a huge swift space cruiser on a big screen makes you think you are there. Watching it on a small screen makes it about as exciting as watching a toy train running around. It's fun for a while but not the same feeling of being there. Instead of getting the rush of adrenalin, the feel of your stomach jumping with every motion, and the urge to duck as the shots coming at you go by — you get a headache from squinty eyes and a furled brow. Rather than the clear presence of the rumblings of giant engines and the screech of passing missiles going from in front of you on one side, to in back of you on the other side, you get garbled noises you have to strain just to identify.

Parts of some of them still work, though. One example is at the beginning of *Close Encounters of the Third Kind*. The movie opens with a dull moaning sound of an orchestra just starting to build and the screen is black as night. All of a sudden the entire orchestra hits a high note while the screen simultaneously turns white. You instantly find yourself in the desert under a bright sun. Breathtaking. Another interesting vantage point is created in *E.T.* when certain of the camera angles are shot from waist level, the point of view of E.T. himself. It really gives you the feeling of being overwhelmed — which is what Steven Spielberg obviously intended. You get a similar feeling when you are with Indiana Jones in *Raiders of the Lost Ark* and that giant boulder starts rolling down through the cave, straight *at you*. It works almost as well on the small screen. Some movie makers know exactly how to get the effects they want, no matter what.

Some don't. In addition some movies are lost due to any kind of translation. The silliest ones are in the films which are poorly dubbed. Big screens just make them even worse. The martial arts films that are run on Saturday afternoon TV are just ridiculous. The sight of two ancient Chinese warriors squaring off to fight can at least grab your attention. Then they talk and ruin the whole thing. The most outlandish is when one has a British cockney accent and the other sounds like he is from Brooklyn. Drama to comedy in 2 seconds. What makes it worse is that the rest of the sounds aren't synchronized. Then the whole thing becomes idiotic. Campy humor transformed to unwatchability. The only consolation is in knowing that the stupid thing wasn't any good in the first place so it's really no loss. Half the time they aren't even in focus. I suppose some things just can't be translated. Others aren't worth the trouble.

You are still probably wondering what, exactly, is meant by "state of consciousness." I promised you a thorough explanation. This chapter will make you as knowledgeable on the subject as you need to be for now. In Volume III there are experiments to get you operating with the concepts. Together, they will make you more knowledgeable than the vast majority of psychologists about how to use states in everyday life. Don't tell them I told you so, though, or they'll want to argue about statistics or some equally noxious (read irrelevant) subject.[1]

A number of terms immediately come to mind that are roughly synonymous with the term "state of consciousness." Frame of mind, state of awareness, mood, etc. all mean pretty much the same thing. Generally when people talk about the subject in useful terms, though, they are talking about what are called in some circles discrete states of consciousness. In other words, states of consciousness that are in some way discernible, definable, and distinguishable from other states of consciousness. The two terms are often abbreviated "SoC" for state of consciousness and "d-SoC" for discrete state of consciousness.[2]

The important thing is that in NLP we have an easy fool-proof method for delineating a particular state of consciousness so that we can use it, and modify it, as we see fit. Also, we have made it much simpler than anyone else to date. This is because we talk about the *experience*, as I have repeated so often, of being in a particular state. We do this on an individual basis which makes the concept useable with people, rather than charts and graphs.

We all go in and out of many states of consciousness all the time. Probably hundreds each day. These are what are called natural states, though this isn't the most precise term. Some of these states are easy to tell from others. Sleep is usually distinguishable from wakefulness. Exceptions to this include certain relatively rare individuals like some epileptics, some drug and alcohol abusers, or a number of college professors and researchers.... But I don't think of sleep and wakefulness as really distinct states. They're different from each other, but each contains many possible states of consciousness. For example, deep sleep differs markedly from dream or REM (Rapid Eye Movement) sleep. Both differ from other lighter sleep stages. We all know this from our experience and it can be shown through EEG studies. Trance states differ from both sleep and wakefulness and also include many varieties. Even hypnosis does not produce a *particular* state. Rather it is a tool for going from one state to another. Like any tool it can be used or abused. The tool can't decide whether the state a person gets to is worthwhile or not. The person has to make that decision based on some, hopefully sensible, criterion. The same is true, of course, for drug states.

These last few examples, hypnosis, drugs, etc. constitute the group generally referred to as "altered states" (ASC). This is a bit of a misnomer though. These may still be just as natural as other more generally occurring states. The path taken to get to them is different from everyday activity so some people generally assume the states to be different. After working with altered states for a number of years, however, these sorts of distinctions begin to blur. The path doesn't necessarily affect its destination. It is possible to induce states, identical in the person's experience and behavior to being on a certain drug, without any drugs being present. Many clinicians, including myself, have done so in working with people who use drugs. Again, I don't know if anyone really is, in some physiologically verifiable way, actually in the drug state. I also don't care. It's the experience and the behavior that count. The use of the state is only to achieve a particular outcome. That, again, is our proverbial bottom line.

This brings us to identifying particular states. Since we're going to do so in terms of experience and behavior we need to have an organized method that easily makes sense. You remember that I said states are the same as 4-tuples. A 4-tuple is made up of the combination of sensory modalities at a particular moment in time: visual, auditory, kinesthetic, olfactory-gustatory (V, A, K, O-G). Then I said we can break down each of these into their respective submodalities. So the stuff that makes up a state of consciousness, in this scheme, is submodalities and sensory modes; the form of content and the representational systems.

The submodality level is the most efficient place to begin looking at how states are built for a variety of reasons. One is that it is the most basic level of awareness in our model.

Another is that it is the smallest "chunk size." That makes it easiest to start with. In addition, you can become skilled at manipulating your internal experience at this level quite quickly. Then you will have much greater control at all the other levels. Submodalities are the basic building blocks of experience.

Changing a submodality in one representational system can effect submodalities in the other representational systems as well. This is provided, of course, that you change the right one. For example, for most people, brightening an internal *visual* image will intensify the *feelings* that go along with that image. Try it for yourself. Remember an image that has a particular feeling attached to it. Perhaps some scene you remember that reminds you of a particular emotion each time you imagine it. I suggest you pick one with an emotion you would like to have be more intense. In other words pick an image that gives you a nice feeling. Now imagine that you have a brightness control knob next to the image in your mind's eye, just like the one on a television set. Imagine turning up the brightness knob and watching the image get brighter as it would on a real TV. Avoid making it so bright that it becomes hard to see or uncomfortable. Pay attention to your feelings at the same time. How do they change? In most people they will become more intense. What happens for you is specific to you as an individual.

The point here is that changing one submodality, brightness of a visual image, has an effect on another submodality, intensity of feeling. These are qualitative as well as quantitative changes, to be sure. They are also totally within your experience and control to play with. And I do mean play with. So much of our communication is based on these changes that it is difficult to describe. In this sense, we have all let others play with us, all our lives. Here is a tool that can help us get the control back.

It should be obvious that even this subtle change of one visual submodality can have far-reaching effects on your experience. Just this one change can help you change your feelings about anything. You only need to experiment with each image, and adjust the content to suit your needs. Much of

Volume III is devoted to these experiments.

The reason I chose a visual submodality to change is because that's easiest for most people at first. It's a function of the visual nature of our society. Internal auditory (sound) changes are just as dramatic, though. You simply need to find which changes will work to create the effects you want.

Here is a good start. Remember the sound of someone's voice that intimidated you when you last heard it. This could be someone you like, or not. It doesn't matter what the situation. The important thing is that you felt some amount of fear or anxiety, or whatever term you wish, when you heard this voice. And when you remember it now you still feel that same feeling.

When you have a clear idea of what the voice sounds like in your head, and how you feel when you hear it internally, change it. Give it the tempo and tonal quality of that famous star: Donald Duck! Still feel intimidated? Doubtful. It is truly difficult to feel afraid or in awe of someone who sounds like a cartoon. The voice could still be saying exactly what it said the first time! It is the form (sound quality) that you changed, not the content (words). Getting the idea?

The key here is in finding the right submodality to change, for you, in a particular situation. You have a great many choices. What you will find is that when you have determined how a particular submodality change affects you, you'll then have a new tool for changing your experience. *That* submodality change will work the same way for you each time you use it. For example, if you find that brightening a particular visual image increases the feelings attached to it, it will work for all your visual images the same way. Brightening the image will make the feelings more intense, dimming it will make them less so. We call the submodalities that work for you *critical submodalities*. Brightness is a critical submodality for you if changing it affects something else, like your feelings. If it doesn't, it is not critical *for you*. We are talking about finding the difference that makes a difference.

Another important thing to remember is that your brain only knows how to make the feelings more intense when you make the pictures brighter. It won't decide, on an unconscious level, whether or not *it is good idea* in each case. It will simply follow instructions. A feeling of pain will get more intense just as well as a feeling of pleasure. That's why I suggested that you pick an image that gives you a good feeling to experiment with first.

Clearly understanding the vast range of this level of analysis is easiest if you can see all the major ones listed and described. That way when I talk about using one or another for some purpose, you can refer back to the list. A significant portion of NLP training is now devoted to this level because of its power and simplicity. Quality time spent here and on the exercises in Volume III will really pay off for you.

Visual Submodalities

Color	Shape	Size	Distance
Location	Brightness	Contrast	Clarity
Focus	Movement/Speed	Direction	Depth
Slides/Motion	Picture	Associated/Disassociated	

Color means which one(s) you see. Is the picture black and white, full color, or a combination? Does some color or colors stand out as central or important somehow?

Shape means shape of the image itself as well as internal shapes that stand out in the picture. The same goes for size, distance, and location.

Brightness we have already covered. It is just the same as on a TV set, i.e. how bright the picture itself actually is. In some cases this may vary inside of an image. Contrast also means the same as it would on a TV. Some people think of this as sharpness. Clarity is similar, but is likely to vary within an image itself. The same goes for focus. Some people have trouble distinguishing these as separate qualities. That is an example of the limiting nature of our use of language, not the experience itself.

Whether you see an internal image as a still shot, like a slide or photograph, or as a motion picture, can be crucial. Also the depth perception of the image. It could be flat and two-dimensional like a photo, or appear to be three-dimensional like a slide, or more dramatically a hologram. If it is a motion picture, the speed and direction of motion(s) could be important. For example, the motion may be exactly as you remember it, if it is a remembered image, or it could be in slow motion. More unusual, it could be going backwards. This can be a very useful change in some circumstances. Another possibility is that the direction has changed in some other way.

Last and perhaps most dramatic is association. An associated image is one in which you see exactly what you would see, through your own eyes, if you were there. In other words, you would not see yourself in the image, just as you do not really see yourself now. A disassociated image is just the opposite. You would see yourself in the image as if you were looking through someone else's eyes. Imagine for a moment that you are in a room with a group of people and you are being videotaped. What you see while you are in the room is an associated image. The playback that you see later from the tape is disassociated, since you see yourself from another point of view. Do you have a more literal idea of what people are telling you when they say they need a different perspective, or a new point of view? They are talking about, often literally, changing from associated to disassociated images in their mind. This can be a most dramatic change as you'll see later.

Auditory Submodalities

Sound/Words	Voice/Whose?	Internal/External	
Location	Distance	Direction	Volume
Pitch	Rhythm	Tempo	Duration
Tone	Timbre		

The first distinction to make is whether you hear sounds, words, or both in your mind. At different times, of course, we can hear a variety of sounds internally just as we can externally. That is another distinction to be made, whether the sound seems to be coming from inside your head or if it seems like it is coming from somewhere on the outside. This becomes especially important when we seem to hear a voice. Some of us seem to hear voices as if they were coming from outside of our own head. Not that we're hallucinating — we know the difference but sometimes the sound seems to be located outside of us. If we hear a voice, a distinction should be made about whose voice it is. We may recognize it as some particular person. Sometimes we won't but it may still be clearly male or female, old or young, or some other characteristic. Remember that all of these distinctions will help us recognize, reproduce, or change the sounds.

Whether the sounds seem to be coming from inside or outside, the precise location can be important. Then of course, the direction from which the sound is coming as well as the apparent distance can usually be determined. The volume can be a function of the distance and direction as well.

Also important are things we generally consider to determine the "quality" of sound. Thinking of musical sounds generally helps make these clear. One of these qualitative characteristics is pitch: how high or low the notes would be on, say, a piano. If the sounds are musical there may also be a rhythm (beat) and tempo (speed). Duration means how long the sound actually lasts, important in some instances but not all. Tone and timbre refer to frequency ranges and distributions. Without getting too technical, think of different brass instruments such as a trumpet and a saxophone. Even while playing the same note the two instruments sound different. They have a different tone and timbre. This is certainly specific enough for our purposes. The reason for including all of these is only to remind you of the different possibilities. As you practice you will automatically consider those most important for you.

Kinesthetic Submodalities

Internal/External		Tactile/Proprioceptive	Intensity
Location	Size	Shape	Moisture
Weight	Pressure	Temperature	Texture
Duration	Frequency	Movement	Rhythm

Again, the first thing you will probably want to consider in kinesthetics, or feelings, is whether they are on the inside or the outside. Tactile means the feeling of touch as opposed to proprioception, which means internal feelings. These include the internal physical sensations of body position, muscle tension etc. Next, the intensity or strength of a feeling is something we are usually quite aware of.

Location is important since we can feel some things in very specific areas of our body or on our skin. Some feelings also seem to have size and shape to them. Moisture is certainly something we can feel on our skin, though usually it is a function of temperature as I mentioned earlier. Besides our skin, our mouths can certainly feel wet or dry, especially during certain emotions or around food.

Generally when we notice our feelings we can sense weight, pressure, and temperature changes. This is true whether the feelings are on the outside, on our skin, or on the inside. We can also feel texture on our skin and some people find this to be one of the first things they notice.

Some feelings also seem to have movement to them. Then we can usually distinguish the qualities of duration (how long), frequency (how often), and rhythm (what pattern) as well. This is especially true of natural functions such as breathing and heart rate. Often becoming aware of these is a powerful experience for people. Feelings have a special place in our behavior and some of these qualities of feeling seem to be the deciding factors in the overall quality of our experience. Obviously, paying special attention to them can make a great difference in both our experiences and our abilities.

This, then, is a description of the major parts that comprise a state of consciousness. If you can identify, in yourself or someone else, as many of these as possible at a certain time, you will have a good description of your, or their, state of consciousness at that time. Since you remember how much of Meta-Cation was devoted to getting you to resource states, you know how important this is. Resources are what make excellence. Knowing how to get them together in a state is a pretty useful thing. This is true in teaching and everything else.

We have all had experiences that were troublesome in one way or another. By the same token we have also had times of relative ease and smoothness. Maybe the ratio of one to the other isn't what we had hoped for. All of us would like to minimize the difficulties and increase the ease with which we do things. If we get to the states in which we perform our best, accomplishing things will be easier. One way that I used in Meta-Cation to help get people to resource states was to rely on previous experiences. When we vividly recall times and places in which we were at our best, we can recreate the state of consciousness as it occurred then. That's one good way of gathering together those same resources. Then we can perform to the same level again. And we'll usually give our self-confidence a boost in the process.

It turns out that a feeling of confidence, connected to a state of competence, can be useful just about anywhere. Feel capable, do well. This doesn't mean that just having the feeling of confidence is enough. We already discussed our friends who felt wonderfully confident and capable, though all the while, they were failing miserably. They needed to dim, and perhaps alter the shade, on their rose-colored glasses just a bit. You can use the submodalities to get the right balance. The feelings we want are often a good place to *start* this adjustment. Once we feel the level of confidence we want, we can add in the specific skills and abilities we need for whatever we're doing.

States of inefficiency, failure, or resignation work the same way. They are still just a collection of submodalities, attached to some content. Once you can identify both a resource state and a "problem" state, in yourself or someone else, you have all you need. The differences in the submodalities will often be drastic in many ways. Simply changing them from the way they are in the lousy (present) state to the way they are in the good (desired) one will help enormously. Then you can use your skills of anchoring and future pacing to make them last.

In this sense you are using your brain much like you would a computer. That analogy is especially apropos here. Your brain can do many things amazingly well. It can process information with fabulous precision, consistently and dependably. It can store it, alter it, and make generalizations from it. On an unconscious level, though, it won't make judgments on that information. As I said earlier, it is important to know what you are intensifying and what you are making weaker.

Every technique in NLP works both ways. For better or worse. That is because they're based on the actual functioning of the brain and its effects on behavior. Your brain will operate based on inherent processes and the rules it has learned about what to do with information. Critical submodalities, as far as anyone can tell, are inherent properties. How they are used depends on your previous life experiences and judgments. You can make your life exquisitely wonderful or exquisitely dismal. Your brain does not care which. It is your responsibility as a functioning human being to teach it worthwhile rules. Then you need to use your brain, within those rules, wisely.

Wise use of your brain includes deciding which states of consciousness you want, when you want them, and what to do with them. The extent to which you practice going from one state to another is the extent to which you will have control over your consciousness. This, in turn, is the extent to which you will have control over your abilities and your experience as well. Once you have gotten used to the idea, and the procedures that go with it, you can share it with the children.

When you get ready to do that you'll discover something truly remarkable. They'll do it much better than you. Though we all adjust our internal submodalities constantly, kids do it with more good sense, creativity, and flexibility than most adults. That's possibly because they haven't had too much education yet. Which states are most effective to get to, of course, depends on what tasks or skills are involved. As an adult and a teacher, your responsibility is to guide the children to those most effective states. Or at least stay out of the way while they get there on their own.

Notes

Chapter 6

1. If you are one, just assume that you hallucinated those two sentences — they really never happened.
2. See *States of Consciousness*, by Charles Tart, New York, Dutton, 1975, chapter 1, for a complete look at this classification scheme.

CHAPTER 7

CHECK THE RECIPE
BEFORE YOU FRY ...

I am a big sports fan, every now and then. Like a lot of us, I have my favorites, my most convenient times to watch, and so on. I do get really excited for certain major events, though. One of these is the Olympics. During the last Summer Olympic Games, ABC ran a story that really caught my eyes and ears. They were describing the latest technology athletes are using to get themselves in the best frame of mind possible for competition. They call this frame of mind the Optimal Performing State. Obviously this is one of the desired states I've been talking about. Athletes all over the place are working with Neuro-Linguistic Programmers to get to their best state, since they know it's one of our specialties.

The example used in the explanation was beautiful. They showed a platform diver standing at the top of the ladder before taking the plunge. They described some of the things the diver might say to himself. They said he might remember an exceptionally good dive he made before, and tell himself he could do it again. He might visualize his next dive as it would be seen by an observer. He might even imagine doing the dive — commentator and famed distance swimmer Diana Nyad mentioned this as especially useful. Or he may go through some other sort of internal process.

The point of the things he does, and the sequence he goes through, is to get him to access his resources effectively. When he has got the ones he needs at his command, he is in his Optimal Performing State. He will have some internal signal that tells him if it's just right. Then, and only then, will he dive.

Athletes have always been superstitious. It has to do with needing to maintain a particular level of concentration. Top athletes will often do some outlandish things to make everything "just right." Baseball players are famous for things like unwashed "lucky" socks, much to the chagrin of their teammates. But many of these things are really effective.

One of the things that works is to go through the same steps each time right before performing something. A great example is the steps a tennis player goes through when he or she is about to serve. I used to teach tennis, and like most teachers learned early on that some things are done best *exactly the same way every time.* Serving is one of them. If you watch John McEnroe serve you can easily see this. He will line his feet up with the baseline — a rather unconventional stance. Then he'll lean forward, bending deeply at the waist. He'll bounce the ball three or four times from this position. Then he will hold the racket and the ball in his hand together and rock a couple of times, shifting his weight from his front foot to his back foot. When he has his balance, he will rock forward one last time, bent at the waist, and touch his racket to the ground. Then he'll go through his actual service motion and deliver one of the most devastating weapons in the game. It is unusual in form, but always the same. (Wouldn't you know, the next time I saw him play after writing this he had changed his serve? Most notably, he lines up his feet somewhat more conventionally. He also seems not to quite touch his racket to the ground now. He still does exactly the same thing each time though.)

We can only guess what is in his head while he is going through this routine. One of the things we do know is that whatever it is, it works. We can also assume that since his behavior is very consistent, his thinking undoubtedly is too. That is the point of these sequences, to get the thinking straight. That is also the point of NLP.

We have spent years figuring out how sequences work. We

have two main models for describing them at this point: strategies and chains. The older of the two, and more involved, is strategies. Fortunately, other psychologists had been working on similar thought structures for some time. A particularly unusual and gifted group came up with a very useful model that they published in 1960.[1] Though they didn't use it in as sophisticated a way then, they did a great job.

All strategies have the same form if they work. Remember, when I mean if they work, I simply mean they end in some result, not necessarily one we'd want. The form is based on the neuro-behavioral model I mentioned called the *T.O.T.E.* model. The letters stand for *T*est, *O*perate, *T*est, *E*xit. This simple model can be used to explain just about any behavior but let's go back to our diver on the platform as an example.

The first Test is the one that is used to determine whether or not the strategy is appropriate to be used at this time. Our diver may not want to use this sequence when ordering a hamburger at Fast Food Heaven. Or, more importantly, the next time he goes on a tour of the Grand Canyon. It is most appropriate when he is about to dive off the platform in competition. So his first test may be, literally, to step onto the platform from the ladder, look around, and ask himself, "Is it time for me to get to my best state for performing this dive?" Hopefully when looking down into the Grand Canyon the answer would be, "No!"

The Operation phase is the sequence that gets the diver from this beginning step, to the desired state. You can think of the present state as whatever he was going through on the way up the ladder. Then comes the first test, then the sequence to the desired state. This may begin as a statement to himself like, "I know I can hit this dive perfectly." Maybe he'll remember the last time he did the dive perfectly in practice and visualize it. Possibly he will go through a series of visualizations. This could begin with a mental image of the best he has ever seen anyone perform this particular dive. He might possibly then say to himself, "I can do that." Then another image, this time of himself on videotape doing the dive. This one is actually quite common. Next he may remember what he actually saw the last time he did the dive — from his own perspective. From this, he may be able to remember exactly how he felt doing the dive just right.

That feeling of doing the dive just right will usually put him into the Optimal Performing State. This is the point at which the second Test in our T.O.T.E. model occurs. The diver might ask himself at this point, "Is this how I feel when I do this dive best?" In this case, he would be using the feeling as the signal for whether the state is right. If he's not sure the feeling is right, his best bet would be to go back through the previous steps until it is.

That is the point of this second Test, to keep him at it until he gets it right, or to let him know that he has it right. If he does, he Exits the program for getting to the desired state, since he got it. Then he dives. If not he keeps going until it is. Graphically it might look something like this:

Test$_1$	Internal question: "Is this the time to use my desired state strategy for this dive?"
	Internal answer: "Yes."
Operation	Visualizes the best version of this dive he's ever seen.
	Says to himself, "I can do that."
	Visualizes himself doing the dive on video-tape.
	"Stepping into the picture," he visualizes exactly what he saw the last time he did the dive perfectly.
Test$_2$	Asks himself, "Is this the right feeling that I need to do this dive the best I can?"
	Pays attention to his feelings at this moment.

> If the answer is "No" he returns to the begin-
> ning of the Operation sequence and repeats it
> until the answer is "Yes."
>
> When the answer is "Yes" he goes to the Exit.

Exit   He leaves the previous sequence — he dives.

Once you have applied this format to a couple of activities it
really gets quite easy. The best part about it is that it is a
"checks and balances" sort of model. You get to be sure you
have finished whatever step you were on before going further.
This is the kind of organization computer programmers use to
design a program. Good writers and speech-makers would use
a similar sequence. It arranges your beginning, end, what
comes in the middle, and when to go from one step to the next
(or not). It is also one of those rare models that is at least as
useful 25 years later as when it was developed. Those aren't too
easy to come by!

The other nice thing about it is that once you have applied it
to an area where change is needed, it often points you in the
right direction immediately. For example, let's imagine we
have a diver who can't quite get to his desired state on the
platform. By simply finding out what sequence he *does* go
through, we may quickly find the reason.[2]

For example, it may be that when he reaches the top of the
ladder, instead of reminding himself that it's time for his
desired state strategy, he does something else. And nothing
else he does could be as useful as the right sequence. One rather
unfortunate possibility that comes to mind is that he will
notice the crowd and wonder if he can perform to their expectations. Maybe he'll fear mistakes or embarrassment. If he starts
thinking about embarrassment enough, for example vividly
remembering his most ridiculous moment in diving, he won't
get to his best state for this dive. He'll most likely feel all the
feelings he had when he was embarrassed. That is how our
brain works. For most of us "what you see is what you get,"
even (especially) in our mind's eye. How well would you

perform with those feelings? His best bet, obviously, would be to start over.

Another possibility is that he gets past this phase but gets stuck in the Operation. Maybe he will visualize the best version of the dive he has ever seen and then respond to this image with: "I'll never be able to do that!" If he believes that, he'll most likely be right. We have all said something like that to ourselves at some time. Maybe we can trudge ahead and do OK. More often, though, our confidence is shot and we need to get it back before going ahead. There are a lot of possible pitfalls in the Operation sequence. Since it is the actual series that takes you from the present state to the desired state, this should be apparent.

The second Test can be tricky as well. Usually if the strategy bogs down here it is because the person doesn't know what he's looking for. He may not know his own feelings well enough to make the determination. Just as often, he may not trust them. Some people will never be quite satisfied with the feeling and continue in an "endless loop" through the Operation. This would be easy to determine with our diver. He'd still be up on the platform until nightfall unless someone dragged him down and took him away.

Sometimes there has never been a second test for the strategy. In that case the person goes through the operation and exits after the first time automatically. This is fine if it works the first time, every time. Life doesn't always comply so neatly. People who work this way are the ones we all know who operate as if the effects of their actions had nothing to do with *them* at all. They do whatever they do because they always did. And they just keep chugging along, making the same mistakes over and over.

Most of the time once someone gets through the first Test, Operation, and second Test, they Exit the program comfortably. Certainly the diver is limited in his choice of alternative directions for travel. In some other strategies, though, it is important that the exit be precise in nature. I know some people who finish projects but never seem to deliver them. This seems to be quite common among writers. Sometimes it's because they are never satisfied with what they wrote. Therefore, they never got past the second test. Sometimes though, once they finish writing they *feel completely finished*. Then, as far as they're concerned, there is nothing more to do. What a pity.

This can also take the form of the person who comes up with great ideas or plans but never implements them. A lot of these people have great strategies for creativity, problem solving, and so forth. Unfortunately, once they have completed the task of figuring out what to do, and Exited the creativity strategy, they find themselves "all dressed up with no place to go." They are called "dreamers" or "planners." Those around them wish they would be "doers." I know I'm not the only person alive who has had to deal with these poor souls. What they actually need, in our T.O.T.E. format, is to have the Exit on their creativity strategy be the First Test on their motivation or completion strategy. That way everything they created would automatically spur them on to the action they so sorely lack. I hope this is beginning to spur you on in thinking about yourself and others, as well as behavior in general.

Once we have determined pretty much what someone does to prevent themselves from getting the outcome they want we have several choices about how to intervene. Often, as in the above examples, good sense and experience will immediately show solutions. Then it is simply a matter of interrupting the existing strategy and putting in new steps. We could simply base these on logically figuring out which ones fit the task.

A different way is to find another strategy that person uses, that works well when they use it. Then we can transfer it over to the area they need it in. Often this can be done in the wink of an eye. Other times some alteration or adaptation is needed for the best result. But using an already existing and successful strategy is usually the easiest for the person doing it. This is because, most of the time, they feel good about the strategy where it works. That makes them comfortable trying it in other areas. Not surprisingly, the person who hasn't connected his creativity to his motivation often *does* have good motivation and completion strategies. He just doesn't use them where and when he needs them.

The way that is most universally effective, as I've hinted several times, is to find someone else who is very effective at whatever the task is. The structure of how we work is much more similar from one person to another than you might think. Granted, we are all unique individuals. It turns out most of the time, though, that a strategy that works, just works. Anyone can use it. If it is used the way that it was intended, in the right time and place, it should result in the same outcome.

The interesting thing about that last statement is that most NLPers rarely transfer a strategy from one person to another without making some changes. Most people's strategies for achieving things, no matter how successful, can be stream-lined and made more efficient in some way. This is not always true, but most of the time it is. This is because we learn to do the vast majority of what we do by trial and error. That is a simple fact of life (if such things really exist). Trial and error will often guide us in useful directions. It will very seldom tell us the *best* way to get where we're going, however. There is such a thing as effectiveness without efficiency. What trial and error will teach us is the *first* way we got there. Then we will do it the same way from then on. We all know lots of people who drive to work by exactly the same route every day. Heaven forbid there should be a detour. Some of them would just have to turn around and go home.

Another way to find strategies is to borrow or steal them from others. This is what is meant by the term "stealing be-havior." Beyond that, with some experience, it is possible to actually artificially design strategies that will work to achieve certain things. They can be made as good or better than ones people already use. You just figure out what steps would be necessary. Then you decide how best to create them. Next you put them in a logical order. Finally you decide what signals the person can use for each Test, how to begin, where and when it should be used, and how to Exit. Then you find a volunteer (subject, victim) to try it with and see how well it works. You can rest assured that it will either work or it won't. Profound, eh?. If it does, fine. If not, proceed as we did before. With a little good sense, patience, and perseverance you'll eventually get it right.

At this point the obvious question is, "How can you make the strategy a part of yourself?" Useful strategies should be as automatic as breathing. This is part of the goal. We want these strategies to be natural, which means unconscious as well. That way they don't occupy our conscious thoughts, becoming another burden. We have enough of those. They should function as if they were completely "transparent," allowing our conscious processes to be used for more important tasks than just being able to function effectively. In Volume III, when I give you exercises using strategies, I'll go through ways to "elicit" and "install" them. You will find that you already know how, but haven't thought about it enough yet.

The other main sequence that we talk about in NLP is the chain. In many ways it is a much simpler form than the strategy. It is structurally a little easier to understand, as well. A chain is simply a series of individual states, or 4-tuples, connected by anchors. The first state triggers the next and so on. Simple. Also, like strategies, these are naturally occurring phenomena. We all have lots of them. We just don't think about our behavior in these terms too often. Also, like everything else, the chain does not care where it takes you. It simply goes. We all have some we enjoy and others we would just as soon be rid of.

An example of one we might want to have, if we don't now, would be something to help us handle anxiety. If every time we feel anxious it triggers an internal awareness, then we remember to take a deep breath, chuckle at our over-reaction, feel a renewed confidence, and finally motivate ourselves to keep trying, we will never be immobilized by anxiety. This is a really nice chain. Let's look at those steps again:

Feel anxiety
Focus attention inward
Remember to breathe
Chuckle at our reaction

Feel renewed self-confidence
Feel motivated

It turns out that many highly successful people go through these steps, or similar ones, each time they feel anxious. In fact many of them don't even remember the initial anxiety that triggered the rest of the steps once they have gone through them! All of us have experienced something similar before. A strange occurrence will initiate some series of events. By the time we have gone through them, we can't remember where the whole thing started. This is how chains work.

Contrast the chain listed above with a chain that starts with anxiety, goes to anger, blame, frustration, hurt feelings, disgust, and surrender. We have probably all seen people, maybe us, go through that one before. It's no fun. The structure is the same as the other one: step one triggers step two, and so on. But the outcome is real different. Think of the effect each of these sequences can have on our relationships with others.

Unfortunately, a lot of evidence suggests that our brains don't much care about the quality of the chains we go through. They just take us through the ones they have been *trained* to go through. As always, it is up to us to train, or retrain, our brains to get the outcomes we want. Then, once we know how it works and have ourselves straightened out, we can train the children.

Compare this form of sequence to strategies. The steps in a strategy are slightly smaller than in a chain. Each one consists of an internal visual image, sound, feeling, smell or taste. The steps in a chain are each a complete 4-tuple. In each type the sequence starts with some event and leads to some outcome.

There is no way I can describe all of the ways to use each of these concepts. The exercises in Volume III will give you a great start in directly experiencing their use, though. At this point it is enough that you understand as much of the whole picture as possible. I have shown you the levels of analysis, broken them down, and discussed the structure of each. Using them is something that can only be learned by doing. Here is another look at those levels:

Beliefs
Contexts
Sequences
States
Sensory Modalities
Submodalities

Submodalities are the form of the content of material we perceive in each sense (representational system). If we can identify each of the major ones within a sense, at a certain time, we will know that experience much better. As the submodalities change, so does our experience of that sense. There are critical submodality changes that affect not only that sense, but the others as well. This is a way of changing our awareness.

That process is what gets us to pay attention to one sense more than the others. It also causes us to go from our awareness of one to the awareness of another, as in a strategy. For example a visual submodality will change causing us to become aware of our feelings more than the picture. Going through these steps, to achieve some outcome, is what using strategies is all about.

Getting all of our senses in a particular condition, all at the same time is what states of consciousness are about. We can use our senses, and their respective submodalities, to get control over those states. This allows us to make sure they're worthwhile going through.

Going from one state to another, in a sequence, is a chain. Again, we can use the basic building blocks of submodalities and senses, or representational systems, to make these the most useful ones. Then, as you'll learn in Volume III, you can use anchors to hook them together in the right order.

Which strategies and chains we use, when and where, is the stuff of contexts. Strategies, states, and chains only become worthwhile when they are neatly packaged in the right time and place. Diving is most fun when it's done from boards into water. This obvious example is deceptive in its simplicity, but it makes the point.

Which states and sequences we use in which contexts, and the reasons for the choices, result in the generalizations we make about life. Though beyond the scope of this book, the ways people sort the world into categories can determine how they do everything else. I think we intuitively realize this. The total packaging of all these levels makes up our belief systems. The job of a teacher is to build these, as well as each level of experience, for children. Knowing the components, and what tools are available, can sure make it easier. Attempting such a task without this knowledge is a little like trying to master a sport without learning the necessary skills, the proper conditioning, the use of the equipment, or the basic rules.

Notes

Chapter 7

1. See G. Miller, E. Galanter, and K. Pribram, *Plans and the Structure of Behavior*, Henry Holt & Co., 1960. This is still extremely enjoyable and worthwhile reading.
2. I stressed this kind of thinking in *Meta-Cation* over and over again (see p. 38 for example). Starting with what you have is always a good idea.

CHAPTER 8

TALK TALK

I figured that since I have written almost two complete volumes on communication, it was about time I discussed language itself. OK, so I'm slow sometimes. In addition to being slow, I also like to approach the subject from its roots: sensory experience. I didn't feel it was worthwhile to do that until I had talked about the levels of sensory experience and their uses and relationships to one another. Now we're ready.

You'll remember in *Meta-Cation* that I gave you some listening exercises. These were designed to get you to hear the representational systems children use in certain circumstances. Then you could change your own predicates to match the ones they use to establish better rapport. From there you can gently change what you're using, say from kinesthetic predicates to visual ones, and they should follow along. That's pacing and leading.

Well, as you may suspect, there are lots of other ways to pace and lead besides representational systems. In fact, everything I have talked about in this book can be used in the same way. You can pace submodalities, sequences, beliefs, and lots more. It only takes practice to hear the ones the children are using. Once you have established adequate rapport, you can pace people's thinking just about anywhere worth going. It is all right there in the language. That means they're telling you everything you could possibly need to know about communicating with them.

Good communicators know this and hear what they need to, automatically. Sometimes they are aware of exactly what they have heard someone say that spurs their own thinking, but not usually. For example, how often have you heard someone say, "There was just something about the way that person talked (moved, sat, looked, etc.) that told me what to do?" Those are the kinds of statements that NLPers try to get to the bottom of. What they really mean is, "That person communicated something crucial to me, but I don't *consciously* know what it was." That's just fine. NLP is here to help them figure out just "what it was." Once that is figured out, it can be used over and over again.

A lot of the time when one of us helps someone else we do it by asking the right questions. I have stressed this often enough to sound ridiculous, but bear with me. The process of asking the right question has structure, just like all other communication. The original work Bandler and Grinder did in developing NLP was based on this one idea: asking the right questions. This work led to the Meta-Model, a tool designed to help you do just that. In *Meta-Cation* the model was outlined in Appendix II. I am repeating it here, piece by piece, but you may want to look at it again.

Let's begin with the assumption that we don't communicate clearly with our words most of the time. Knowing that, the Meta-Model is meant to help out by showing you the parts that aren't clear. It is based on the principles of human modeling, and transformational grammar from the study of linguistics. One of the most important principles of human modeling is that when information is transferred, there are three likely pitfalls: deletion, distortion, and generalization. Knowing the Meta-Model will help you to fill in missing (deleted) pieces, clear up distortions, and more precisely specify generalizations.

Transformational grammar is based on the study of how meaning is transformed into words. We call the words, or language, the *surface structure*. The actual meaning, or experience, underlying the words is the *deep structure*. So the Meta-

Model is built to help you get at the underlying deep structure by clarifying information given in the surface structure. This may sound a little *too* deep, but it's really quite simple.

The Model itself is divided into three major sections: Gathering Information, Limitations to an Individual's Model, and Semantic Ill-Formedness. Within each of these there are several major classifications that are more specific, making a total of 12 patterns. Each of these is a way in which one person can give information to another person, in words. For each pattern there is a corresponding *response* that will help ensure that the deep structure — the real meaning — wasn't lost in the words. I will give you each of the 12 patterns as they appear in Appendix II of *Meta-Cation*, followed by a brief explanation or comment. Also, it is important to remember that these patterns aren't *bad* or *wrong* ways of using language. They just aren't as clear as they could be. The examples are normal sentences we all use all the time. So are the responses. Simply pay attention to how the particular response helps clarify the particular example sentence given in each case. That is what I mean by asking the *right* questions.

The first major division is Gathering Information. Five of the 12 patterns are contained in this division. They're real important and basic.

First is:

1. *Simple Deletion*:
   When some object, person or event (noun phrases or noun arguments) has been left out of the surface structure.

Example: I'm really uncomfortable.

Response: Uncomfortable about what specifically?

This is pretty straightforward. Something is missing from the example sentence. The response, like all of the responses in the Meta-Model, is a question. It simply asks for the missing information. We all do this when we are unsure of what another person means — and it matters to us. Too often, though, we *think* we know what the other person meant and act as if we understand. Much of the time it probably doesn't matter. Every once in a while, though, it does and we end up embarrassed or worse. It can matter at the most inopportune times.

Speaking of things that matter, the second pattern is:

2. *Lack of Referential Index*:
When an object or person (noun) that is being referred to is unspecific.

Example: They never believe me.

Response: Who specifically never believes you?

Example: That doesn't matter.

Response: What specifically doesn't matter?

Again this is sensible and obvious. (I know: "What specifically is sensible and obvious?"). Also, again, it is something we often overlook when we are talking with others that could make our understanding of each other more accurate. One helpful way to remember the pattern is to listen for pronouns that are ambiguous. Then ask people to specify them ("Which people, Sid, come on ...?"). Your conversations will go better.

The last, but not least, of the deletion patterns is:

3. *Comparatives Deletion*:
When a referent is deleted during a comparison (i.e. good-better-best; more-less; most-least).

Example: It's *better* not to force the issue.

Response: Better for whom? Compared to what?

A lot of people do these most. They can really get you into more trouble than they are worth. It's much better to respond to them as often as possible to avoid too many misunderstandings. I'm sure you agree with me, and understand the pattern — at least enough for now.

Notice that you've encountered this next pattern before:

4. *Unspecified Verbs*:

Verbs which are not entirely explicit where sometimes the action needs to be made more specific.

Example: He really frustrates me.

Response: Frustrates you how specifically?

If you remember tear-out page 7, on page 163 of *Meta-Cation*, you'll remember the list of predicates I gave you. I have repeated it in Appendix I. Ponder the list of unspecified verbs — it will help you become more aware of how this pattern operates. This will allow you to understand it more fully and benefit from the experience in such a way that you'll recognize these unspecified verbs naturally and correct them in your own and other people's behavior. They often show up in run-on sentences....

This next pattern deserves close attention:

5. *Nominalizations*:

When an ongoing process is represented as a static entity in a way which may distort its meaning.

Example: I can't stand her insensitivity.

Response: Her sensing what about whom? and how specifically?

I hope you have a clear understanding and an appreciation

for this pattern. I know people who communicate most of their thoughts in nominalizations. I find them damn near impossible to understand. I find myself really working to understand their understanding of what they're talking about. One of the standard NLP ways to remember this pattern is to ask yourself, "Can I put that noun in a wheelbarrow?" You can't with "understanding". It should be a verb — a process word — not a noun. Or put another way, it isn't something you *have*, rather it is something you *do*. Our language is so full of these I wonder how we have any comprehension at all ...

The next major division is called Limitations to an Individual's Model. This means that these particular language patterns tell you something about how a person limits their own model of, or thinking about, the world. The responses can help the person expand their "boundaries" as well as helping you to better understand the limitations they place upon themselves. These limitations are usually established through people's style of thinking.

You already know the first of this group:

6. *Presuppositions*:

When something is implicitly assumed in the other person's communication which may, if taken for granted, cause limitations to a person's choices about the experience.

Example: If you knew how much I suffered, you wouldn't act this way.

Presuppositions: 1) I suffer 2) you act this way and 3) you don't know.

Response: 1) How specifically are you suffering? 2) How specifically am I reacting? 3) How do you know that I don't know?

I mentioned that many people in NLP have their favorite

level of analysis, mine being submodalities. Well this is my favorite Meta-Model pattern — for obvious reasons. It is certainly the most elaborate, with 29 separate varieties identified.[1] I mentioned these earlier and I'm sure there is no need to reiterate how important and dangerous our assumptions and presuppositions can be. It is equally important to recognize that almost every sentence you can come up with will generally have several presuppositions built into it. They are unavoidable. Like a lot of other things in life, being aware of them can help us a great deal. But that probably goes without saying.

The next, relatively imperative, pattern is:

7. *Modal Operators of Possibility and Necessity*:
Statements identifying rules about or limits to an individual's behavior (i.e., possibility = can/can't, it's possible/impossible, will/won't, may/may not; necessity = should/shouldn't, must/must not, have to, etc.).

Example: 1) possibility: I can't relax.

Response: What stops you?

Example: 2) necessity: I *shouldn't* let anyone know what I feel about that.

Response: What would happen if you did?

It's possible that you have already realized the necessity of using this pattern effectively. If you haven't until now, you should. When I hear people tell me what I have to do, I usually respond, "The only two 'have to's' for me are death and taxes, and I'm working on both." Still I am aware that I put limits on my thinking and, especially, my beliefs. We all do. The best way to protect ourselves might be to remember that we must constantly be on the lookout for our own self-defeating limits.

If you've kept up to this point, you'll find the next one easy:

8. *Complex Equivalence*:
When two experiences or events come to stand for each other but may not necessarily be synonymous.

Example: She's always yelling at me ... She hates me.

Response: Does her yelling at you always mean that she hates you? Have you ever yelled at anyone that you didn't hate?

This pattern is quite easy so I'm sure you understand it perfectly. Actually these types of equivalences aren't really *complex* in their structure. They're simple: this = that. What is complex is the thinking that produces them. It's also silly a lot of the time, but then so are we all. If you pay attention to how people make these equivalences, they will tell you a great deal about how they construct beliefs and other generalizations. That is really what these are: generalizations constructed out of *some* sort of logic or experience. *What* sort you have to guess at until you ask more questions to learn about it. The responses that seem to work best to these are counter-examples. In other words, give the person an example of the two things they have stated as equivalent, *not* being equivalent. But that's obvious, so you'll be more careful about these from now on.

The last major division is called Semantic Ill-Formedness. These really are just that: sentences that are not well formed, semantically. Something is wrong with their inherent logic and form. Again, they will tell you a good deal about the kind of thinking the person is using at that moment.

The first of this group will really make you sit up and take notice:

9. *Cause-Effect*:
When an individual makes a causal linkage between their experience or response to some outside stimulus that is not necessarily

directly connected, or where the connection is not clear.

Example: This lecture makes me bored.

Response: How specifically does it *make* you bored?

People who use this pattern to excess make me a little bit crazy. The notion of personal responsibility is tied up in this pattern. Most of the questions in response to cause-effect statements boil down to "Who's in control here? Are you running your life, or is the 'world' running it for you?" As I have said, I am a stickler for responsibility so this one is important to me. When I hear it too much from one person, it often makes me forget my sense of humor.

I know exactly what you're going to think of this next pattern:

10. *Mind-Reading*:

When an individual claims to know what another individual is thinking without having received any specific communication from the second individual.

Example: Henry never considers my feelings.

Response: How do you know that Henry never considers your feelings?

I know some of you think you *really can* read people's minds. Maybe you can, but it makes for sloppy communication more often than not. It also makes people mad — especially when you're wrong. If all the so-called psychic people who have told me what *I think* were really psychic, they'd know better than to tell me what I think. That isn't to say they are always wrong, just usually. And most of the ones who are right could still use their talent in more useful ways. But they know what I think about that ...

This next pattern is really the most valuable one to know:

11. *Lost Performative*:

> Statements and judgments that an individual considers to be true about the world which may be generalizations based on the individual's own experience. (Lost performatives are characterized by words like: good, bad, crazy, sick, right, wrong, true, false, etc.)

Example: It's bad to be inconsistent about what you think.

Response: Bad for whom? How do you know that it is bad to be inconsistent?

It's bad to make value judgments like these that have lost performatives in them — that's what makes them the most important. The actual lost "performative" is the person who originally said that it (whatever) was true. You can think of these statements as rules of life made up by someone, the performer, who is no longer available. A good typical response to a statement with a heavy value judgment in it is, "Who says so?" That usually brings the person to the point where they have to internally challenge their own beliefs, in trying to justify them. Any time you can get someone to do that, it's a really good thing.

You should always be on the lookout for this last pattern:

12. *Universal Quantifiers*:

> Words which generalize a few experiences to be a whole class of experience (characterized by words like: all, every, always, never, etc.).

Example: She never listens to me.

Response: She *never* listens to you? How do you know that she *never* listens to you?

I am, of course, always vigilant never to fall into the universal quantifier trap. When you hear these, they are often a sign that someone is feeling pretty desperate. They come out a lot when people are under pressure. You'll hear things like, "I'll *never* get out of this mess," or "I *always* get treated worse than *everybody* else." Never say never. And always watch out for those sweeping generalizations. That's what I always say.

So these are the twelve patterns of the Meta-Model. I'm sure all of them looked familiar to you, as a normal, functioning, communicating, human being ("Human how specifically, Sid?"). And learning them can be fun. Or it can be a pain. If you run around correcting, or challenging, everything people say, soon you'll find yourself getting pretty lonely ... So if you want to practice some of these, begin by listening for them in people's language. Get used to identifying them, *silently*, inside your head as people speak. When you feel confident that you know them well enough (whatever that means), then try responding appropriately to people. Remember you already use these patterns anyway. But try to do so in as gentle a way as possible. Then you can avoid getting people angry with you. A fight is not the goal of this model.

Really, the most valuable lesson from the Meta-Model is to use it on yourself. If you have it built into your thinking, it will make you communicate much better — I know, "better than what ...?" Better than you do now, that's what (you can't get away with that on me!). "But Sid," I hear you asking slyly, "you use all of those 'bad examples' all through these books!" "No kidding," Sid responds smugly. You wouldn't want to read them if I didn't. Remember the Meta-Model assumes that our language is full of deletions, distortions, and generalizations. It doesn't assume that they're bad, though, just imperfect. And nobody likes a perfect person ... Seriously, though, I could write with much greater precision and I know it. We could all speak with more as well. But the world would be a pretty dull place and we would sound like a bunch of robots if we tried to be perfect. The secret is to decide, based on your understanding and experience (I know, nominalizations) of people (any people you want, that's which), when you need to be more precise, or not. When we are around people we are close to, and have good rapport with, we can comfortably assume a lot. It makes life more efficient and fun. With these folks, we need to save the *techniques* for times when we need especially clear communication. Overuse can give the opposite effect.

I think the Meta-Model is a great set of rules to guide your thinking by. Remember that language is a reflection of what is in our minds. If our words come out like a tossed salad, well ... So listen to your language when you talk with people, and especially when you teach. Find out what improvements you can make in yourself as a person and a teacher.

Also, there is another set of questions that I think teachers should have available for themselves at all times. Besides the Meta-Model patterns, these will help to guide your thinking as you interact with children. They are true "meta-questions." In other words, questions outside of the normal interactions you would have with people. They are ones you ask yourself inside your head to get you thinking in more useful ways.

One of these is, "How is it possible for this to occur?" The "this" can be anything. It is a good question to ask when you are in any situation you don't understand. Being that you work with children, I am sure you have at least a few situations like that. For example, when a child asks a question, or acts in a way that does not seem to relate at all to what is going on around him, this is a good time for this question. By asking it, you look beyond the fact that he is "out of context" and figure out how he got there. If you come up with a good answer to the question in your head, it will be easier to bring him back into the context you want him in. It's a much more graceful approach than looking at him like he's crazy, or telling him you think he could use a neurological work-up ...

Another closely related question to this one is, "When and where would this behavior naturally occur?" It is a direct question, to yourself, about what context the child is in at one of these confusing times. Sometimes this can tell you where "that crazy idea" came from. The answer may also tell you a lot about how this child thinks that you wouldn't otherwise figure out. This is also an important question when using strategies in NLP, but that's a topic for another book (Volume III).

The most interesting question of this type for me is, "What exactly am *I* doing (saying, asking, thinking, etc.) that got this child to respond in this way?" This is the one that gives you back the responsibility for creating whatever you get. Remember one of our presuppositions in the NLP model is: The meaning of your communication is the response you get, regardless of your intention. This question is a great one for boosting your self-awareness (though not necessarily your ego) as well as your personal responsibility.

All three of the above questions rest on the notion that everything somebody does makes sense somehow. Your job is to figure out how. I am sure you can think of lots of similar questions to these that will help you think more clearly about what you're doing. They can also get you out of whatever jams you find yourself in. Most importantly, perhaps, they will help you clarify your own presuppositions when you are communicating with others.

Speaking of those, I think it is time to mention a couple more things about presuppositions. I already said they were my favorite Meta-Model pattern. That is because learning about them has been so important to me personally, as well as to those I teach. Again, we all have some, applicable to whatever situations we find ourselves in. The NLP model is no different. It has underlying assumptions that make the rest of it hold together. Here is a list of the major ones:

1. The map *is not* the territory.
2. All behavior has some "positive" intention, whether or not it is apparent.
3. The meaning of any communication is the response it elicits, regardless of the communicator's intent.
4. The mind/body relationship is cybernetic; a change in one part of the system will create changes in other parts.
5. There are no mistakes, only feedback.
6. All the information you need can be obtained through clear and open sensory channels.

7. A change agent (read teacher) needs three characteristics:
   1. Flexibility of behavior, to elicit any response.
   2. The sensory acuity to notice the response(s) to that behavior.
   3. The good judgment to know whether the responses are worthwhile eliciting.
8. The law of requisite variety: The part of any system with the most options in its behavior will be the part that's in control of the system.
9. There is no such thing as a dangerous or unethical process or technique, only dangerous and unethical users/people. It is up to us to know the difference and act accordingly.

Those presuppositions are important. Look them over carefully and think about them. The questions I have given you should have gotten you thinking about them by now anyway. See if you share these basic assumptions about communication and people. If you disagree with any of them, why not try it a new way for a change? It could be an interesting experiment for you. It may also lead you to some more interesting questions you can ask yourself from time to time.

Speaking of interesting questions, have you ever wondered how many ways there are to answer a question? Teachers, like the rest of humanity, tend to think in linear terms. What I mean by that is that when asked a question, they will generally just answer it. Stimulus — response. That's OK some of the time, but not always. In fact it can really hamper learning greatly. I believe that the most important thing you can do in teaching is to ask yourself and the children the best questions you can. Second to that comes giving the children the best answers you possibly can. Occasionally a direct answer to a direct question is best. Other times it's the worst.

Think about discovery. I already said that it's the way we learn best. A direct answer to a direct question often wipes out any chance for discovery, or real learning. It just gives information. There are so many more interesting and valuable ways of fielding questions. Especially if you pay attention to the structure of the question and, perhaps, ask yourself some of the ones I gave you before. A good one is, "How could this child ask me this question, based on what we're doing?" Maybe the answer to this will tell you something about how the child is organizing his or her thinking. Then you can give an answer that will be more than just another piece of information to be lost or forgotten later.

Questions are a tool. Using tools properly can make things easier, better, faster, etc. This is just as true in the classroom as it would be in a workshop. Like in the law of requisite variety, above, more choices in fielding questions will give you more control over the actual learning in the classroom. As a partial answer to my question about how many ways there are to answer questions, here is a list that I came up with off the top of my head:

1. Answer the question directly.
2. Answer the question indirectly.
3. Set up an experiment or exercise that will guide the child to find his or her own answer.
4. Answer the question *with* a question designed to: A) gather more information about the child's question B) find out what the child thinks or already knows or C) lead the child to the answer through your question(s).
5. Refuse to answer: A) with or B) without stating your reason.
6. Defer the question or answer to a more appropriate time or place.
7. Evade or ignore the question.
8. Thank the child for the question and go on to why it was such a good question: A) with or B) without giving an answer.
9. Say you don't know the answer (whether true or false) and tell the child to find it himself if he can: A) with or B) without further guidance.
10. Change the question to a better one and answer that one instead.

I am sure that if you look over the list you can come up with examples where each one is appropriate, or not. Also, I make no claim that the list is complete. Add to it if you can. If you ask yourself the above questions like, "How is this possible ...?" etc., I think they will guide you toward better choices in using all of your options — or at least a more interesting classroom experience. That's got to be worth something.

Language has many levels. This is obvious. Thinking about those levels consciously, however, can make you a much better communicator. I have talked about questions and answers. I've described the levels of experience that I use to organize my thinking. And I have demonstrated, throughout these first two volumes, many different ways to use language effectively. I can't stress enough that our language is based on our experience of the world. That is why I talked about experiencing the world first, and language later. It's the right order.

But my explanations of the world of experience are all done through language. This is primarily because I haven't yet figured out how to write without it. Hopefully these explanations have made sense to you, on whatever level you needed them to. That is one of the reasons I use so many stories.

Metaphor, or the art of storytelling, is one of the best ways in the world to teach people anything. I've said this before. I consider it to be the highest, most sophisticated, use of language — when it is done well. That means when it affects people in some useful way. That is what these books are about: how to affect people in useful ways. Everything described in them can be learned, understood, taught, used, etc., through stories. You can change people's submodalities, give them a new strategy, anchor, chain, or anything else you can think of. You need only know how to construct and deliver stories properly.

The advantage to using stories is that they give the teller and the listener more choices about communicating, perceiving, and understanding. The stories that are in these books are, of course, designed to teach you specific things. They are also designed to trigger your thinking in specific ways. And there are even more things they are designed to do. Like shake up your perception of reality. I, of course, haven't removed your ability to choose how to understand or use my stories. You always have that.

One of the other nice things about using stories is that you can get many different messages across simultaneously. And they can be taken together, or separately. Some of these are obvious, and aimed at your conscious thought processes. Others are not. Metaphors can be completely obvious at times. They can also be thinly disguised or completely disguised. A really good storyteller is able to do all three at once. You might spend a little time looking back over the stories in these first two volumes. Maybe on a second or third reading you will find more in them than you did the first time. You are not likely to find all there is however.

Metaphor construction is a fascinating subject. It is also beyond where I want to go in this series. That's not because it is more difficult or complicated — it's not. I just want you to learn more about experience and how to alter it, piece by piece, before going into higher levels of analysis and communication. Besides, there is a very good book on the subject available already.[2] At this stage I think allowing yourself to experience the stories in these volumes is plenty. When you're ready you'll get more training.

One particular metaphor I have been telling you about throughout this series, though, is the metaphor of language. Remember that language is a model of experience. It is not the same as the experience itself. The map is not the territory. Language is only a description, however imperfect, of experience.

By the same token, NLP is only a metaphor. It is a model of language, communication, and experience. So in a sense, it is a series of metaphors about metaphors. These stories from the NLP model may or may not be true. I don't care. They are very valuable either way. You will find this to be so when you go through the exercises in Volume III. Besides, metaphors don't have to be believed to be worthwhile. They only need to be experienced. That is really what matters in the land of maps and territories. With that said, I will now say something you don't generally find at the end of a book:

Let's get started.

Notes

Chapter 8

1. See *The Structure of Magic, Volume I,* By Richard Bandler and John Grinder, Science and Behavior Books, Inc., Palo Alto, Ca., 1975, Appendix B.
2. See *Therapeutic Metaphors*, by David Gordon, Meta Publications, Cupertino, Ca., 1978.

APPENDIX

APPENDIX I

PREDICATES, REPRESENTATIONAL SYSTEMS, & RAPPORT

Here is a list of common verbs categorized into representational systems. They will be helpful as a *guide* in listening to someone and discovering which representational system(s) they *favor at that time*. They will also be helpful to you in practicing to *expand* your speech to include sensory systems you may not normally use. The unspecified verbs are included to remind you that not all speech is *sensory* specific. Remember, these words will indicate which portion of sensory experience a person is primarily *aware of* while he or she is speaking.

Keep in mind that this list is only a guide — it is not complete. Feel free to add to it as necessary.

VISUAL	AUDITORY	KINES-THETIC	UNSPECI-FIED
see	listen	bite	seem
view	hear	burst	be
observe	overhear	bend	aware
witness	sound	bind	have
sight	quiet	break	think
spot	order	fall	believe
look	ask	catch	allow
glimpse	beg	fight	become

VISUAL	AUDITORY	KINES-THETIC	UNSPECI-FIED
glance	ring	go	be able
peer	chime	grasp	have to
peek	yell	grab	must
peep	scream	hold	want
survey	sing	hit	shall
eye	speak	climb	know
examine	talk	run	do
inspect	shout	struggle	make
gaze	whisper	throw	understand
stare	groan	walk	create
glare	moan	jump	contemplate
pale	whine	push	ponder
find	buzz	feel	desire
read	call	grip	appreciate
show	click	handle	sense

Remember also that using the *same* representational systems another person is using will help you to *establish rapport* with that person more quickly and easily. This is a natural phenomenon that occurs all around us. It is one way of "speaking the same language as" another person. Any time you can do that it will increase your ability to communicate — in a useful way — with someone else. *Practice makes perfect.* First get used to hearing the different representational systems, then get in the habit of switching your own to match others'.

APPENDIX II

EYE MOVEMENT PATTERNS
& ACCESSING CUES

The representational system(s) a person uses while speaking gives you information about what sensory system they are primarily aware of while they speak. But, they *may or may not* have that information *stored* in the *same representational system* in their mind. One way of finding out how this information is stored, and therefore *accessed* from memory, is by watching the direction of the person's gaze as they speak. These eye movements are called *accessing cues*.

Most people have had the experience of asking someone a question to which the person said, "Let me *see* ..." How often does the person actually move their eyes so that they are looking in a direction *up and to their left*? Literally, that person is seeing an *internal visual image*. That is also why they say, "Let me *see*" rather than, "Let me hear, feel," etc. But, following that upward visual eye movement, the person may then speak to you about what they hear or feel. This means that they have the information stored as a picture in their memory, even though their *representation* of that information to you can be as a feeling or something they have heard.

It is important to remember, however, that *people don't generally know* that they are going through these processes. For example, the person who looks up and to their left, and then tells you about how an experience felt, will generally only be aware of the feelings they are describing. They will seldom realize that they were preceded by an internal picture.

Most effective communicators seem to somehow "know" about these processes. They will often tailor their explanations to *match the internal accessing* of the person they are talking with. In other words, if they notice that the person seems to "think in pictures," they will *change their explanations* to include words that indicate visual representations. They seem to "paint the picture" for the other person. The same is true for sounds, feelings, etc.

Following is a chart showing the eye movement accessing cues. Again, practice will make noticing these cues natural and automatic. Using this chart along with the list of predicates can *greatly increase* your ability to establish rapport and *communicate effectively with anyone.* Remember, this chart is based on a "normally organized" *right-handed* person. For some people (primarily left-handed) the left and right sides of this chart need to be reversed.

Visual accessing cues for a "normally organized" right-handed person.

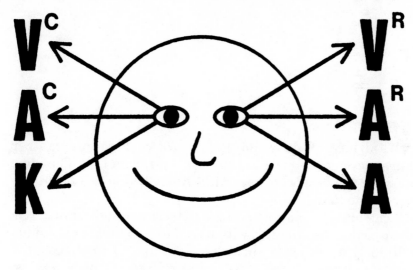

V^c   Visual constructed images.   **V^r**   Visual remembered (eidetic) images.

(Eyes defocused and unmoving also indicates visual accessing.)

A^c   Auditory constructed sounds or words.

A^r   Auditory remembered sounds or words.

K   Kinesthetic feelings (also smell and taste).

A   Auditory sounds or words.

APPENDIX III

ANCHORING

We all have off-days and on-days. We would certainly rather have the ones where we are really on and at our best. The same goes for the people we deal with. *Anchoring is the technique used to do that.*

Remember, anchoring is simple Classical Conditioning. It is the pairing of a stimulus with a response so that the stimulus will elicit the response whenever it is presented. In this case the *response* we want is a state of mind, or *state of consciousness.* We need only get into that state and set up the signal: the *anchor.* Remember also that an anchor can be a touch, sound or word, something we see, smell or taste. Touch anchors are the easiest to learn with since they are the easiest to duplicate. Once we are in the state we want, we need only establish the particular touch that will be our anchor for that state. The example used in *Meta-Cation* was touching the thumb to the forefinger on the right hand. Then for each subsequent anchor we set up, we can use the thumb and another finger, for a total of eight anchors, using this method.

Remember the following rules in using anchoring:

1. Make each anchor distinct from anything else you normally do. *Make it unique.* In other words, if you touch your thumb to your forefinger quite often don't use that as an anchor. It will be contaminated by all the other states you are in when you do it.

2. Make sure you are really in the state you want anchored, not just thinking about what it should be like. *You will anchor whatever state you are in when you set up the anchor* — it may be one of thinking about the state you really want, rather than experiencing it. That won't help you much.

3. Anchors can be *collapsed* on each other. The result will be *a third state*, different from either of the original ones. Make sure that the one you want to have is stronger than the one you want to be rid of.

4. *It may take several tries* to get the anchor to work. This is especially true when you are first learning. Be patient, and give yourself a reasonable number of attempts.

5. The more internal awareness you have the easier it will be to ensure success. You'll know if you are in the desired state or not.

6. The same rules apply for anchoring others. The better your sensory acuity the easier it will be to distinguish between the various states another person goes through. Use your senses and good judgement in using anchors with others.

7. Test your work at all times. Make sure you anchored what you want in yourself or others.

APPENDIX IV
RECOMMENDED BOOKS FOR FURTHER STUDY

There are a number of books on NLP readily available. Some are much easier reading than others. Some should be read only in the right order — in other words after you have read some others. All of the books in the first section are quite readable, however. For a complete list of all related materials, including articles, research papers, books, tapes, and dissertations, contact one of the organizations listed.

Books recommended for schoolteachers:

Jacobson, Sid. *Meta-Cation: Prescriptions For Some Ailing Educational Processes.* Cupertino, Ca., Meta Publications, 1983.

Jacobson, Sid. *Meta-Cation, Vol. II: New Improved Formulas For Thinking About Thinking.* Cupertino, Ca., Meta Publications, 1986.

Jacobson, Sid. *Meta-Cation, Vol. III: Powerful Applications For Strong Relief.* Cupertino, Ca., Meta Publications, 1986.

Harper, Linda. *Classroom Magic — Effective Teaching Made Easy.* Troy, Michigan, Twiggs Communications, 1982.

Cleveland, Dr. Bernard F. *Master Teaching Techniques.* Stone Mountain, Ga., The Connecting Link Press, 1984.

Dilts, Robert. *Applications of Neuro-Linguistic Programming: A Practical Guide to Communication, Learning, and Change.* Cupertino, Ca., Meta Publications, 1983.

Reese, Maryann, Reese, Ed, Van Nagel, C., Siudzinski, Robert. *Megateaching and Learning: Neuro-Linguistic Programming Applied to Education*. Southern Institute Press, Inc. 1985.

Gordon, David. *Therapeutic Metaphors: Helping Others Through the Looking Glass*. Cupertino, Ca., Meta Publications, 1978.

Books primarily aimed at psychotherapists and counselors:

Bandler, Richard, and John Grinder. *The Structure of Magic, Vols. I & II*. Palo Alto, Ca., Science and Behavior Books, 1975.

Bandler, Richard, and John Grinder. *Patterns of the Hypnotic Techniques of Milton H. Erickson, M.D., Vols. I & II*. Cupertino, Ca., Meta Publications, 1975.

Bandler, Richard, and John Grinder. *Frogs Into Princes*. Moab, Utah, Real People Press, 1979.

Bandler, Richard, and John Grinder. *Trance-formations: Neuro-Linguistic Programming and the Structure of Hypnosis*. Moab, Utah, Real People Press, 1981.

Bandler, Richard, and John Grinder. *Reframing: Neuro-Linguistic Programming and the Transformation of Meaning*. Moab, Utah, Real People Press, 1982.

Bandler, Richard, and John Grinder, Virginia Satir. *Changing With Families*. Palo Alto, Ca., Science and Behavior Books, 1976.

Bandler, Richard. *Using Your Brain for a Change*. Moab, Utah, Real People Press, 1985.

Bandler, Richard. *Magic In Action*. Cupertino, Ca., Meta Publications, 1984.

Lankton, Steve. *Practical Magic: The Clinical Applications of Neuro-Linguistic Programming*. Cupertino, Ca., Meta Publications, 1979.

Gordon, David and Maribeth Meyers-Anderson. *Phoenix: Therapeutic Patterns of Milton H. Erickson*. Cupertino, Ca., Meta Publications, 1981.

Books of general interest:

Dilts, Robert, et. al. *Neuro-Linguistic Programming, Vol. I: The Study of the Structure of Subjective Experience.* Cupertino, Ca., Meta Publications, 1980.

Dilts, Robert. *Roots of Neuro-Linguistic Programming.* Cupertino, Ca., Meta Publications, 1983.

BIBLIOGRAPHY

Bandler, Richard and John Grinder. *The Structure of Magic, Volume I.* Science and Behavior Books, Inc., Palo Alto, Ca., 1975.

Dilts, Robert. "Applications of NLP in Health," in *Applications of Neuro-Linguistic Programming.* Meta Publications, Cupertino, Ca., 1983.

Caldecott, Leonie. "Liv Ullman: Making Choices," *New Age Journal.* July, 1985.

Gordon, David. *Therapeutic Metaphors.* Meta Publications, Cupertino, Ca., 1978.

Goetz, Michael. *Adventure.* Michael Goetz, 1982. (This version of this computer game is NOT in the Public Domain, though it is available from some of the same distributors.)

Miller, G., E. Galanter, and K. Pribram. *Plans and the Structure of Behavior.* Henry Holt & Co., 1960.

Drucker, Peter. *Adventures Of A Bystander.* New York, Harper & Row, 1979.

Tart, Charles. *States of Consciousness.* New York, Dutton, 1975.

Watzlawick, Paul. *How Real Is Real?.* New York, Random House, 1976.

META-CATION
VOLUME III

Powerful Applications For Strong Relief

by
Sid Jacobson

CONTENTS

INTRODUCTION:
META TEACHING TEACHING

Shortly after I bought my computer, I thought I knew a little something about what made it work. I spent a week learning word processing, my checkbook program, and my mailing list. I even played with the spreadsheet financial programs, just for fun. As I got more into using these things I felt like I knew less and less all the time. Obviously that wasn't true, I just felt like it. I got to the point, primarily with word processing, where I thought I knew enough so that I didn't want to know any more. I could write letters and text just fine. I could even get them printed out, looking pretty much the way I wanted. I thought, "This is just a tool, I don't need to know how it really works."

But every once in a while I would want to do something more advanced. One of these things was my own typesetting for advertising and publicity. Each new task required new learning. At some point I decided that I was being foolish. It was silly to use a truly powerful technological tool at half speed. So I began looking into the manuals more closely. Soon I found myself looking for new and sophisticated things to do with my marvelous machine. When I would get stuck, instead of thinking, "Well, I don't really need to do it that way — I can get by with just ..." I started thinking, "I know there is a neat, clean, interesting way to get this done — and it will work better than settling for ..." The more I did this the more I learned.

Within a few more months I was looking for new software —

something I thought I would *never* do. I use a Kaypro 4 and it came with plenty of free software, capable of doing just about anything a small businessman or writer could ever want. Or so I thought.

Then I discovered the Public Domain. Free software! It is written by people who really care about advancing the technology and helping others. You generally just pay about $10 to $12 for the floppy disk, shipping, and handling, etc. The actual information on the disk is free. And it comes chock full of amazing stuff. There is some written for just about every machine you can find and tons for a popular one like mine. All designed to do lots of strange little things. Some of them, of course, seem useless, others incomprehensible. Some disks, however, are truly wonderful. For every half dozen programs I got that I thought were ridiculous, there was at least one real gem. I use a couple of them so habitually now that I wonder how I did without them. Less efficiently I think. Certainly with more effort and less fun. I even discovered a few that are marvelously helpful, especially in getting machines to communicate with each other. Some do it by getting them to talk over the phone. Others actually redo software so that one machine can translate, understand, and even change another machine's information.

Best of all, there are a few little jewels that are designed to get you out of trouble when you screw up. One of these actually will get back stuff you thought you erased. I learned that just because the machine said you erased your brilliant creation from the disk, it was just kidding. You really only hid it by removing the labels. This particular program can find it for you and bring it back in its original state, right there in front of you.

It's really comforting to know that someone spent the time to come up with a way for you to cover up, and recover from, your mistakes easily and gracefully. And do things, quickly and easily, that you never would have dreamed of. Those people should get medals.

There were a number of exercises in *Meta-Cation* designed to get you using the skills of a novice NLPer. There was also a lot of other stuff in those exercises. The same goes for the ones here. But before you do these new ones, I suggest you review the ones in *Meta-Cation* again. Everything in this book builds on the previous two volumes. Because of this, you will need to be comfortable with anchors, representational systems, and accessing cues. You will also need to be able to establish a significant level of rapport with children to be able to do some of the more advanced things. The sharper your senses are the better you'll do. More on this later.

In addition you will need perseverance. Some of the experiments in this book are going to be difficult for you. I can't tell you which ones because everyone is different. Some that you find hard others will find easy, and vice versa. Take each difficulty as a new learning about yourself and you will grow from it. That is what this book is for.

In addition, they will take some time. Considerable time in some cases. I am conscious when I say that of a likely response from many teachers of, "We don't have time!" I know many people believe that. But some learning takes time. So I suggest you think of this in a different way. Think of everything in this book as a long-term investment, to be added to *slowly*. For some people every new book becomes a race to the end. If you're one of those people, I suggest you treat this book as a new experiment in itself. See how much time you can take with it. Try and make it last as long as you can. It will enhance your investment and your learning. I want to relieve the stresses and strains that go with teaching, not add to them. So pace yourself. If it takes you a year to get through these experiments, I don't think that is too long. For some people it will certainly be too short.

The experiments here are based on the NLP principles in Volume II. The more carefully you read that volume, the more you will understand about the processes. Whether you really understand, from a theoretical point of view, why the procedures work is not very important to me. Not that it isn't important at all, just not very. This book is designed to get you to do things you probably didn't think were possible. They are. The more diligently and systematically you approach each experiment, the better you will learn. Each one will directly improve you in some way. The ones involving working with children will also improve them, directly. They will improve both of you indirectly in many more ways, however. I won't even ask you to trust me on that. I think if you have come this far in this series you already realize that the information and technology we have is very special. Throughout this volume I will refer to the two previous ones to keep you oriented to the NLP model as a whole.

I also want to comment on the various ways people read books of this kind. Some people will just scan through quickly and put another notch on their "books read" belt. This will be of some value in this case, but not so much. Others will carefully hang on each word, as if they were gold, until they have thoroughly understood all of them — and skip the exercises. They will, of course, gain more than the person who skims over the material quickly. Quite a bit more actually. But they will still be defeating the purpose of the book. Then there are those who jump from place to place hoping to find their favorite topic covered. This, I find, usually means the spots where their favorite opinions are most eloquently agreed with. If you attempt that with this book you will probably find yourself completely lost in short order. There is almost nothing in this volume that does not rest heavily on what came before it. On purpose.

This is a teaching book. More accurately, perhaps, a guide book. But it is designed to guide your behavior first, and your thinking second. Think about that for a moment. I said in Volume II that I believe very strongly in learning by discovery. That means through behavior and experience. Not by agreeing or disagreeing with the theory that you guess is lying just beneath the instructions. By the same token I also believe that good writing in itself can guide you to experiences you will learn from.

Hopefully I have written good experiments for you to do. They are much more involved than the ones in Volume I. That is one of the reasons for Volume II — to give you some base to work from. You will remember that I commented in that book that I teach differently than I write. I usually teach by giving experiments and drills first, explanation later. I wish that was viable in book form. I don't think it is. A book is still a book and I can't be there to clean up any messes I make. So I attempt to clean them up before and during, rather than after, in this series. That is not to say there is no pure discovery here. There is. It is just framed differently than it would be if we were physically together.

I invite you to glean what you can from the organization of the book and the exercises within it. I have tried to be a model of good teaching as much as possible throughout. I hope you feel that it comes through and is helpful to you. I know that writing is one of my best learning methods. I certainly have learned a great deal in writing this series. I hope that comes through also.

Good teaching grows out of good learning. Good learning grows out of learning how to learn. Learning how to learn comes directly from experiment and discovery. When we understand how learning works inside of experience, we can generate experience that leads to good learning. That's a pretty fair definition of experiment and discovery. The two can't be separated. Just teaching someone else's material, without knowing it on the inside, in experience, creates mediocre learning. That is not to say that exploring new territory isn't worthwhile, just that it has to be connected to internal experience at some point in the process. I hope my connections work well for you.

I also hope I have successfully combined all of these principles within this book. Though I don't think books are a particularly good way to learn NLP, they definitely have their function. I also consider it a worthy challenge, for both of us, to prove that I am wrong about how much NLP you can learn from books. I hope some of you will let me know how we have done.

One final note. In an effort to avoid contributing to the sexist nature of our language, and the awkward nature of continually constructing sentences with "he or she," "him or her," etc., I have attempted to alternate male and female pronouns for each exercise. If the first one in a section refers to working with a boy, the next one does so with a girl. In cases where the exercises involve two children, I refer to one of each. Remember that I am not suggesting that you should do certain exercises with girls and others with boys. I am simply trying to respond to those who feel that our language is biased regarding gender. I agree that it is, and I invite anyone to come up with workable solutions. Until then, I do the best I can.

CHAPTER 1

TOURING A FEW STATES

You learned something about anchoring states in *Meta-Cation*. Of course when you were anchoring these states you could only guess about their true nature, based on your good judgment and observation. When we use words like "motivation," "excitement," or whatever, we're not being very precise. That is simply a function of our words. *We* may know what we mean, but only by our internal experience of each of those states. The next step is to enhance the descriptive words by including that internal experience. This is easy, now. In Volume II, I introduced a vocabulary for determining just how one state differs from another: submodalities.

In addition to writing books, I do a variety of workshops. One of these is on "stress management." I call it "Stress for Success" just to be obnoxious. What I do is much different from anyone else as far as I can tell. Since you have had the guts to undertake this exploration, I'll give you some of it — no extra charge.

Quite simply, I have each person in the room identify one of their problem stressful situations. Then I split them into groups and pass out the following sheet:

Work Sheet For Identifying States of Consciousness

Give a content description of the situation and any images you notice inside. In other words, in a couple of sentences describe what the pictures and sounds are in your head:

Under each of the following sections, make whatever notes you will need to guide you through the changes you want to make.

Visual Submodalities

Color	Shape	Size	Distance
Location	Brightness	Contrast	Clarity
Focus	Movement/Speed	Direction	Depth
Slides/Motion	Picture	Associated/Disassociated	

Auditory Submodalities

Sound/Words	Voice/Whose?	Internal/External	
Location	Distance	Direction	Volume
Pitch	Rhythm	Tempo	Duration
Tone	Timbre		

Kinesthetic Submodalities

Internal/External		Tactile/Proprioceptive	Intensity
Location	Size	Shape	Moisture
Weight	Pressure	Temperature	Texture
Duration	Frequency	Movement	Rhythm

This is a description of your state of consciousness at this point in this situation. If you pay attention to the feelings they will help you know if the visual images and sounds are what you want. Systematically changing the visual and auditory submodalities will, of course, help you change the feelings until you have them the way you want them. It is always a good idea to have an anchor for any state that is especially pleasant or useful.

This should look pretty familiar by now. If you need review on any of the submodalities, check back in Volume II. Also, this sheet is in the back of the book, conveniently set up for you to photocopy — make lots of copies, you'll use them. You have already experimented a little with submodalities, but now it is time to get used to finding out which ones are critical for you, and how you use them. If you sometimes suffer from symptoms of stress, this is for you.

Your States, Experiment #1

Step 1

Remember a time when you felt you were in a state of real stress. This could be teaching or anywhere else. You'll know you have it when you feel the same pressures you did then. Don't worry, you'll get rid of it soon enough. Use the sheet above, or a copy of the one in the back of the book, as a guide and write a couple of descriptive sentences about the situation and your internal experience.

Step 2

Next concentrate on the internal pictures you have of that memory. Again, using the above list as a guide, make some notes to yourself about each of the visual submodalities as you watch the image. Be as complete as you possibly can for now. If you have trouble determining some of them, do your best. When you have some sort of note on each, go on to the next step.

Step 3

Now listen for any sounds or voices you remember as you look at the image. Go to the auditory submodality list and make notes to yourself as you did for the visuals. Be as complete as possible.

Step 4

Do the same thing for the feelings, using the kinesthetic submodality list as a guide. Be especially careful to note your feelings in this stressful situation.

Step 5

Get up and walk around for a minute. We call this a break state. If necessary, eat a cookie, you deserve it. You want to shake off whatever effects remembering that state had on you. Everybody is different. You now have, however, a good description of at least one state of stress you know how to do. The next task is to learn how *not* to.

Step 6

Now remember a time when you were extremely efficient, energetic, and pleased. I know you have had one, you can't fool me. It may have been a time at work when everything was going really smoothly and you felt in control of the situation.

Step 7

Write a brief description of the situation you remember, as you did with the other one.

Step 8

Go through the visual submodalities as you did before, making notes on each.

Step 9

Repeat this with the auditory and kinesthetic submodalities as you did before. When you have finished you will have a description of a state of effectiveness. Take another break if you wish, or savor this state for a few minutes, whichever you prefer.

Step 10

Now comes the interesting part. Compare your notes on each of these states, the stressful one and the effective one. They will certainly be different. Notice which of the submodalities are different and which are pretty much the same in each state. Make any notes you think may be useful.

Step 11

Go back to the stressful state you were in and recall the images vividly.

Step 12

When you get to that state, look at your list of the visual submodalities of the *effective* state. One at a time, change the ones you have in this stressful state so that they are just like they would be in the effective state. Use your notes and your memory.

In other words, let's say that in the effective state, the visual image was somewhat dimmer than in the stressful one. You would then dim your present image, the one of the stressful situation, until it is at the same level of brightness as it was in the effective state. Repeat this with distance. If the image seemed to be several feet further from you in the effective state, move your present image away from you to that spot. The same for location, size, color, and so on. Take your time, this may take some getting used to.

Remember to only *change the form*, not the content of the images. Content changes constitute cheating (I couldn't control myself).

Step 13

Do the same with the auditory submodalities. If the voices are softer in the effective state, make them softer in the stressful state. If they seem lower in pitch in the effective state, lower them in the stressful one as well. Do the same with distance, location, etc.

Step 14

When you have changed all of the visual and auditory submodalities of the stressful state so that they match the ones in the effective state, spend a few minutes paying attention to how you feel. Undoubtedly it is different than when you started.

One of the interesting things about doing this kind of work for a number of years is the opportunity it gives you to collect patterns. I am very careful about making generalizations, but I do notice certain things occurring over and over again. "Stress," to me, is no longer as useful a word as it was. Its unique meaning has been killed by overuse. Still, most of us know what we mean for ourselves when we use words like "overwhelmed," "frazzled," "tense," "burned out," and all the other idioms we have come up with. They aren't any better than stress, but at least they add variety and color. More than the actual states do as far as I can tell.

It seems we can, for most people, tell them exactly how to build a state of stress based on a few crucial submodalities. I am not sure anyone would really want to, but if they did we know how. It doesn't seem to matter what the situation, certain internal processes, all at the same time, can feel uncomfortably stressful to anyone. Try out the following list for yourself. First, pick any scene, no matter how mundane. Then change it so that it conforms to a few of the following characteristics:

Too many images in a small space (or field of vision)

Images moving in different directions, too fast, or at different speeds

Images that are too close

Images that are too large or too bright

Sounds that are too close, loud, or shrill

Too many sounds or voices at once

Sounds or voices of unpleasant tonalities

Each of these is a matter of degree and of individual preference. This is one area in which people are clearly different and unique. However, each of the items listed above is a common way people create anxiety, tension, and a feeling of being overwhelmed. You can make just as much of a mess with the pictures and sounds in your head as you can help yourself with them. Don't stay in a state like this for very long, even to experiment with. Be as gentle with your visual and auditory images as you would be with your feelings. Even better, be as gentle as you would like *others* to be with your feelings. We don't need martyrs in education, they don't last very long.

Some people have a really hard time seeing and hearing their internal images. It does not mean they are broken. If you have had difficulty, don't worry. You will need to practice. You're having the images, to be sure, but you are just not used to paying *conscious* attention to them. I bring this up now because, for some people, this is a cause of concern. They read my instructions and think they have brain damage or something. Then they know how to build a state of stress much better than I do.

More common are people who say they have trouble concentrating on, or holding, an image for any length of time. It becomes just as difficult for them to describe the submodalities of an internal experience as for those who "don't see pictures" inside. Fleeting images are fairly common. In fact, for just about everyone, some images are hard to hold. If you find that yours fit this description, again, don't worry. With practice you will be able to handle the images just fine. In the meantime, do the best you can with the descriptions.

Strangely, or not, "pretending" to follow the instructions

often seems to work fine for people who have trouble seeing and hearing the images inside. If you think about it, though, this makes sense and really isn't strange at all. Remember that these techniques are all based on normal brain functioning in the first place. So your brain understands the instructions perfectly on some unconscious level. Therefore, it can go through the procedures on that same unconscious level with no trouble. In fact it may actually be laughing at you since you don't know what is going on. Brains do those sorts of things sometimes. In sum, it is worthwhile doing these first few experiments even if you have some difficulty following, or knowing if you're following, the instructions perfectly.

Done with diligence, changing the submodalities changes your state to the one you *want*. That's if you change the right ones. You probably noticed that changing some of them had a very powerful effect, while others had little at all. Remember the ones that made a difference. Those are your *critical submodalities*. They should work the same for you with everything. List these critical submodalities on a sheet of paper, or mark them on your state sheet. You'll want a list while you are learning to use them. After that you'll know them so well you can forget about taking notes. Just like school, eh?

Speaking of school, there are some other states I'd like you to explore in the same way. Comparing states is fascinating and will teach you a lot about yourself and how your brain works. Knowing which ones to compare can make it even more interesting and fun. And once you know yourself well enough, you'll get to inflict yourself on a child. Won't that be fun!

Your States, Experiment #2

Step 1

The next state I want you to explore is one of intense interest and curiosity. Remember a time when you were engrossed in something that riveted your attention, perhaps for several hours at a time.

Step 2

Use the lists above and make notes regarding each of the visual, auditory, and kinesthetic submodalities, along with a brief description of the situation in which the state occurred. Make sure you have your list as complete as you can get it. You may want this state again some time.

Step 3

Next, break out of that state. Now remember a state of sheer, utter, screaming boredom. I am sure you can remember a few — you went to college.

Step 4

Make your notes describing this state as thoroughly as before. The object is to learn how you *do* boredom.

Step 5

Now look at the list you made of *critical* visual submodalities after the first exercise. Choose one of these and change it so that, while in your bored state, you have this one submodality the same as when you are in that curious and interested state. For example, if distance is critical, change the internal visual image so that it appears to be at the same distance from you in the boring state as it was in the interesting one. Notice any changes in your feelings.

Step 6

Now change this one back so that it's the way it's supposed to be when you are fabulously bored. Pick another of the critical submodalities from your list and change it. Again notice any effects, then change it back to the way it was.

Step 7

Continue this until you have tried it with each of the critical visual submodalities on your list.

Step 8

Now do the same thing with the auditory submodalities, changing each one that is critical, then reversing the change, one at a time. Notice the effects on your feelings in each case.

Step 9

Once you have experimented with each of your critical visual and auditory submodalities, change all of them at once. Make the ones in the boring state match the ones in the interesting state. Remember, leave the content of the pictures and sounds alone, just change the form. Check your feelings when you are done — ultimately they are what matter to most of us.

I hope you are thinking about ways to control your own interest level in different situations. I also hope you are thinking about how daydreaming works. It is more than just imagining you were somewhere else. It can be a natural defense. Used constructively, it may allow you to pay attention to what is going on, while still absorbing the content of whatever is boring you. You can really alter your feelings about this content or situation by changing the quality of the form inside your head.

I think we have all played with these things from time to time. I know I have imagined people talking with different voice tones than their own for my own twisted amusement. I have also imagined people being smaller and further away from me when I really didn't care to be near them. These are form changes, not content. They were the same people saying the same things, unfortunately in some cases. But my experience of them was made more tolerable, even pleasant, by my internal creative license. That is the license nobody can revoke.

Even more interesting than comparing boredom and interest is comparing confusion and understanding. Both of these states are extremely useful in the right context. We only notice them when they aren't, however. Confusion is easy to recognize because most of us don't like it. There are times, while learning just about anything, that we have to go through it. We usually ask questions, read further, or explore until it is gone. We usually notice its absence when we have what we consider to be "understanding."

I, and most of us in NLP, think this can be a dangerous trap. The understanding we often reach is the same as my "understanding" of my computer early on. Enough to get by with, but not enough to create from. Worse off are those of us who just have to be "RIGHT." What a shame. What a shambles it makes of our relationships. And what a message it gives to our children.

Your States, Experiment #3

Step 1

First I want you to distinguish between two clearly qualitatively different states of confusion. The first is the kind where you have just found something that is so different from your previous experience that you don't even begin to know how to categorize it. A real stumper. The kind of state that gets you so lost that you have to find a new starting place to get back to normal. The kind where Mr. Spock says, "There is nothing in the known universe to explain such a phenomenon, Captain." We'll call this one state number 1.

The second is the kind where you know something about the new information, but not quite enough. Perhaps you're playing your favorite trivia game and you can't remember if the capital of Montana is Trenton or Boise. But you know there is a capital, and you could probably figure out where to look it up, given the slightest bit of thought. Or when you're writing something and you can't remember how a word is spelled, so you try it all three ways but none looks any better than the other. Maybe you are at a party with a large group of people and can't quite remember who was married to whom, when. Or if that couple, glaring at each other from opposite corners of the room, are already divorced or just practicing. These are less jolting forms of confusion, though for some of us they can be nearly as mind-bending as the first kind.

Begin by identifying an example of one of each of these states for yourself, state number 1 and state number 2.

Step 2

Now, for each, go through the lists of submodalities and fully describe each state, one at a time. Remember not to stay too long in either one of them, lest you never finish the exercise.

Step 3

Next compare the submodalities, especially the critical ones, as before. Notice any similarities as well as glaring differences.

Step 4

Now we'll distinguish between and identify two different states of understanding. The first is the kind of "almost" knowing something I talked about earlier. Like when you have to take a history exam and you know the basic facts and the sequence they fall in and you know it's an essay test and you'll only have an hour so you know you can get through an hour's worth of the most important things without having to really know any details and besides you got a B on the midterm and it's your last semester and you already know what you're doing after school is out and your professor is really an easy grader and as long as you avoid really obvious screw-ups — like run-on sentences — you'll do OK so ... I think you get the idea. This is state number 3.

The other kind is the one where you absolutely know how it

works, whatever it is. You could make up the test, you learned it so well. Something you learned deeply in your experience and just thinking about it brings on a flood of examples. You have explained it to others and used the concept successfully many times. One of those areas of knowledge in which your expertise is exceeded only by your humility ... Call this state number 4.

Take an example of each of these four states, and go through a submodality sheet with each. If you choose to stay in one of them longer than the other, you might try the latter, number 4.

Step 5

Now you have four states fully identified on your submodality sheets. Compare the critical submodalities of each and note any apparent patterns.

Step 6

Now we'll get mildly weird. Take state number 1, the one of utter, total, blithering confusion. Change the critical submodalities of this one so that they are like the ones in the more mild confusion state, number 2. Notice any changes in your feelings or thoughts when you have finished.

Step 7

Now take it one step further. Change these same submodalities again, so that they match the ones in the basic "sort of understanding" state, number 3. Again make any notes to yourself and pay attention to your thoughts and feelings.

Step 8

Now go that last step and change the critical submodalities in the images and sounds so that they match your state of total and complete understanding, number 4. When you have finished pay close attention to your thoughts and feelings for a few minutes.

You have taken a state of complete confusion and, in a graduated way, changed it so that it matches the form of a state of complete understanding. Hopefully you realized somewhere along the way that you have probably done this for most of your life in one way or another. Here, though, we completely ignored the content of these experiences, concentrating only on form. What effect did it have on you? Remember everyone is different, but everyone will be affected somehow.

Your States, Experiment #4

Step 1

Now we'll get largely weird. I intend to take you on a journey you did not expect, using those same four states. Begin by taking your original total understanding state, number 4. This time I want you to go the other way, and match the critical submodalities in number 4 to the ones in number 3. Notice any changes.

Step 2

Next take it a step further and match the critical submodalities to those of number 2, mild confusion. Again see how you feel and think.

Step 3

Go the last mile and change it all the way so that the critical submodalities match those of number 1. Allow yourself to maintain this state for a few minutes. Pay particular attention to your thought processes. Try and remember what it was you knew so well when you started off in this state.

Step 4

When you have had enough, slowly take it back, step by step, to the way it was originally. Get it back to "normal" and see how you feel.

When doing experiments like these many people have strange and powerful experiences. Knowing these particular states of consciousness can tell us more about how we learn and understand, or not, than anything I have come across.

Some people have a really bizarre time with that last experiment. At the first change — taking something they know well, and changing their state of consciousness to match that of something they know less well — they begin to doubt their own knowledge and expertise. How often do we all do *that* to ourselves?! When they go the next step to a state of mild confusion, sometimes they really get worried. Now they're not sure if they ever knew what they were doing. The last step really throws them. They can actually be convinced they never learned this idea, whatever it was. They are just as confused about something they know absolutely, as they are about things that they don't know, absolutely. And it is just as fascinating to watch them go back through the steps the other way. You can almost see them recovering information, bit by bit. Knowing those steps can help immensely in learning new information. It's an internal sort of "knowing" that is hard to explain adequately, but it's the kind that really counts. Save your notes on these last two experiments. We're going to use them again.

As I promised, once you have sufficiently experimented with yourself, you'll have the opportunity to do the same things with children. I was serious about doing the ones with yourself, first, too. If you have not fully explored these states yourself, and done the experiments, it isn't fair that you work with children in this way yet. That isn't just a guilt trip. Besides, you'll likely miss important things and make it hard on both of you, if you haven't had the experience — or at least tried to the best of your ability. Most distasteful of all, when you present it to the child you won't know what you're talking about.

Also, I mentioned earlier that you need to be very good at several things before doing these experiments. The necessary prerequisites are:

RAPPORT   Establishing and maintaining rapport. This is very important because of the strangeness of these procedures compared to what you normally do with children. As you talk to the child, put everything in a framework of helping him to enjoy school and learn better.

ANCHORS   You need to be comfortable with anchoring children while you're working with them. In each experiment, you will first want to establish good comfortable rapport with the child. Then you should have an anchor for this feeling of comfort and safety. That way if the child should become upset or remember something too unpleasant, you can fire the anchor and bring him back into the state he began in. For review, see *Meta-Cation* pages 109-114.

AWARENESS   You need to have your eyes and ears with you and functioning at all times. Also your good judgment. If you detect any serious discomfort on the part of the child, stop, use your anchors for comfort, and do whatever else needs to be done.

CLARITY   You need to be clear in your communication so that the child understands what you are talking about. Read the directions to each experiment carefully ahead of time. You may want to practice explaining some of what you will do before you begin.

PATIENCE   Last and most important, you need to be patient with the child. You will be asking him to do things that no one has ever asked of him before. Be sensitive to the nature of these procedures. You will be working at a pace that is comfortable for both you and the child.

Others' States, Experiment #1

Step 1

Find a child you are comfortable experimenting with. This exercise will take a little time, so allow accordingly. As in all the others when working with another person, you will begin by explaining to the child that you want to help him with something. In this case it is how to handle boredom and be more interested in school work. You will also establish rapport and set up an anchor for a comfortable easy state before going on.

Step 2

Next tell him that you want to find out how he thinks about being interested and being bored. You may also mention that you have done what you are about to with yourself already and that it's fun. If you share with him what your experience was like he may be more interested — it's a good habit to get into. Don't tell too much though, just give a general idea of where you're going. Leave a little for him to find out on his own.

Step 3

Begin with the boring state. Use one of your photocopied state sheets. It will be more comfortable for you. Ask the child to remember the last time he was really bored in class. Don't take it personally, this is an experiment. When he gets to the state, anchor it *with a different anchor than the one you are* using for comfort. You can use this anchor to help him stay in the state for now. Later you may use it to get him back to this state.

Step 4

Ask him to describe the situation and make a note to yourself about the content.

Step 5

Next, tell him you want to know certain things about the picture in his head when he is bored like this. You might remind him of the brightness knob on a TV set. Then ask him to tell you how bright the picture is. Tell him to imagine, in addition, a TV with lots of extra controls, for distance, color, etc. You may need to ask for a comparison to something you can both see for each one. For example, "Is it as bright as the daylight outside now?" Repeat this with each of the other visual submodalities. Make a note about each one.

Step 6

Repeat this with each of the auditory and kinesthetic submodalities as well. Essentially, you are doing the same thing with this child that you did with yourself. One advantage this time, though, is that you can observe him while he pays attention to his own internal experience. You'll be able to see his eye movements and any other physical changes while he gives you the information you want. This will also force you to ask good questions.

Step 7

When you have gotten the information on this state, take a short break. Fire the comfort anchor, if you need it, to get him back to normal.

Step 8

Repeat the above steps with a state of interest and curiosity. Help him into the state, anchor it *differently,* and gather the information. Remember to be patient and clear in your instructions.

Step 9

When you have both states clearly mapped out, take another short break. Compare the two sheets and notice which submodalities are most different. You can probably assume that these are the critical ones for *him.*

Step 10

Just as you did with yourself, have the child go back to the state of boredom. Use the anchor for that state to help you if you need it. One at a time have him change each of the submodalities you think may be critical, i.e. the ones that are different in the two states. Again, you want him to change these so that they match the ones in the more interesting state.

Do them one at a time, and remind him to change each one back before going to the next. This way you will be able to verify that changing them makes some difference. Do this by asking for feedback *and using your eyes and ears.*

Step 11

Now help him change the state of boredom completely. Ask him to change all the critical submodalities so that they match the ones in the state of interest. He may need to do them slowly, one by one. Ask, watch, and listen for the changes.

Step 12

Discuss the results. Again share with him what happened for you. Any differences between you are just that. Remind him that we are all different in some ways and this is one of them. Talk about ways he might use this for himself. You should already have thought of several.

Sometimes you will want to work with several states when helping someone, rather than just one or two. Everything isn't black and white of course. As I said earlier, in my Stress For Success workshop I do some unusual things. One is that I give people a chance to explore more than just a stressful state. I have them determine a state of real efficiency as well. But I also think it is a good idea to have a relaxing state to escape to when the time is right.

I believe the trick to handling the symptoms of stress and burnout is in knowing when to use each of these two alternatives to stress: efficiency and relaxation. If you're too relaxed you might not do much work. I sure don't want to if I am very relaxed. I reserve that state for the appropriate (though I hate that word) times. Otherwise, the work I am avoiding will pile up — and so will my level of stress. When I have a lot of work to do I use one of my several states of real efficiency. That is what they are for. I have also had to learn to shut those off so as not to overdo it. I am no fun to be around when I haven't had some time for myself, away from the never-ending work load.

Others' States, Experiment #2

Step 1

Pick another child, one you feel would benefit from help handling stress. Explain this to the child, while establishing good rapport, comfort, and an anchor for this comfortable state.

Step 2

Pull out yet another of your work sheets on states. Ask this child to remember the last time she was under a great deal of stress. Use whatever terms she'll understand. Anchor this state when she gets into it.

Step 2 — Alternative

This step can be done in another way. If you feel it is appropriate with this child, you can do Step 1 and stop. Save Step 2 for when she has already worked herself into a state of stress on her own. That way you can avoid putting her into any more discomfort than she is already doing to herself. Also, you'll have established an anchor to get her to a calmer, more comfortable state if you need to.

Step 3

Ask her the questions that will give you the information you need about visual submodalities. Repeat with auditory and kinesthetics. In this case, she may immediately be aware of one or two in each representational system. This is common in highly emotional states. Don't force her to go through all of them. It is better to get a few quickly, and get her out of that state. The ones she gives you will probably be more than enough to help her with. This is not always the case, but usually it is.

Step 4

Once you have this state mapped out, you can go on to more pleasant ones with her. You might say something like, "I'll bet you'd feel a lot better if you could just relax." She just might do it. At any rate, the next state to get her to is her relaxed state. Ask her to remember a really nice one. You could describe one for her and help her into it that way if it helps. You had plenty of opportunity to do each of these in *Meta-Cation*.

Step 5

Use another sheet to fill out the details of this state. Make sure you are as complete as you need to be; it's good practice anyway. This is a state you may want to let her enjoy for a while.

Step 6

Talk with her about how it is important to be comfortable like in the relaxed state, but also to be able to have lots of energy to get things done. Describe an "in-between" state of effectiveness for her. Make sure she understands and ask if she has ever had one like that. If so get her into that one, anchor it, and go through the submodalities again. If not, go to the Step 6 — Alternative.

Step 6 — Alternative

This child may not have ever built the state you want for her at this point. Undoubtedly she has come close, but you may want to give her a new one. Look at the submodalities of the two states you have just mapped out: stress and relaxation. Notice which ones are very different. Again you can assume that these are the critical ones.

Get her back into the relaxed state. Slowly change the submodalities you think may be critical until they are closer to, *but not the same as* they were in the stressful state. Check with her each step of the way to make sure she is comfortable. The goal is to give her some of the energy that goes with the stress, while maintaining enjoyment. This is where the two of you get to be creative and experiment, one submodality at a time. Anchor the state when you have it the way you want it.

Step 7

Now talk with her about the different states. Let her know she can substitute either the relaxed state or the pleasant/energetic/productive one whenever she feels pressured. Show her that she changed herself by changing certain of the qualities of her pictures and sounds in her head. If you want, you can certainly show her how to use the anchors. This is the time to remember and use your skills of future-pacing. If you need to review, see *Meta-Cation*, pages 29-32 and 110-117.

The problem with confusion is not that it exists. The problem is that we have never been taught how to use it. For most people confusion is "bad." It denotes an inability to make up your mind, a weakness in intelligence, or laziness. This is the case only when we let it breed on itself and send us into the "endless loop." That is the proverbial circle with no way out, for those of you not hip to computer jargon.

As I said earlier, confusion is a necessary part of learning. At least that is the reigning NLP view. I don't know if it is true, but it makes me feel a whole lot better. Let's pretend it's gospel. What I do know is that confusion can be a good thing. If nothing else it gets us out of our prearranged expectations and into the real world of random chance, Murphy's Law, and dumb luck — good or bad. More important, it can get us going in new directions. Some people think of confusion as a "doorway to a new reality." Maybe someday I'll be clever enough to think up stuff like that. In the meantime, I use and respect confusion, and help others to do the same.

Others' States, Experiment #3

Step 1

For this exercise, I want you to wait until you have a child who is really confused and lost in some area. For most teachers this waiting period could be as lengthy as ten minutes. Also, you will need a little time to do this experiment.

Step 2

When you find the child in this naturally occurring state, tell him you wish to do an experiment that can be a lot of fun. You want to teach him how neat (terrific, interesting, cool, or the idiom of your choosing) life can be when you're confused.

Step 3

Pull out one of your state sheets, or wing it if you feel ready. Anchor the state. Go through the visual, auditory, and kinesthetic submodalities making appropriate notes. It will probably be obvious to you, by this time, which ones are making the child uncomfortable. Interrupt him however you need to, and get him out of the state.

Step 4

Remind him of something he knows well. In other words get him into his state of "understanding" like you did with yourself earlier. Anything he knows thoroughly will do, school-related or otherwise. It may be interesting for you to use whatever he last understood clearly, on his way to his present confused state.

Step 5

Anchor this state of understanding and take him through describing the submodalities. Make notes as you need to.

Step 6

Teach him the difference between the two states. Explain as much or as little as you think best. Get him to understand critical submodalities; it will help you understand them better as well. Tell him how knowing this has helped you.

Step 7

Now you get to experiment on your own. Between the two of you, figure out what he might do when he gets into the confused state so that *it will help him to learn*. Use the submodalities, anchoring, and future pacing however you think they will work best.

I'm asking you to be a bit creative here. I can't give you

step-by-step instructions forever. Sooner or later you have to do things based on why and how they work, not by the numbers. As long as you use what you know from previous experiments, you'll do fine.

States of consciousness have become the basis of just about everything I do in working with people. That is because it has become so easy, natural, and fun for me to use them. Once I really understood, as much as anyone now does, how they worked, I felt like I had a much better understanding of how people work. So, human behavior isn't so mysterious as it once was for me. This new perspective has made me a lot more comfortable in many different situations. It has also given me the confidence that, with a little effort and good judgment, I can help people solve just about any problem. Beyond that, I also feel confident that this kind of understanding is what will move the field of education forward, in the direction it needs to go. And there is so much more we can do, just with sub-modalities and states ...

CHAPTER 2

TO ASSOCIATE, OR NOT ...

Several years ago one of my instructors, Richard Bandler, gave me a tremendous compliment. Since he hardly ever gives any of those to anybody, I was quite pleased with myself. I was also a little puzzled. I didn't think what I had done was so special at all.

A little background. About six years ago we had an NLP convention, with lots of workshops and demonstrations. Richard was talking about love and commitment in relationships. He had just discovered a very important part of how it worked. Like any normal person I was fascinated. So was everyone else. He demonstrated a technique he had devised based on his findings, with a married couple in the room. He had them do something inside their heads and describe what it was like. They described some pictures, some associated and some disassociated. They were right on target with what he had said. He also demonstrated this particular pattern with several other people in different situations. Most notable was a recently de-programmed ex-cult member. His experiences with devotion and commitment followed suit with these notions Richard was presenting. It was all based on visual associated images and disassociated ones.

He finished his demonstration by outlining the technique for people who were in the business of marital counseling. I was doing a good bit of that kind of work at the time so I listened closely. He emphasized, as I have done with you repeatedly, that the technique would work *either way*. It could be used to get two people more strongly committed to one another. But if you weren't careful, and you did it in the other direction, it could break them up. Counselor beware.

About six months later a woman came to see me who had been in a lousy relationship for years. "For seven years this guy has been treating me like _____ ," she complained. Given her descriptions of his behavior I had to agree. "If only I wasn't so attached and dependent on him. I guess I just love him too much to let go," was the statement that lit my internal light bulb. I said, "I have just the thing."

I remembered Richard's warnings about not using the technique in the opposite direction from the way he taught it or the results could be disastrous for the relationship. In this case I felt the situation was reversed. Why not reverse the technique? I didn't feel right about just doing it though, so I told my client the whole story. I said I didn't feel this should be my decision, because I knew it would work. "None of this maybe stuff," I told her. "This is it." She was a very intelligent woman, more so than I, I felt. She could make up her own mind. "Let's get on with it," was all she said.

Needless to say it worked like a charm. In fact, it took about 15 minutes and worked so perfectly it was a little scary. But that is how all these things work when you use them right.

That is what Richard complimented me about. He said, "You are one of the very few people I know who actually uses the techniques the way they work. Most people just throw them around and hope for the best." I said I thought that what I had done was perfectly logical and natural. It would have been obvious to anybody who knew how it worked. He gave me one of his sly "come on, grow up" looks that said I was being ridiculous. Then he complained, with appropriate venom in his voice, about the throngs who *always* want everything handed to them in nice tidy packages, who *never* exercise their brains, apply things in new ways, extend themselves into new territories ... etc., etc., etc.

Association in Your Image, Experiment #1

Step 1

Remember a time when you had an argument with someone that still gives you the same feelings when you think about it. If not an argument, perhaps an uncomfortable scene of some sort. You'll know you have the right one when you feel exactly like you did at the time of the incident — cruddy.

Step 2

Now you are only going to examine one visual submodality: association. Undoubtedly, if you have those same feelings again, you are associated in the image. In other words you see the scene from the same point of view, through your own eyes, as you did then.

If you find you are disassociated, ask yourself an important question. Are you feeling the same feelings you had at the time, or are you having feelings *about* the incident? Feelings about something are usually different, though not necessarily any more pleasant, than the original actual feelings. If you find that you are disassociated in this scene, pick another.

Step 3

When you have the right associated image, and the feelings, change it to a disassociated image. To do this you need only imagine how you would have looked in the situation to some other impartial person. You need to see yourself in the image, as someone else would have seen you.

There are, of course, lots of possible points of view. You could imagine looking in the window from outside. You could see yourself from above, below, or in back of yourself, or anywhere else that is different than your original point of view. As long as you see yourself. For creativity think of the different camera angles a movie producer would use when shooting a dramatic scene.

Step 4

When you can clearly see yourself from another point of view, pay attention to your feelings. They will be different if you have "flipped" the picture. Which one do you like better? Flip the pictures back and forth from associated to disassociated for comparison a few times. Leave it the way you like best and remind yourself to think of it this way from now on. You have my permission to anchor it and future pace yourself if you'd like.

Association in Your Image, Experiment #2

Step 1

Now pick a memory that is very pleasant for you; one that brings back all the original feelings you had when you went through this experience.

Step 2

Undoubtedly, as in the last case, if you have the *same* feelings you had then, you will find that this is an associated image. It is as if you are there again. Pay close attention to the image and the feelings that go with it.

Step 3

Now flip this picture so that it is disassociated, just as you did before. Notice the difference in the feelings. Now which do you like better? Try it both ways a few times and decide. Again leave it the way you like best and future-pace yourself.

The point here is that to get the feelings as they were at the time, the picture needs to be an associated one. This is one of those neurological quirks that makes us human. Using it can really help us in a variety of ways, too. Obviously, knowing whether we want the feeling the same way is a good start. It is a decision we have to make for ourselves. As usual the principle involved, and our brains, don't care if we delight, or torture, ourselves.

This seems to be a good place to make another observation about visual images and what people seem to do with them. Every once in a while I'll ask someone to remember a pleasant experience. They'll obediently look up and to the left, their face will momentarily brighten, then they'll frown and burst into tears. It was a little disconcerting the first few times. There are several possible reasons for this in such a case. The first and most usual is that they found, instead of a pleasant memory, an awful one. That is easy to correct. I just interrupt them and tell them to find another. It usually does the trick. Then there are the people who cry tears of joy. I don't worry about them. Even when I do it myself, though, I wonder where this idea ever came from.

Every once in a while though, someone will have found just the right memory. But instead of holding it as a still image, they have it stored in their memory like a movie. Remember that is one of the other visual submodalities we look for. In and of itself, it doesn't really matter how the memories are stored. Like everything else, however, certain other things are affected by which ones are stored which way. In the cases we're talking about here, the initial delight is the delightful portion of the film they are watching in their head. The lousy part is the ending. That's the part where they had to come back to their miserable home after the wonderful vacation. Or the part where the romance ended and they got left with the mortgage and weekly visitation rights. Worst of all is the end of a wonderful experience, of any kind, that the person is absolutely convinced they can *never have again*. I get depressed just hearing about those. Explaining the process to them is enough to help usually. Then I carefully instruct them to *hold the picture as a still shot at the good part* and anchor if necessary. Easy enough when you find out how it works.

Association in Your Image, Experiment #3

Step 1

Remember a situation that you handled badly in some way. It could have been in the classroom or not. The important thing is that when you remember this situation, you know you should have done something else. Just to make it interesting, if possible, remember one you still haven't figured out a solution for.

Step 2

Now run it as a movie in your head, start to finish, as you saw it then: associated. You'll certainly get those feelings back, but don't worry, we'll fix them soon enough.

Step 3

Now go back to the beginning of your little movie, and disassociate. Run the movie from start to finish, disassociated, from whatever point of view you can most easily imagine. For effect do this five or six times, from a different vantage point each time. You are the director of your internal movies — why not make them interesting?

Step 4

As you do each of these, see if some solutions to this situation appear. Things look different, and are different, from different points of view. If need be, imagine this scene from the point of view of the other people involved. That's usually an eye-opener.

Step 5

When you have a couple of alternative ways you could have handled this situation, reassociate. Run the movie again, using one of your solutions and see how it feels. Try each solution until you come up with the one that feels best to you. Then you might congratulate yourself on learning a new way of behaving. You'll probably never have to screw up *like that* again. Whew!

Running movies associated and disassociated is a great way to use hindsight constructively. What good are unpleasant experiences if you can't learn from them? The more creatively you go about the process of learning, the more creative the solutions. You might want to repeat the above experiment with a lot of memories. Who knows, you might change for the better in more ways than one.

In addition to hindsight, this is a great technique for foresight. I think we all rehearse future events that are important to us in our minds. To get the most out of it, why not rehearse from several points of view? For example, writers often imagine themselves as each of their possible readers. It is part of the writing process that helps give them the perspective they need. Public speakers do the same. I do this constantly when I am getting ready to teach someone something. It saves a lot of embarrassment later. I suggest you try the next experiment when you feel comfortable dealing with moving images from both associated and disassociated viewpoints.

Association in Your Image, Experiment #4

Step 1

I mentioned sometime earlier that it can even be useful to run movies backward. This is terrific for one thing in particular. We have all had the experience of "the straw that broke the camel's back." Remember a time when you allowed events to slowly build up to an explosion, one in which you wound up in a temper tantrum of some sort. Again, you can't fool me. I know you've had a few of those before.

Step 2

Now run the movie of this series of events forward, associated, and see if it brings on the feeling of building up to an eruption again. Often it will. Control yourself at least long enough to complete this experiment.

Step 3

Do it again, but this time run the movie *backward*, from the end to the beginning. Do it *disassociated*. Make sure of several things during the procedure:

1. It is *not* a series of still shots that you are "leafing through" from the end to the beginning. It needs to be a movie. If you have ever seen film or videotape rewind you know what I am talking about.
2. By the same token, you are not to run a short segment forward, then back up and run the one in front of it forward. Only rewind.
3. You need to go continuously. Do not stop, even if you seem to be skipping over parts. Remember, your brain knows what it is doing. Whether it knows why is anyone's guess.
4. If you find you have broken any of the above commandments, start over.

All of these are things that people have done when I was instructing them in this. Any of them can mess the whole thing up, so be as sure as possible about what you are doing.

Step 4

When you have done that, do it again. This time though, run it *backward associated*. This may take a little practice but it is worth it. Imagine you are actually doing everything in the sequence in the opposite direction.

Step 5

When you have successfully run the movie in reverse, once disassociated and once associated, run it forward again. It may come out either associated, disassociated, or some combination. Let your brain do what it wants this time.

Step 6

Check your feelings now as you watch this incident. Different? Just for fun, try to get back the original feelings as they were the first time. Can you do it?

Now, of course, you get to experiment with some children. Many people find these association experiments to be the easiest and most rewarding of all. You will find, as is often the case, that the children are very fluid at this. Kids visualize much better than most adults. They also will relish the chance to play with their internal images, without getting in trouble. You can tell them this is permissible daydreaming.

Association in the Image of Others, Experiment #1

Step 1

Again wait, for this experiment, until you find one of your children in some sort of emotional distress that you need to deal with anyway. Depending on your situation, this could be first thing tomorrow morning, or sometime later. When you have the child in custody, tell her you would like to show her a trick that should make her feel better. Calm her as much as you need to, to be able to work with her.

Step 2

Explain the difference between associated and disassociated images in language she'll understand. Tell her that you would like to teach her to see herself from another point of view. You may say, "I wonder what you would look like from up on the ceiling," or "I'd like to show you how you look to other people," or some alternative phrase of your own choosing.

Choose one that you think she'll understand and appreciate. If she is terribly self-conscious about what other people think of her, be cautious about suggesting she see herself as others do. She may already be constructing images of herself as ugly, foolish, or worse. If you pick up some signal that this is what is going on, simply use your best judgment. This experiment could really help her in a case like this. But you need to be sure the image she constructs doesn't cause more harm than good. You'll know by what she says and does how best to proceed.

Step 3

Next tell her to close her eyes and imagine what she would look like from this other vantage point. Use your eyes and ears. You will undoubtedly notice when she has the image changed to a nice disassociated viewpoint — she'll change as well.

Step 4

Ask her to concentrate on the picture in her mind. Have her, at the same time, pay attention to how she feels. Undoubtedly she'll feel better.

Step 5

Practice several different points of view with her. Discuss ways and times she might use this flipping of pictures for her own benefit. In other words, future-pace.

I hope you are getting the hang of association and disassociation. Before going on, think about what you have learned with this first child. How were your explanations? Did you run into any unexpected difficulties? How about expected ones, like the self-consciousness I mentioned? Spend a little time digesting what you know about how this works, and how to communicate it to the next child.

Association in the Image of Others, Experiment #2

Step 1

For this experiment pick a child you think needs to learn to be a happier person. I'm sure finding one will not be a difficult task.

Step 2

When you can spend some time with the child, tell him you want to find out how he organizes the pictures in his head. You're doing a survey and you think you may know how to help him be a happier human.

Step 3

Ask him to remember a really happy time in his life. Explain associated and disassociated images to him and find out how this one is stored.

This is another one of those times when you may get a child who draws a blank. If kids, or we, are unhappy, it can be difficult to remember nicer times. Remember state-dependent learning from Volume I? If the child is really in a lousy state, he will probably be able to remember lots of other lousy ones. Vividly.

Use your skills if this is the case. You may need to suggest possible nice experiences to him. You may need to interrupt him and get him on some other subject for a while. Perhaps you have an anchor established with this child that could help. If so, use that. With a little work, he'll be able to remember a good time.

Step 4

Next have him find a relatively unhappy one. That should be easy. Don't pick his worst personal tragedy if you can avoid it.

Just use some time he didn't like. Find out if this one is associated or disassociated.

Step 5

Have him go through each of these two images. Teach him to flip each so that he can have them associated or disassociated at will. Ask him how he feels in each.

Step 6

Have him choose his favorite way of seeing each image. He will probably choose to have the pleasant memory associated and the unpleasant one disassociated. If so, congratulate him on making a wise decision for himself. He should be proud to take this good care of his feelings.

If not, suggest that he should. If need be, give him permission to feel as good as he wants to about these experiences. This is not a joke. Some children honestly believe they are supposed to feel bad about certain memories. Stress the importance of having control of your own brain and using it to make yourself the best person you can. Remind him that this means being happy also. Ask him to experiment doing it this way for a while, just to see how it turns out. Sometimes it helps to remind people that there will be plenty of stuff to feel bad about later. Why waste time now?

Step 7

Future-pace. Talk about all the many experiences we have in life and how we can remember them. Tell him that if he has the nasty ones stored in his brain so that they still hurt, he is just wasting energy he could use for something better. If he does this, and has the nice ones stored so that they don't bring back the good feelings — i.e. disassociated — he won't have any memories to make him feel good. That is how people make themselves unhappy.

You might spend some time doing a bit of this yourself. It makes such a difference in the way people perceive the world that no superlative is strong enough. If you are giving advice this good to children, you owe it to them to take it yourself. Remember you are their model, like it or not.

Association in the Image of Others, Experiment #3

Step 1

For this experiment, find a child you notice is about to make "that same mistake again." The one she always seems to do on automatic pilot, whatever it is. These are usually easy to spot.

Step 2

Interrupt her gently and rescue her from whatever the situation is. Tell her you want her to be able to see herself in a new way. One that will help her to avoid the same problems over and over. That is literally what you are going to do.

Step 3

Describe the situation as you see it, step by step. How she starts, and how she continues — every time — to make the same mess. Remember to be sympathetic. If she thinks you are scolding her, it may make it harder for her to do what you ask.

Step 4

Ask her to imagine the scene from your perspective. You can even have her imagine she is watching herself on videotape along with you. Guide her view so that she remains disassociated from it at all times. You can easily anchor this to do so.

As a helpful alternative, you can have her imagine she is you. Then role-play her, the way she acts when she goes through this. Sometimes a bit of artistic exaggeration helps (in other words, ham it up). Tell her to watch and she will see you the way you see her. Then have her imagine what *she* would look like in your place.

Step 5

After going through it once, tell her you want her to watch it again. This time, though, you want her to make whatever changes in the movie she thinks would help "that girl" (her). Again, you might consider the role-play demonstration I mentioned in the last step.

Step 6

You should repeat step 5 several times for practice. Also you will want her to have several different options about what to do.

Step 7

Future-pace. Tell her you will let her know every now and then when you think it would be a good idea to "rerun that tape," or any others. And tell her it would be a good idea to do this herself immediately after messing up anything. That way she can learn from life.

Association and disassociation are the submodalities we have been using the longest in NLP. They are so natural and powerful that you can help just about anybody, with anything, just using them well. That is why, out of all the submodalities I chose association to experiment with separately. Also it is well to remember what I said about making ourselves happy and unhappy by choosing which way to store our visual images. I was neither kidding nor exaggerating.

I know we have just scratched the surface on this one. Fortunately this powerful concept is also very simple. Once you feel you have a good grasp of how it works, repeat these experiments a few times. Then you can add to them, combine them, or make up your own. Combine them with the other sub-modalities and watch what happens. Once you know how anything like this works, the number of ways you use it is limited only by your imagination.

CHAPTER 3

CARRIED OVER THE THRESHOLD

We have all had the experience I mentioned earlier of things slowly building up and then — snap! It turns out that there is a field in science devoted to studying just such occurrences. It is called "catastrophe theory." Delightful, eh? OK, so we won't call it that. In NLP we call this phenomenon "going over threshold." Sounds more pleasant. These things don't always turn out bad anyway. Sure we have all had camel's backs, broken by weighty straws — just before we got in a fight with someone. But we have also had "the last piece of the puzzle" that completed something important for us. We build up to new learnings just as we do to old problems.

Would you like to take a wild guess about how it works in our heads? This time I really will let you discover most of this on your own.

Your Thresholds, Experiment #1

Step 1

Take a visual image you have that brings up mildly unpleasant feelings. Just pay attention to the picture and the feelings, we'll ignore sounds for now.

Step 2

Remember which visual submodalities are critical for you. Pick out your favorite to experiment with.

Step 3

Slowly change this one so that the feeling gets stronger, more intense. In other words, if bringing pictures closer makes them stronger, bring it closer. You should feel your feelings getting more *unpleasant* as you do this. You are just verifying that this works here.

Step 4

Now take it back to normal, the way it was when you first got it.

Step 5

Next you are going to repeat step three, but keep going all the way until something changes dramatically.

An easy-to-understand example is brightness. You can make a picture so bright in your head that it turns completely white. Remembering films you've seen of nuclear detonations is a good way to understand this. And do it quickly. It takes no more than 2-3 seconds if you just do it without pondering. Remember to change the image in the direction that causes the feelings to become *more* intense. In other words, for a moment it will get worse before it goes over the threshold.

Sometimes it helps to give people verbal descriptions to help them understand each possible threshold. Some submodalities don't make sense in these terms, but many do. Here are some descriptions of going over threshold, visually, that seem to help:

Color   Increase the intensity of colors until they "bleed" into each other and the image is no longer identifiable. Or decrease to black and white and then all the way to a dull, even, gray slate. Decreasing seldom turns out to be very effective, but try it anyway.

Size   Increase until the picture is so large that you can't see enough of it to identify. Or decrease it until it disappears. Decreasing is seldom effective.

Distance   Bring it so close that it seems to go through or past you, losing its identity as it does so. Or move it so far away that you can no longer see it, though this too is seldom effective.

Brightness Increase it until the picture turns pure white. Or decrease it until it fades to black. Decreasing is only sometimes effective but definitely worth trying.

Contrast   This can only be decreased until the picture fades out of resolution and becomes indistinguishable. The same is true for clarity and focus. Try and see.

Speed   You can only increase the speed of the motion until it becomes a blur and is indistinguishable. Slowing down to a still shot may change the feelings but that is not the same as going over a threshold.

Step 6

What happened? If you felt, all of a sudden, the intense feeling vanish, that is as it should be. If it only got more intense, and you didn't seem to go over any sort of threshold, just put it back the way it was. Forget about the threshold of that submodality for now.

Step 7

If it seemed to go over threshold, try and bring back the picture again, exactly as it was. Not close — exactly — and with the same feelings.

If you seem unable to do this, congratulations. You have one less image to bother you. If you are able to recover the exact image, with all of its original feelings, it means you didn't really go over the threshold. Try again. If it doesn't work a second time, forget it for now.

Note: When I say exact, I mean *exact*. Some people have stored many similar images of particular events in their lives — especially unpleasant ones. This, of course, adds many choices about how to conjure up the unpleasantness. More on this soon.

Step 8

Now pick another image that, like the first, brings on mildly unpleasant feelings. Go through the above steps, but use a *different* submodality that is critical for you.

Step 9

Repeat this with each of the submodalities on the above list. Use a different internal picture each time. You should be able to produce the effect of going over some sort of threshold with at least one, and most likely, several of them. Each one you have success for should work with any image.

Step 10

You may have been unable to get one or more images over threshold. Go back to these now and use one of the submodalities you found most effective. Use it to remove the image from your existence.

Practice this until it works well for you. It will, even if it is difficult at first. This is the level of analysis at which individual differences are commonly found. That doesn't mean thresholds don't work for some people. They work for everyone. You just need to find *which* work for you best. This is what our brains do every time we make any kind of change. They do it so quickly and completely that the submodality change itself is invariably beyond our awareness. This is as it should be. It happens so often, that if we were consciously aware of it, we wouldn't notice much of anything else.

You may need to try a number of images to get fluid doing this consciously. It can be a cumbersome process on the conscious level, like many processes that are naturally unconscious. You may also want to experiment with each of the above list of submodalities several times. For some people, my descriptions aren't much help, either. That is partly my limitation and partly one of effectively converting raw experience into language. If you can come up with different or better ways of describing these changes I'd love to hear about them. I'm not all that satisfied with these myself.

The reason I commented that some of the ones on the list are not very effective is simple. Say, for example, you move an image so far away that you can no longer see it. If you think about what you have actually done, you'll realize that it isn't really gone. It hasn't actually changed, just moved. Most people can move it back into sight again, along with the bad feelings. This is not universally true, so it is still worth experimenting with. If you can make this or the other ones I commented on work, great. If not, don't worry.

This is the reason location is not even on the list. Many people will move a picture out of sight, and therefore out of mind, by imagining it is behind them. Then I say, "Well, move it back again," and they do. Back come the feelings. So in these cases the change may only be temporary. As long as someone *can* give themselves the image again, they *can* give themselves the unpleasant feelings. That is OK, but what we are working for here is to wipe out the picture altogether, permanently. We are actually going beyond the realm of personal choice.

I know some people don't think it is a good idea to take choices away from people. In general I agree. But there are a few things I would just as soon not have the choice to do. I'm sure you can think of a few for yourself. In fact, and I am aware of my biases, there are some things I wish no one had the option to do. Maybe you can guess what a few of them are.

Now we're going to do the same thing as before, only with auditory submodalities. Most people find these trickier. I'm convinced that this is for no other reason than that we use our auditory sense so much more poorly than our visual. This experiment should help remedy that unfortunate characteristic.

Your Thresholds, Experiment #2

Step 1

Begin by picking an experience you clearly remember. One with distinctive people, who have distinctive voices, is usually easiest at first.

Step 2

Next listen internally to those voices, tones, and other sounds. Pay attention to the feelings these create in you. Pull out or remember your list of critical auditory submodalities.

Step 3

Pick one of these and use it to increase the intensity of the feeling here. Then bring it back to normal. If this worked adequately, go on. If not, use another submodality and change this one so that the feeling gets more intense, and then back again. For most people it is easiest to do this with voices when first learning. After a while, all other sounds become just as easy.

Step 4

Now take this one over threshold and find out what happens to your feeling. Here, again is a helpful list of descriptions of how to take auditory submodalities over threshold:

Sound/Words	Changing a sound into words can be fascinating. For some people, the particular sound, especially if it was unusual, never comes back again. The reverse is possible but unlikely.
Voice	Changing a voice so that it matches that of some other person (or duck) is sometimes very effective. For some people it seems to stay that way for good.
Internal/ External	Moving a voice from the inside of your head to the outside may help, and actually remain changed. The same is true of the reverse, but in both cases people can usually change them back again.
Distance	Again, you can only move the voice so far away that it disappears. This is sometimes effective.
Volume	You can make a sound so loud that it becomes just a meaningless roar. By the same token, you can soften it so that you can no longer hear it at all. Softening is seldom effective for the reasons mentioned above.
Pitch	You can either increase or decrease the pitch so that the sound is a high squeal or a low moan, neither recognizable as the original. For some people this one will work either way.

Tone   Both this and timbre can be changed so that the sound is no longer recognizable as the original. It sometimes helps to think of the sound of one musical instrument gradually changing to that of a vastly different one.

Step 5

Again, if the voice or sound went over threshold, you won't be able to make it come back as it was. Repeat this with a variety of voices and sounds that create specific, unpleasant feelings. Try each of the above list of submodalities to find which ones are most effective for you. Remember the test is whether or not you can bring back the original sound, just the way it was, and retrieve the same unpleasant feelings with it. If you can, you aren't done.

Again, the thought of permanently changing visual and auditory images on the inside bothers some people. Keep in mind that we are not talking about shutting off feelings. We are only breaking up certain images that cause certain feelings. Specificity is the key, along with your good judgment. Be sure to use both.

Many people say, "But gee, I can still get a picture back and feel bad about it." When pressed, it is always a slightly different picture. As I mentioned a few pages ago, many of us construct lots of images, pictures and sounds to make ourselves feel lousy. It's no great skill. Some of us make lots of them for important — whatever that means — experiences. This only means that the above exercises need to be repeated *with each image*. They only work one at a time. Believe it or not, one at a time is how they were constructed to begin with. Our unconscious minds can do this at fabulous speeds, for better and worse. That is why there can be so many images that seem the same. They are really close approximations.

Also, it is important to repeat that any change is not the same as going over a threshold. Some are permanent and some aren't. Just getting angry is not the same as 25 stored up angers going that last final step and bursting your bubble. By the same token, each solved math problem does not necessarily represent new learning, though it may only take one to finally get the idea across. Moving in a direction is different than going all the way.

One of the things I get asked about a lot is how to help kids who are obsessive. This is especially in cases where the child has had some really traumatic experience he or she can't seem to shake. It is really painful to watch a hurting child and not know what to do. Here are some very good ways to start to help, and at the same time, teach the child about change itself.

Others' Thresholds, Experiment #1

Step 1

For this experiment choose a child who seems to be stuck on some event in his mind. Don't go for a major trauma *unless he is already in the midst of it* and you have to do something anyway. I don't want you jumping in to do magic until you've had some practice. Start relatively small and begin with a good strong anchor for comfort and safety. Use your skills to get the child into a good state to experiment in.

Step 2

Tell the child what you have noticed about his behavior and what you think might be going through his head, if you can do this without being intrusive. You'll know, or he'll let you know. Avoid making value judgments as much as possible. They'll only get in your way. *Don't argue* about whether your observations are accurate. It is seldom worth the effort and the evasiveness it creates.

Step 3

Next tell him you know a way to turn off the pictures and the feelings they cause. Also, that you need his help. Tell him you want to work as a team. You do.

Step 4

Explain as much about submodalities and thresholds, or as little, as you need to. Tell him it works for everybody, even you.

Step 5

Start with an emotionally neutral image first. Tell him you just want to demonstrate it the first time. While you have him go through each of the visual submodalities, ask him how he feels as he increases or decreases each. Find out which ones are critical.

Step 6

When you have a few, or at least one, definitely critical submodality, help him to take it over threshold. Then make sure he *can't* bring back the image.

Step 7

When you are sure you have a good critical submodality, and he knows how to use it, bring up the problem behavior again. Tell him you would like to help him do the same thing with this (these) nasty picture(s) in his head.

Step 8

Now, have the child take the image over threshold. If at any point you think this is too intense for this child, stop, break the state, and use the anchor for comfort and safety — that's why you have it. You should always have this kind of anchor available when dealing with any kind of traumatic or painful experience.

Also, in my experience with this technique, there have been occasions when people do something that makes the procedure difficult. Instead of just increasing the brightness, let's say, quickly and smoothly, they go real slow. Something about trauma seems to slow some people down. Others speed up, everyone's different. That is why we sometimes hear people say that, for example during a car accident, everything seemed to move in slow motion. Others will say it happened so fast they don't remember it at all. This phenomenon is called time distortion.

If this child is one of those who slows things down, the memories may be in slow motion. This can cause him to slow down everything while he is thinking about it. We don't want that. We want people to finish quickly. It usually helps to have them practice on mundane images for a few minutes, at the speed they need to use. It should be obvious to you just by observing if you need to do something like this. The child will let you know.

Step 9

After he has taken the image over threshold, have him try to bring it back again. The same rules apply that did for you. If he can bring exactly the same one back, it didn't go over threshold. Be very clear on this with him.

He may have many similar images that, for him, are the same. Rather than getting into an argument about it, it is better to tell him to do it again. You can tell him it may take him several tries to get it right. Practice makes perfect. Also, it may help to have him go through it with any similar images. Remember, this only works one image at a time.

Step 10

Future-pace. Explain as much or as little as necessary. The same goes for advice giving. Often the less said, the better. A few compliments never hurt though.

Others' Thresholds, Experiment #2

Step 1

Now find another child in the same condition as the first. This time, though, using your sensory acuity, the eye movements and other accessing cues, as well as your good judgment, pick a child who is stuck on sounds or voices in her head. Establish an anchor for comfort and good feelings.

Step 2

Tell the child about the behavior you have noticed. Avoid value judgments and opinions. Tell her you want to help and explain as necessary. You should be great at this by now.

Step 3

From here on it is the same as the last experiment, only with sounds. Begin by experimenting and demonstrating with relatively mundane sounds and voices. When you have established which submodalities are critical, and the child is able to take at least one of these over threshold successfully, go on.

Step 4

With your comfort anchor ready at all times, have the child go back to the unpleasant sounds. Using the critical submodalities you have found for her, have her take them over threshold. Repeat this and practice as much as necessary.

Step 5

Future-pace. Discuss the procedure and whatever else you think might be worthwhile with her. Praise her whenever possible.

All else being equal, this is the quickest and most powerful technique there is for making changes. That is because it is exactly what our brains do. Gathering information about which submodalities to use simply shows us more precisely how our brain does it. Some people take more practice than others, but this will work for *everyone*. It is worthwhile to get in the habit of. After a while it will be as natural as talking. The same is true in working on yourself.

I'd also like to remind you of something. We have only used visual and auditory submodalities to change feelings. Most of the time that is what we want to do. But let's not forget that changing submodalities of feelings will change the visuals and auditories also. Any change in one component, i.e. sensory mode, will affect the entire system, i.e. person. It will do it by affecting the other modes as well. This is one of the reasons I have suggested watching body posture. You can watch the child change his posture when he changes his internal images. By the same token, you can just tell him to change his posture. Ask him what happens to the images — you may be surprised.

I had an interesting, though admittedly rare, occurrence in a workshop. I was doing a demonstration with one of my students, a career teacher. We were playing with submodalities to change the feelings around an experience he had had a number of years ago. He mentioned that he had had tinnitus — ringing in the ears — since being "blown up" in the Korean War. By adjusting the submodalities in all three representational systems for a number of images, we made some significant changes. He not only relieved the unpleasant feelings completely, but the tinnitus went away as well. His description the next day was that "the floodgates just opened up" and enabled him to make a number of other remarkable changes immediately afterward.

I said in *Meta-Cation* that we could wipe out stress-related illness and a lot of other noxious stuff in a generation if we use our heads. These are lessons in using our heads. It's just as simple to devise fun experiments for a whole class to do together, as it is to work with one child at a time. Just remember to start with easy, pleasant images. *Avoid trauma* when working with classrooms or groups of children. That is when individual attention is called for. Be creative and make the experiments fun. I suggest you review Volume II, Chapter 4, on the Discovery method, as a guide. Remember there is no right or wrong way to teach these things. Just get it to work for everyone. It will save you, the children, and society a lot of grief later on.

CHAPTER 4

SYSTEMATIC ORDER

I shouldn't have to repeat that individual things don't just happen. They usually have something come before them. And invariably they cause something else as well. One of those common facts of life is that figuring out the patterns and orders of people's behaviors is quite a bit more complex than any single event, logarithmically more complex. I don't mean that much more difficult, just more complicated. Difficulty and complexity are not the same. A bicycle is much more complicated to operate than a chair, though you sit on both. Once you get the hang of a bike it's pretty easy. But it's still much more complicated to operate. It's also more fun.

I also believe that only so much can be learned about sequences — strategies and chains — from a book. In fact I haven't met anyone who was able to do anything with either of them without some discussion, demonstration, and practice. On the other hand, they haven't been covered this systematically yet. In fact, chains haven't been covered in print yet at all, as far as I know. The only attempts at covering strategies in book form are *NLP, Vol I*, by Robert Dilts, and *Practical Magic*, by Steve Lankton. Both would be worth your time. But they, too, could only do so much and we have learned a lot since those texts were written. The subject deserves much more than I am going to do here. I suggest you read those other books and find an NLP training program to help you along when you want to learn more.

I have already described strategies for you in Volume II. Remember they are sequences of internal events that lead to some outcome. The internal events themselves are each a representational system. So we may see a picture, then hear some words, then have a feeling, and then act in some way. The picture, words, and feeling, or V → A → K in NLP code, are the events. The action is the outcome. To make the T.O.T.E. complete we need to know what triggered the picture at the beginning, where and when. Remember T.O.T.E. stands for Test, Operate, Test, Exit and provides a framework for us to work within.

Also remember that most of what happens in a strategy is not apparent to the person using it. It often seems like one single event, rather than the series it actually is. None of us could consciously function with any efficiency at all if this were not the case. For that reason it is invariably easier to observe in other people, while learning. We would miss too many of the steps in our own to be able to learn effectively. That is not to say that you can't find out about, or change, yours, just that it is easier to start with others'.

One of the things that makes this easiest is the accessing cues, particularly eye movements. If you are not *very* comfortable recognizing these I suggest you review *Meta-Cation*, pages 38-49, 94-101, and the Tear Out Page 151. The picture on the Tear Out will help refresh your memory *before you begin*. This is one of those times, I'm afraid, where using it as a cheat sheet will cause you real problems. You need to be able to recognize eye movement accessing immediately and automatically to do the exercises here. That is why this is Volume III.

The eye movements will tell you the order in which the events, i.e. representational systems (rep systems from now on), happen. That is just about all they're good for. But for that they are very good indeed. For example, in the above V → A → K strategy, you would be able to see, usually, three distinct eye movements. For most people these would be:

V	Eyes gazing up and to the left, or ahead and defocused, for a remembered image
A	Eyes gazing down and to the left, or scanning to the left or right across the midline
K	Eyes gazing straight down, or down and to the right

It is important to remember that these can happen very quickly. That is why the cheat sheet is more trouble than help for this. One glance away to check your notes and you can miss *a lot*. Also, you must remember that everyone's eye movements are not organized exactly the same. I stressed heavily in *Meta-Cation* that you have to check for each person you deal with, to find out how they are organized. Sometimes it is easiest to assume they are normally organized as in the charts, and then find out if you are wrong. Working backwards can save time in this case but you still must check. You *can* use the questions on the Tear Out Page for doing this determination. That is exactly what they are intended for.

Also remember the rules for eye movement watching. First and foremost, *do not glare at the children*. You'll just make them uncomfortable. Second, pay attention to what you're doing, as well as the child. This means ask decent questions that will give you the information you want, not prevent it. Avoid moving your hands or body in ways that will distract them when you want them doing something inside their heads. I have seen lots of people do unusual hand movements that get children's attention, and get them to look in odd directions. Then they tell me about the strange organization of the child's eye movements. Really! The same is true for talking to the child while he or she is doing something internal. There is a time for this to be sure. But there is also a time to shut up.

What you want to do first is strategy elicitation. As I said in *Meta-Cation*, this means nothing more than finding out what the child does. Eliciting strategies is easy, but takes a bit of time, practice, and patience to do well. All of the other rules about working with children apply also. We are going to avoid any traumatic situations here, however. Remember to read the experiments carefully before you begin. There is a lot in them.

Children's Strategies, Experiment #1

Step 1

Begin with a simple concept. This could be cooperating with other children, spelling, enjoying a particular class, etc. Don't go for an understanding of quantum mechanics, Shakespeare, French, or the epistemological considerations of paradigm shifts. Save those for next week. Just pick something that most of the children in your class handle just fine.

Step 2

Next, pick two children: one who understands this idea thoroughly, and one who is totally lost. Again this shouldn't be too difficult.

Step 3

Start with the one who knows what he's doing. Tell him you are exploring how some people understand things and some don't. It's the truth. Determine how his eyes move in relation to the pattern you know for "normally" organized right-handed people.

Step 4

When you know how his eye movements work, bring up the subject you know he understands well. Tell him you have noticed this is something he is especially good at. You want him to tell you how he does it inside his head so that you can help teach others better.

In gathering information, you have to use your head and your logic. If you are talking about spelling, for the standard

NLP example, you should probably ask what happens in his head when you say a word, during a test. This is logical and will help you because you already have the time, place, and what triggers his activity: the sound of the word during the test.

If you are looking at cooperation, you might mention an incident you think he handled really well. That will set the time and place for you. You still have to pick the logical starting point however, based on your observations at the time.

Let's imagine the following scenario: perhaps some other child said something that caused a disagreement. Then you noticed him responding in a way that helped smooth things over and get some task accomplished. You might say, "I noticed when she said something, you paused for a moment, then turned and suggested an alternative. What happened inside your head when she said that?" That is how specific, and how general, your questions should be. That question does two things. First it sets the time and place, i.e. the context, so the child knows what you're talking about. That's specific. Second, and just as important, it *does not* ask what he saw, felt, believed, or anything else that could lead his thinking away from what he actually did. It is open-ended, in other words general, enough to let him tell you and show you that.

Set the context and ask for what you want. At this point your job is to watch his eye movements and listen to his description. When he has finished, and not before, make any notes you need to. This is where things can get a little tricky because there are many possible responses. In addition, the verbal responses may or may not match the eye movements.

For example, let's say you asked about spelling. In response to your eloquently phrased question he says, "I dunno, what?" That is a typical "kid" response. If something like this is what you get, you have several options:

1. One is to ask more specific questions. Sometimes it takes a few before he'll understand what you want. Remember, no one has asked him anything like this before.

2. You could also give examples from your own experience of your thought processes. But use something different from spelling. You might say, "Sometimes I talk to myself when I am thinking, but other times I just make pictures in my head, or have feelings." If you do this, make sure you don't inadvertently lead his answers. You don't want him to try to please you with smart answers, you want the strategy he uses.

3. The best way to get better information is to have him go through the process of spelling a word. If you can get him to describe for you what he is doing at each step, that plus your observations will give you the best possible information.

Another possible response is that what he *does*, and what he *says* he does, appear to you to be *different*. This is quite likely. Let's say you have just asked about spelling, or even asked him to spell a word. The first thing he does is look up and to his left. Then he briefly looks down and to his right, then immediately back up and to the left. What he says is, "I just spell the word and I know it's right because it feels right." Obviously to you, he is visualizing the word, but he is not aware of it. Probably he checked his picture against his feelings, just to make sure. This is quite common in spelling, and lots of other stuff. Some people make all their decisions based on how it feels. That isn't all they do, but it could be all they are *aware* of.

You have several choices in a case like this:

1. You can just guess at what he actually does, based on your observations. Believe what you see first and what he says second. You will sometimes have no other choice but to do some guessing. You stand to miss some things if you don't dig a little deeper though.

2. You can ask him to repeat what he does, the Operation, several times. This will give you the chance to be sure of what you see and hear.

3. You can always share what you see with him and tell him what you think it means. Again, avoid value judgments. Explain to him that people are likely to only know part of what they do. You're just telling him so he can check to see if you are right or not. You might say something as simple as, "I noticed you looked as if you had a picture of the spelling word in your mind's eye. Why don't you spell another word for me and see if that's possible?" Use your judgment about this child and how you think he'll respond.

A final possibility, though rare, is that the child will tell you and show you exactly what he does. The first time you ask him, he'll tell you and his words will match his actions perfectly. Consider yourself fortunate when this happens.

Step 5

Now take a break and dismiss the child back to whatever he was doing before you so rudely interrupted him. Your job now is to ask yourself some questions:

1. Do you know at exactly what point the Operation begins? In other words, what is the *first Test* that starts the strategy going? In spelling it should be the sound of the word, as we said earlier, but in other activities it will be something else.

2. Do you have all the steps that you think constitute the *Operation* phase?

3. Does this make logical sense? For example, if the task was spelling, and all you think the child did was talk to himself and have feelings, you should ask yourself if this would work. As I've said often enough, English words are not spelled the way they sound. If this child is a good speller, he has to have a visual image of the word at some point to be able to get it right. You should *apply this same*

kind of logic to all other strategies as well.

4. Do you know what the *second Test* is? In the above child who had a feeling that told him the word was correct, that feeling is the second Test. That is how he knows he has found the right spelling. What is it for this strategy?

5. Can you map out this strategy so that you know, step by step, how it works? Can you go through these steps and get the same result yourself? That is usually a good check on your logic.

6. Based on the answers to these questions, do you need to ask the child to do this a few more times for you? It's OK, go ahead!

You are done with this step in the process when you have satisfactory answers to each of those questions. Remember, this is a complex task. It isn't really hard, but there are a lot of things, and different possible responses, involved in gathering the information. Each time you do this you will get much better at it — it only takes practice.

Step 6

Now that you have finished with child number 1 it is time to go to work with the other one. You now have exactly the same task. You want to find out how she does what she does. But since you know that, whatever it is, it doesn't work, you can start differently. Tell her you want to find out exactly what she does in this case so that you can help her to do it better. Go through all the steps of eliciting her strategy that you went through above. All the same advice and rules apply.

When you have finished look at the questions again. Make sure you have satisfactory answers for each. Remember to take your time and be patient with the child and with yourself.

Step 7

Now compare the strategies of the two children. You already know which one gets the worthwhile outcome and which one doesn't. Use the questions to determine where the second one falls down. Decide what needs to be different based on the first one. This is like correcting math tests by using one that is 100% correct as a guide. You can compare the ways the problems were done and usually see immediately how any mistakes were made. Even though we have to allow for different ways of accomplishing the same things, some universals usually exist.

Let's use a different example than spelling. Let's say that your first child is good at solving disputes. We can imagine a strategy that might work as follows:

1. A(external)   He hears two people arguing. That is the first Test so he knows it is time for this strategy.

2. A(external)   He listens carefully to their words for a moment.

3. A(internal — constructed)
He then looks down and to his left and repeats the words in his own voice, inside his head.

4. K(internal)   Next he looks down and to his right and checks his feelings in response to these words spoken to himself.

5. V(internal — remembered)
Then he looks up and to his left and recalls a picture of a time when he felt this way before. It's a still picture of two people arguing.

6. A(internal — remembered)
He gets the image and looks down and to his left to hear the words, as a check that this is really a similar experience.

7. V(internal — remembered)
Now he looks back up and to the left and sees the old memory as a movie going forward. He watches to see how it finally was solved.

8. A(internal — remembered)
Then he again looks down and to the left and hears the words of the solution and how it was arrived at.

9. V(internal — constructed)
Next he looks up and to his right and creates a movie of himself, disassociated. He sees himself talking to the children having the dispute now, and providing his solution.

10. K(internal) He again looks down and to his right to find out how he feels about this image. He feels good about it. That is his internal check that says he has completed the "finding a solution" part of the strategy — the Operation.

11. V(internal — constructed)
Now he imagines stepping into the movie. He reassociates.

12. K(internal) Immediately he feels ready to tell the other children what he thinks will work. That is his second Test. Since he feels good about it he knows he has successfully completed the strategy.

13. Outcome He exits the strategy and says what is on his mind to the others.

   I purposely chose a somewhat more elaborate strategy than spelling just so you could see the logic in some other form of activity. Also to liven things up a bit. If the ones you elicited are anywhere near this complete, you are doing far better than I did when I was first learning. To be honest, there is quite a bit left out of this one. But the important features are there for you to get an idea of what we're driving at. Being elaborate and detailed isn't nearly as important as getting the hang of the concept of strategies. As I said, I am not trying to get you to be an expert. Just attempting something like this is terrific. Congratulate yourself on your bravery for giving it a go.

I am also avoiding using the official NLP code for strategies because I think it is too cumbersome to learn when you are just trying to start to think about these things. I do want you to know that there is a complete "calculus" for all of this. When you read *NLP, Vol. I* you'll see how it works.

But back to our second child and our comparison. Let's say that you have asked her how she handles disputes like the one above. What you get from her is the following:

1. A(external)   She hears two people arguing.

2. A(external)   She listens to their words for a moment.

3. A(internal — constructed)
   She then looks down and to her left and repeats the words in her own voice, inside her head.

4. K(internal)   Next she looks down and to her right and checks her feelings in response to these words spoken to herself.

5. V(internal)   Now she remembers a time when she felt this way before. She sees a still shot of two people arguing.

6. K(internal)   Next she checks her feelings again, and notices she is getting frustrated.

7. V(internal)   She looks back at the picture to avoid the

feelings. Then she again sees the two people in her still shot. It hasn't changed.

8. K(internal)   So she checks her feelings again. Now she is getting more frustrated because she has just given herself the same jolt from that nasty picture — a second time.

9. V → K → V → K → ...
Continues in this "loop" going from the feelings to the picture looking for relief. She doesn't get it since it isn't there to be gotten. This goes on until she can't stand the feelings anymore and has to leave the scene.

If you compare the two strategies, you'll immediately notice that the first five steps are essentially the same. Step 6 is where they get different. The boy double-checks to make sure his experience compares closely with the one at hand. Then he runs it as a movie to the happy ending. For the strategy to be effective, if it weren't a good ending, he would have to discard this image in favor of another. What makes the strategy work for him is that he then imagines what it would be like to duplicate that past experience in this new situation.

The girl, on the other hand, gets stuck here. She doesn't check to see if the experiences are similar. She also leaves the visual image as a still shot, so that there is no change, and therefore no possible solution in it. Then she begins to feel bad. Because she simply alternates between the unpleasant unchanging picture and her feelings, she is in trouble. There is no relief except to wait until the feelings are bad enough to have to do *something*. So she escapes.

I wish I could say this was all just hypothetical. Both of these strategies, in various forms, are extremely common. The first one, or something like it, should be taught as a matter of course. The second one needs to be eradicated. There are children all over this country who freeze up when presented with other people in conflict. It isn't that they have no resources for handling the situation. They just get stuck on old unpleasant memories, of other unrelated conflicts, and get caught in the feelings. This is a very nasty loop to be stuck in. Worst of all is that there is so much conflict around them all the time. That means they go through it a lot. The more they practice — guess what? For all the ones you *notice* going through some thing like this, there are others who have learned to make stone faces to avoid ridicule, or worse. They are in just as much pain, but it's private pain.

The solution is plainly obvious if you look at the strategy that works. Simply, the girl needs to have access to more than the first memory that comes up. First she needs to decide on whether it fits with the current predicament. Next she needs to find one with a solution she can see. She is much more likely to get that if she can change the still shot to a movie. Most conflicts get settled — eventually. Arguments may take some time and some grief, but sooner or later there is some kind of peace. Teaching this girl to access several pictures, run them as movies, and pick one that feels OK to her will do her a world of good.

Applying this kind of thinking to all your work with children will help you and them tremendously.

Step 8

When you have figured out how the second strategy goes haywire, spend some more time with the child. Tell her that you think you have figured out how to help her. What you want her to do is think about this, whatever it is, in a new way. Then, as clearly as possible, explain to her how to do it differently.

Have her practice the new steps, slowly and carefully, in her head. It may help to ask if she has gone through those kinds of steps for anything else. Sometimes children are aware enough to know. Another alternative is to suggest other times when you, logically, believe she may have used a similar strategy to the one you want her to have.

Anchor and future-pace any way you think will help. If she feels good about the new strategy she is more likely to use and practice it. Be creative in your explanation of what you want her to do. Keep in mind that examples and modeling always help. Feel free to demonstrate it, complete with eye movements. Practice with her as much as you need to.

Children's Strategies, Experiment #2

Step 1

Pick another child who is exceptionally good at some simple task.

Step 2

Tell him you want to know all there is to know about how he thinks about this in his head, just as you did with the last one.

Step 3

Go through the steps you did last time to elicit the information about the sequence. Watch the eye movements. Listen to his description. Use your logic. Answer the questions to make sure you have it straight.

Step 4

Now you are going to go a step deeper into understanding strategies. Take out one of your state sheets. Fill in the appropriate section on submodalities for each step in the strategy. You will also want to know the content of each rep system. In other words, what is the picture of, if you don't already know.

This is no more difficult than you did when you were eliciting states to begin with. For example, let's look at the successful strategy the boy who could solve disputes had again. For each of the steps you would, of course, only fill in the submodalities of that rep system. For example in step 3:

3. A(internal — constructed)
>   He then looks down and to his left and repeats
>   the words in his own voice, inside his head.

We know he is hearing his own voice, and that he is repeating the words he heard the others say. We also want to know if his voice sounded like it was inside his own head, or outside. Internal only means it is in his internal experience as opposed to someone actually talking to him from the outside. If he imagines the voice as if it were coming from a place outside of himself, where? How far away? What kind of tone? Was it clear, strong, and resonant, or more like a whisper? Did he repeat the words at the same rate he heard them or faster? There is a lot we can know just about this one step.

Let's look at step 9:

9. V(internal — constructed)
>   Next he looks up and to his right and creates a
>   movie of himself, disassociated. He sees him-
>   self talking to the children having the dispute
>   now, and providing his solution.

We know he is seeing a moving picture, disassociated, of himself talking to the other children. I would want to know one important piece of content in a case like this: Are they responding in the image? If they are ignoring him, getting angry, or telling him he is a jerk in his movie, I don't think he's likely to get those good feelings that come in step 10 and say what is on his mind afterwards. Just a hunch, but I'll bet he is imagining a favorable response and that helps give him the good feeling.

Also, but I'd want to check, I'll bet he runs the movie pretty fast. If not they'd all be waiting to solve this problem for the rest of the week. He goes from the beginning to the solution probably in less than 5 seconds. That is generally how these things work. He may even skip sections, or flip through quickly like flipping the pages in a book. In addition I would bet the picture is fairly bright, the colors clear and vivid, and he is at least as big as the other kids, maybe bigger, in the visual image. When you have asked these questions of enough people, as I've said ad nauseum, you find a few patterns.

Let's look at step 12:

12. K(internal) Immediately he feels ready to tell the other children what he thinks will work. That is his second Test. Since he feels good about it he knows he has successfully completed the strategy.

All we know here is that he feels "ready" and "good." Those are not submodalities. If we're smart we'll pretend we don't know what they mean at all. Here you get a chance to start from scratch and go through all of the kinesthetic submodalities to find out what gets him to go ahead and talk to the other kids. If you think about it logically, this is a pretty brave thing to do. He is interfering in other people's affairs, so he has to feel pretty confident. But since I don't know what brave or confident are either, I still have some work to do.

A few guesses would be that he is breathing comfortably but high in his chest, he feels his hands lifting, and perhaps a slight lean forward. In addition he may feel a bit light on his feet if he is standing. These are still only my relatively educated guesses. I still don't know about temperature changes, if he feels cool anywhere, or warm. I don't know if he feels any tension in his stomach, chest, or throat, though I wouldn't be at all surprised.

So there are plenty of things you can find out from watching and asking about submodalities that go beyond the mere sequence of events. Collect as much information as you can gather, at each step you have identified, and look it over really well. The sooner you get to see lots of different patterns, the sooner you'll begin to notice some of them recurring over and over again.

Step 5

Now you get to really explore new territory. There is one

important thing I have failed to mention in all of this. During all the time in this volume or the others did you ever wonder what happens in the arrows that go between rep systems? You know, in $V \rightarrow A \rightarrow K \rightarrow$ ...? Did you ever stop to think what makes the picture lead to the sounds and the sounds lead to the feelings? Right now you have enough information right in front of you, to take one more step and find out.

If you have asked good questions and gathered good information, you have probably made this child quite aware of the workings of this strategy in himself. Ask him if he can tell you. A good question is something like, "What happens just before that picture turns into a feeling?" Or, "Do you know what happens inside to that picture that causes you, all of a sudden, to become aware of the feeling?" Ask questions like this for *every step* in the strategy. The answers will be different at each step.

It is worth your while to explore this on your own for a while before I tell you about it. Again it is one of the many things in NLP that has been right there in front of people all along. It took a long time for anyone to notice it, though. Find out for yourself, as best you can, how it works before going further. If you can discover the pattern, you'll get to feel a lot smarter than I ever have.

Hopefully, during the last step, you discovered the answer in the submodality changes. There are a lot of possibilities and I won't go into very many of them yet. I do want to give you some examples, though, so that in the next experiment you can use these changes. Let's look back at our young friend who helps solve disputes. This time, though, let's look at a sequence to see how these things go from one to the next. We'll start at steps 5, 6, & 7:

5. V(internal — remembered)
    Then he looks up and to his left and recalls a picture of a time when he felt this way before. It's a still picture of two people arguing.

6. A(internal — remembered)

    He gets the image and looks down and to his
    left to hear the words, as a check that this is
    really a similar experience.

7. V(internal — remembered)

    Now he looks back up and to the left and sees
    the old memory as a movie going forward. He
    watches to see how it finally was solved.

We know several things about step 5 before exploring any
further. He finds a picture because it goes with the feeling he
already has. How he makes the comparison we won't worry
about for the moment. We know the content is two people
arguing and that it is a still shot. Let's assume that it is neither
too close, big, or bright, nor is it perfectly focused, just for our
example. All of these, by the way, are likely in a strategy like
this. If they were too close, big, or bright he would probably get
uncomfortable like the little girl did in her strategy. That
wouldn't propel him on to the next step in checking the picture
for accuracy. More likely he would get stuck in the unpleasant
feelings or avoid the whole thing.

You may ask, "Why not perfectly focused?" (he said, knowingly). Because he has probably quickly flipped through some
sort of internal "catalog" of pictures that go with these feelings
or similar ones. Each selection comes up quickly enough to
make it fast and efficient. Think of going through a card file
and focusing just enough on the first line to know what each
card is, but no more. To focus completely on each card enough
to read it would waste a great deal of time. The same would be
true of flipping through a book, or scanning down the page of a
dictionary or phone book. If this is something we have done
enough, we have trained ourselves to allow only pertinent
information to catch our attention.

"What is 'pertinent' information? What do you mean 'catch'
our attention?" (he heard them scowl). Well, pertinent information is usually something that matches something else. In
other words (he continued quickly to avoid being lynched) if we

are looking across the tops of, or down, the pages of a dictionary, we are probably simultaneously holding some mental
image of the word we're looking for. What we notice is the one
that most closely matches that image. That one suddenly
comes into focus. In response to the visual match, we feel
something that stops the movement of our eyes. That may be a
momentary "catch" in our breathing, or a muscle twitch in our
face or hands. Or we could hear the word being clearly pronounced in our own internal voices, or in the voice of the person
who last said it. These are common, but not the only possibilities. Try it yourself.

This is probably how he knows it is the right picture. He has
done some matching. We have all seen the visual tricks used by
movie and TV directors to change scenes. Particularly the one
in which one picture slowly fades out and the other fades in
over it. After a few seconds the first picture is completely gone
and the second has come all the way into focus. This is what we
often do inside our heads. With the image he was holding as a
guide to sort with, he could try some new ones. Perhaps he'll
superimpose the closest match over the one he was holding in
his mind. If they match closely enough, that may be when the
new one clears up for him, replacing the old. Movie directors
know what works. What works is what matches the brain's
own patterns. Again, we are talking about a semi-mythical
child, so the process is semi-mythical as well. But if this is the
scenario, when the new image becomes perfectly clear, that is
the time to check the words.

This is a good example because it's *very* common. We have
all said at some point in our lives that something "just became
clear" to us. Language is not constructed out of accidents. It is
based on internal experience. So the *change in the submodality is what causes the change in the modality*. In other
words, the clearing up of the picture in effect says, "Now we
have finished with this picture — on to the internal voice as a
check."

So he goes on to step 6. All we know about this step is that he
is checking the words that go with the new image against this
current situation. "Maybe he is matching the words in his

image against the ones being said now," I can internally hear you utter. The answer is: you bet! But how does he do that? Well he does it, in all probability, with more than just the words. First he had to run the movie forward just a bit, to get the words going. From there he probably matched as many tones and inflections as possible. Remember, words aren't all that passes between people, especially when they're arguing. Ignoring small missiles and other blunt instruments, we also have the myriad ways in which words are said. Or maybe shouted. Sometimes the actual words are fairly innocuous. He'll probably make comparisons based on several different submodalities — that's what they're for.

Since we're being hypothetical, let's say that he'll know the situation matches when the rhythm of four or five words in a row, inside his head, matches the rhythm of those same words he just heard. Just to march you forward with this a bit (groan, yourself), when the rhythms match just right, he looks up to get the pictures moving with them. Don't think this is farfetched! Imagine listening to really jumping music while looking at a *still* picture of people (not) dancing. See if you don't try to move them in your mind's eye. If not, remember you are only as old as you move.

So again, the changing submodality determines when it is time to move on to the next step. Let's look at a different point in the sequence: steps 9, 10, & 11.

9. V(internal — constructed)

> Next he looks up and to his right and creates a movie of himself, disassociated. He sees himself talking to the children having the dispute now, and providing his solution.

10. K(internal) He again looks down and to his right to find out how he feels about this image. He feels good about it. That is his internal check that says he has completed the "finding a solution" part of the strategy — the Operation.

11. V(internal — constructed)
> Now he imagines stepping into the movie. He reassociates.

Step 9 is an interesting one. Here he directs his own internal movie. How is it constructed? Probably from pieces of lots of others he has stored in his head. Not very mysterious. He probably does lots of quick superimposing, comparing, editing, cutting and splicing, etc. Why a movie? Because how else would he know what to do from start to finish? A series of still shots could work, but not as well.

The most interesting question would be: Why a disassociated image? Self-preservation. Remember that in a disassociated image you only have feelings *about* what you see. In case it doesn't look too good to you, no real damage. This is only a "test pattern" anyway — just like on TV. It doesn't have to be perfect, it's still on the drawing board. If it were an associated image and it ended in disaster, it could feel just as bad as a *real* disaster. That is how people so effectively create anxiety for themselves. They run associated disastrous movies. It works perfectly. If this is a really good strategy, you can bet that it doesn't have any glitches in it like that.

But how would he know he had it right? In other words, when is it time to go on to the next step? Well, there are several possibilities. Most likely, the movie will stop when there is no more of it to run. This isn't as dumb as it sounds. He could imagine running a long argument with these other kids. He might try every solution he has ever heard, in response to their challenges. This would of course involve a whole other strategy and slow things down. But this could also cause the strategy to fail. Remember he has to check his feelings in step 10 to know if his constructed image is worth trying. If he never comes up with a workable one it never will. Think of all the times we come up with good ideas, and then immediately imagine other people talking us out of them. Then we wind up feeling lousy. Certainly he is capable of this as well. He may just try his initial solution, imagine it working the first time, and see the movie stop. Then he can double-check the feelings in the next step.

Another possibility is the longer the movie runs, with more dialog and information passing, the clearer it gets. This is another common feature of people's visualized movies. When it clears to a certain point, just like in step 5, it's done. It could even slowly gain more color also, starting in black and white, and going to vivid sharp colorful images. When he goes to step 10 these images will certainly give him more intense feelings than dull, unclear, black and white ones.

As usual the only way to know the answers to any of these questions would be to explore it with him. Undoubtedly as you read these possibilities you try some of them in your head. Hopefully the whole concept of changing submodalities, to go from one sensory mode to another, is making more sense for you.

Let's go on to step 10 and see what could happen there.

10. K(internal)   He again looks down and to his right to find out how he feels about this image. He feels good about it. That is his internal check that says he has completed the "finding a solution" part of the strategy — the Operation.

We know he is paying attention to the feelings of the disassociated movie, to see if they are good enough to try. Remember his feelings will be *about* the image, but not the same as they would be if he were associated *in* the image. So he makes a value judgment here, based on the look of the image from the outside, and how it feels to him. But, again, how will he know if the feeling is "right?"

Of course, there are lots of ways he could know. Perhaps the feeling will get more intense as he pays attention to it, the image still clearly in his mind. Always keep in mind that the unconscious still holds the image for him so it can easily still be affecting the feelings. The part of the strategy, here the feelings, that we are concentrating on is the part that is most in consciousness. You can think of the unconscious "feeding" the feelings with the picture if you like. So in this case the intensity could increase to a certain point, then go *over the threshold.* That's right, over threshold. That is what we have been talking about the whole time. Each one of these changes is the same kind that we made in the threshold experiments. I just wanted you to have the chance to figure that out on your own before I blabbed. The difference here is that the threshold propels the strategy forward to the next step.

And remember also that thresholds can happen in lots of ways. A common one is by changing the location of a feeling. How many times have we had a feeling "well up" so that our "heart feels like it is in our throats?" Well it isn't really. But the feeling, of tension or whatever, has risen from our stomach or chest up to our throat. Maybe in this child's strategy, when the feeling gets to a certain height in his chest, he goes to the next step. This is one of the most common patterns I know of. And it fits with the next step in this strategy perfectly.

In step number 11, he changes the image back to an associated one.

11. V(internal — constructed)
                Now he imagines stepping into the movie. He
                reassociates.

Maybe you noticed that I didn't include association and disassociation in the chapter on thresholds. That is because going from one to the other really doesn't take something over threshold. It works a slightly different way as far as I can tell. The switch from one to the other provides a simultaneous switch in feelings. It is more of a content change than a submodality change. This is logical. If you think about it, all disassociated images are constructed images, to start with. As such they are probably manufactured by the left side of the brain, then stored in the right. But a newly manufactured image is quite different than a remembered one. The feelings certainly work differently. So I think of switching from a disassociated image to an associated one as switching to a *different* picture, at least in this sense.

Also, it is the associated image that gets us to do something. We can't be disassociated physically, we can only imagine it. Doing so can be a good check on our behavior, provided that it doesn't prevent necessary feelings. Next we reassociate and get on with it. It is hard to be motivated from a disassociated state, the feelings usually aren't quite right. But going from a disassociated image to an associated one can be *highly* motivating.

Let's look at the last 5 steps of the strategy, again, as a package.

9. V(internal — constructed)

    Next he looks up and to his right and creates a movie of himself, disassociated. He sees himself talking to the children having the dispute now, and providing his solution.

10. K(internal) He again looks down and to his right to find out how he feels about this image. He feels good about it. That is his internal check that says he has completed the "finding a solution" part of the strategy — the Operation.

11. V(internal — constructed)

    Now he imagines stepping into the movie. He reassociates.

12. K(internal) Immediately he feels ready to tell the other children what he thinks will work. That is his second Test. Since he feels good about it he knows he has successfully completed the strategy.

13. Outcome He exits the strategy and says what is on his mind to the others.

This is what I was talking about as motivation. This particular sequence is called a New Behavior Generator. That's what it does. The primary feature involves "stepping into the picture" to get the feelings. The feelings lead to the action. There is another nice feature, also. I already hinted that between steps 9 and 10 there is some leeway. He can come up with as many movies as he wants before he gets it right. That is why he checks them with his feelings. If it doesn't feel right, don't do it, to alter an old saying. So this is one of those "loops" I have talked about. In this case, a loop is a real good thing to have. It may take a little work and creativity, more images or whatever, to get a workable solution to the dispute. But until he has a good one, at least one that feels right, he may as well keep his mouth shut. I'm sure you can think of children, and adults, who have yet to learn this sound principle of good sense and survival.

But if he does have a good idea, why keep it to himself? So if it feels right, he steps into the picture. This gives him the impetus to do something. That is also the second test in the strategy. Nice and tidy.

I wanted you to see this as *part* of another strategy. It needs to be part of lots of strategies for some people. I seem to remember mentioning friends who continually come up with brilliant ideas they're still sitting on. If this were tacked on to the end of their "brilliant idea" strategy, they'd accomplish a lot more. Also, it would be a good check on what they created. Looking at something new or unusual from different points of view is almost always helpful. Hint, hint.

Children's Strategies, Experiment #3

Step 1

Now you will get to operate on all this new knowledge, and learn something about creativity to boot. Pick two children, one very creative and one not.

Step 2

Start with the one who is creative. Choose a specific thing

she did that you thought was especially unusual. Tell her you thought so and you'd like to know how she came up with such an unusual creation.

Then elicit the entire strategy. Remember not to ask about creativity in general. There are many kinds and you want a specific strategy. So ask about a specific instance. Also, start with the sequence, like you did before. Then gather the appropriate submodality information about each step. Third, find out how each threshold took her from one step to the next. Doing it in that order will be easier than trying to do it all at once. If you need to look back over previous discussions, go ahead.

When you feel that you have the strategy, look at these questions to see if you have adequately elicited the whole thing. Note the obvious alterations that have been made from the earlier list.

1. Do you know at exactly what point the strategy begins? In other words, what is the *first Test* that starts the strategy going?

2. Do you have all the steps that you think constitute the *Operation* phase?

3. Does the strategy make logical sense? Would this operation work to accomplish this task? Can you justify each step as a necessity? If not, do you know where the extraneous ones are? Do you know why they are unnecessary? Can you surmise any that *must* be there that you have not so far detected?

4. Do you know what the *second Test* is? What is it for this strategy and how does it work to make the strategy effective?

5. Can you map out this strategy so that you know, step by step, how it gets from the beginning to the outcome? Can you write out the sequence so that it is understandable to you?

6. Do you know the important submodalities, especially the critical ones at each step in this strategy?

7. Do you know what submodality changes cause the strategy to go from one step to the next? How each threshold works?

8. Can you go through this strategy and get it to work for you as well or better than the child? That is usually a good check on your logic.

9. Based on the answers to these questions, do you need to ask the child to do this a few more times for you?

Step 3

When you are sure you have the strategy down, and have gone over the questions, look at it for a minute. Then ask yourself these questions. They will help you understand creativity and strategies in general.

1. Does it have some motivation or excitement in it that gets the child to act?

2. It is often assumed that creativity is based on what is already known. Already existing information is just re-arranged, altered, connected in new ways, and so forth. What steps allow the child to make something new out of what he had to start with?

3. What role do comparisons, like the ones in the earlier strategies we discussed, play in this one?

4. Do you notice anything unusual in the submodalities? Do you detect out-of-the-ordinary states of consciousness at some point(s)?

5. If there are extraneous pieces, can you get the child to

remove them? Does the strategy still work? If not at least as well as before, put them back!

6. Does the strategy resemble some things that you do? If not, would you like to steal it immediately? You have my permission.

Step 4

Once you have done all that, go find the other child. Tell him you want to help him with his ability to be creative.

Step 5

Elicit from him a strategy that did not work for some kind of creative act. If you assigned the class some task that the other child used the working strategy on, and this one failed at, use that one. That way you know that the task, and therefore the context of the two strategies, is the same.

Remember to completely elicit this strategy, just as you did the others, even though it did not work. Answer all the questions just as thoroughly. Strategies that do not work for what they are intended aren't necessarily bad. There are several possibilities:

1. The strategy has some minor flaw that can be easily corrected.

2. With a little work, it would be marvelous and unique. One you would be proud to steal.

3. It is one that works great in some other context. Maybe the child feels good using it because it works so well sometimes and he gets reinforced for it. Or even that it could work in another context for something else, and you could teach him to use it for that.

4. It is useless here, and as far as you can tell, everywhere else.

Step 6

Make a decision about how to help this child. You have three choices:

1. You can give him the other child's strategy.

2. You can help him fix the one he has.

3. You can help him construct a totally new one based on what you now know about creativity.

Remember to coach him thoroughly, use whatever anchors and explanations you need, and help him practice.

Step 7

Test the strategy he now has to make sure it works. Assign him some task *that is similar to, or the same as, the original.* Remember this is a strategy that was used for something specific to begin with. Stay in context.

This is actually much easier than it sounds. If you have given him a new strategy, it should be automatic. He should just do the task, much better than he did originally. He may or may not notice how much better he does. Sometimes people are suddenly successful and really don't notice it. If this is the case, it means he uses the new strategy so smoothly and naturally that he doesn't realize anything out of the ordinary is happening. That would be an indication that the two of you did a fabulous job. On the other hand, if he isn't noticeably better, he still doesn't have the strategy right. Practice some more.

I mentioned at the beginning of this chapter that it is easiest to begin with others when exploring strategies. Obviously you can use all of your senses, the eye movement patterns, physical responses, logic, and creativity when working with a child. You can use some of those when working with yourself, but not all. Hopefully, by this time, you understand some of the structure of strategies. Also, you know what needs to be in them to make them work, and what gets in the way. That's enough to begin to look inside yourself.

Your Strategies, Experiment #1

Step 1

The most interesting way to start to understand what you do in your head is through the same kind of comparisons you have been doing with the children. I want to start with the process of reading because it is so central to education, teaching and learning. My hunch is that you read in more than one way, depending on the material. I have that hunch because I haven't found any educated people who don't.

First, because it is more fun, let's look at how you read for enjoyment or relaxation. Perhaps you read magazines, newspapers, or trashy novels. Maybe you read science fiction or the classics. Maybe cereal boxes. Whatever. Pick something you enjoy reading and sit down somewhere quiet with it. You'll need your notes, lists, and questions.

Step 2

Ask yourself when and where you would usually be doing this. Different people read at different times. Some only before dinner right after they get home from work. Some at bedtime every night. You want to know what the context of your strategy is. Also, which things you would read for enjoyment and which you would not. And you want to know what starts the strategy, in other words the *first Test*.

For example, I am one of those people who compulsively picks up whatever is within reach that has writing on it. So I put something worthwhile everywhere I could possibly land in my house. It's not as neat, but it serves my compulsion well. Also, I enjoy reading anything that remotely interests me, so the stacks of things in each spot are pretty varied. So I know the context of my strategy.

What constitutes the *first Test* in my strategy is, literally, seeing something with writing on it that I can reach. Only being engaged in some other activity, and not always that, will prevent me from picking something up and reading it. This is the kind of information you need to know about yourself.

Step 3

Next you want to know what you do when you read. This includes everything from how you hold the book, to how your eyes move across the page, to what you do inside your head. I'll let you figure this out as well as you can before suggesting any possibilities.

Step 4

When you think you know the sequence of events, what submodalities and thresholds are involved, and what makes it work, spend some time thinking about the *second Test*. This is interesting because it is the first strategy I have suggested to you that doesn't have such an obvious end point. This is partly because what we are exploring is a recreation activity. How do you know when you have had enough?

Step 5

When you have the whole strategy mapped out, look it over. Ask yourself the relevant questions about a complete strategy again. You'll find another set in Appendix V.

Step 6

Now you are going to repeat the above. Concentrate this time on technical material. I assume that if you are reading this book, you read some other technical material as well. Especially good for this exercise would be something on math or science though. Nothing like a little particle physics to get the cobwebs out of the old noodle...

Step 7

Make sure you understand everything you need to about this strategy. Where and when you do this sort of reading is important. "Only when held captive and under threat of torture," is *not* an answer. Also, how the operation works, or not, etc. Answer those questions for yourself.

Step 8

Now compare and contrast (I know, I cringe at those words myself) the two reading strategies. For a lot of people they are *very* different. Find out what you can about yourself.

For example, most people will make themselves quite comfortable when reading for pleasure. They will sit in their favorite chair or recliner, or lounge sprawled on a comfortable sofa. Or even prop themselves up with eighteen pillows, fluffy slippers, their favorite beverage, behind locked doors — safe from the outside world and even the slightest hint of intrusion into their ecstasy.

Many of these same intelligent people will do something entirely different with technical or "assigned" reading. They have miraculously convinced themselves that they can only learn new material sitting upright in a hard straight-backed chair, at an old wooden desk, under bad light. And they mustn't stop until they have "accomplished something." Yeah, like a headache. No wonder learning new things is so hard. In what context could people have possibly learned to do this to themselves? I wonder.

I wish I were exaggerating. I have helped too many people with this to believe that I am. I used to coach lots of people who went back to school later in life. Most of them just needed to learn to do it differently than they did the first time.

Don't think the differences in the strategies stop there. I mentioned in Volume II that reading is like movie-making. You take the material written in the book, translate it into sensory information, and construct an internal movie of this for later replay/recall. If you're smart you will have it filed under lots of different codes, i.e. anchors, so that it is easily accessible. There are lots of marvelous opportunities here for creating pain and inefficiency.

If you have mastered your best reading strategies, you have certain states of consciousness in which the operations are performed. I find that many people tend to alter these far too radically from one kind of reading to the other. If you are constantly uncomfortable you won't learn very well. Pretty soon the thought of learning something will bring on the discomfort. What a cheerful thought that is. Wouldn't it be nice to be able to use the best parts of both strategies to make them each more enjoyable and effective?

Step 9

That is what I want you to do now. Look at any places in either strategy that you think could be improved. See if you can take strengths from one strategy and put them right into the other. Comfort is a good place to start. After reading some of the following tips, I'm sure you'll have some more ideas:

1. Speed in reading comes from a combination of things:

   Moving your eyes across the words faster than you can say them. If you hear each word in your head, the way you were initially taught in school, you won't be able to read faster than you can talk.

   Being able to fill in enough of your images with fewer words, i.e. seeing whole scenes flash by quickly, without having to fill in all the details. This requires some sort of filtering out to get the nouns and verbs first, and the other words only when necessary.

   Having the turn of the page be a part of the strategy, rather than an interruption. Many people can speed read for two pages, then the turn of the page itself anchors in their old slow strategy. Some speed reading courses teach you to turn the pages in a different way than you used to.

Not having to be perfect the first time through. Many speed readers will tell you they scan the first time just for the general idea. Then they go back for as much detail as they need. Often they will read something five or six times to get what they need. This will depend on how much they want, how technical the material is, and how well it is written. *No one* really speed reads a chemistry text full of formulas and gets it all the first time, with the exception of certain people who *really* have total "photographic" recall. Even they usually don't have the concepts, either. They just know how to get the information back from their brains so they can figure it out later.

Being able to speed up or slow down at will. This is a plus if you can read quickly when you understand enough and slow down when you need more detail. It will allow you to go through in fewer passes.

2. Comprehension also means more than one activity:

Making your movie with enough accurate detail. This means including enough details as well as not adding your own if they change the meaning. Creative license is admissible only when reading for your own pleasure, not someone else's.

Being able to relate one internal movie to another. Sometimes switching to visual still shots helps in comparing images, like in our discussion of children's strategies. This can also mean holding a still shot while running the new movie along side it as you read. This may include a memory of a similar piece you read previously, that you mentally refer to in making sense of the present piece. I don't have a better explanation than that, but if you try it I think you'll know what I mean.

Reading the words in a logical order when you have trouble. Just as with speed, start with nouns. These will give you still pictures. Verbs will add motion and relationships between the stills, bringing them together, and making it into a movie. Adjectives and other words will add in the other crucial submodalities for you.

3. Enjoyment comes from several things on several levels:

Physical comfort.

The right submodalities in the internal movie, visually and auditorily. This is, of course, a personal matter. But a review of a list you have seen before should help you understand. Any of these will detract from your comfort and enjoyment.

Too many images in a small space (or field of vision)

Images moving in different directions, too fast, or at different speeds

Images that are too close

Images that are too large or too bright

Sounds that are too close, loud, or shrill

Too many sounds or voices at once

Sounds or voices of unpleasant tonalities

In addition to these, in reading, not enough can be as bad as too much. When people don't understand something they tend to make themselves uncomfortable. I think we all know where that was most effectively anchored. Be that as it may, pictures with "holes" in them, or lack of clarity, are common when we don't quite get what we are reading. You have probably figured out by now that if we just worked on repairing those submodalities it would make us more comfortable. But remember we want to fill in the gaps with accurate information. We want comfort *and* learning.

A sense of reading for its own sake. This is my opinion but I really like to learn. I also like enjoyment. I have the belief that I will get both from just about anything I read. So I automatically go into a pleasant state of consciousness whenever I read. It took me a long time to get there, though. I had a lot of old anchors and memories that connected reading and drudgery. I had to overcome those before I could enjoy it. If you have some old anchors like those, you might use what you have learned to do something about them. You might do the same to remove old unpleasant memories about reading for some children as well. Or at least don't give them any new ones.

After all that talk about knowledge, comprehension, and understanding, I thought it might be good to continue in the same vein. Sometimes, no matter how hard you try, what you are reading is barely comprehensible. That is almost invariably due to poor writing (I am letting myself in for it but I'm game). Anyway, having good strategies for understanding can often save you from agonizing reading. So again, let's compare a couple of your strategies.

Your Strategies, Experiment #2

Step 1

Pick something you have read that you understand quite easily. Next find something that is difficult for you.

Step 2

Now start with what you know well. An interesting way to do

this is to begin by thinking of a different topic altogether. Then, quickly, switch to the one you have chosen to work on. As you do this, do you immediately make a picture in your head? Perhaps you say a key word to yourself, or have a feeling. Pay attention to how you access the information to start with; that will tell you something about how you store it.

Step 3

Now go through your internal knowledge of this topic and see how it is organized. You have done this with children by now so you know what you are looking for. Map out your strategy as well as possible. Answer the appropriate strategy questions and be sure you know how you do this. What you want is to find out *how* you are able to know this material.

Step 4

Next take the information you have read and had difficulty with. Find out how you have this stored and organized. Elicit your own strategy. Do so thoroughly and answer the questions, just as before. Find out as much as you can.

Step 5

At the risk of sounding like a broken record, compare the two strategies. You know something about how understanding itself works now — you've elicited strategies from yourself and others. Decide what needs to be different about the topic you have trouble with.

Certainly some things will be obvious right away. This is especially so if you have answered the questions about whether these strategies make logical sense for the task at hand. You might look over those tips on reading again to spur your thinking. I'm sure you'll find some similarities between reading and storing information, and understanding it. I sure hope so!

Step 6

Make whatever repairs you think are necessary in understanding the topic that has given you difficulty in the past.

Your Strategies, Experiment #3

Step 1

Now let's take the next logical step: teaching. You have explored reading and understanding, so why not? This time pick three subjects. Make them very specific. Rather than teaching "math" for example, let's explore how you teach one math concept, or how to do one kind of equation. That is more than enough to begin with. You can think of some equivalent-size piece for any subject you teach.

The first needs to be one you do quite well. This means you can teach it to *anyone*. For the second look at something you have done less than a good job of teaching. The third will be something new, that you have not taught before. If you are the kind of teacher who reads this book I think you'll have a long list of those waiting to be tried.

Step 2

Start with the one you do well. Go through, in your mind, how you teach this. A very interesting place to start is in how you understand it. You don't need to go through your entire understanding strategy, but think about it for a few minutes, it will help.

Step 3

Map out the strategy. Make sure you have all of your external steps listed along with your internal ones. What I mean is, what do you write on the board, for example, while you are saying something to yourself in your mind? And what picture did you have on the inside before you gave a certain explanation?

My guess is that if you are really good at teaching this you know something else as well: how the children respond at each step. That is one of the things that makes teaching really slick. When you can anticipate the questions you are about to get, and you have the answer all ready to give, teaching goes very smoothly. Other times someone will ask you something you have never been asked before, but you know just what they need to understand. I am also willing to bet that you have just the right blend of discovery/experience and explanation. You may also find that you follow some of the discovery steps I mentioned in Volume II. This is all hypothetical, of course. When you know what you do, check yourself with the strategy questions to make sure.

Step 4

Now do the same thing with the subject you don't teach as well. Map out what you do including any important descriptions of floundering, sweating, hoping, etc. Maybe it will help to get out some of the frustration. Undoubtedly you won't find too many of the characteristics I mentioned above. Use your strategy questions to be sure you know, in excruciating detail, how you mess this up.

Step 5

Now compare the two strategies you have so far. The differences will probably be plain. Figure out how to repair the second one, based on useful information from the first. Then do it.

There is only one good way to test your effectiveness here. Teach this at your earliest possible convenience and find out how well you do. You may surprise and amaze yourself at your new-found competence. In the meantime, go on to the next step.

Step 6

Now look at the subject you have yet to teach. You have a good example of one that you do well. You also, at this point, have a bad example, and its repaired version, whether you have tested it or not. Your task here is to design the steps you would take to teach this new subject, based on your new knowledge.

It is often best to practice explaining this in your head first. Then jot down the steps you went through and see what you have. Then you can figure out what needs to be added, subtracted, or changed. You may even try jotting down a list of questions or problems you anticipate from the kids. See if you can guess where each will come. Use the three strategies you already have as guides while you do this. And answer the strategy questions when you are done.

Again, I only know of one good way to test this. When you go to teach this, remember that it can be a fun new experience for you and the kids.

I said at the beginning of this chapter that learning to use strategies from a book is a formidable task. I hope the experiments were clear and concise enough to make it worthwhile. I also hope the lists, questions, and tips helped to guide you as you learned. These are much more advanced experiments than I would normally do with beginners. They are a real stretch, even for some people who have had some training. Trying them is the only way to get them to work. Even if you feel less than successful, you will have undoubtedly learned a great deal of useful information. This can only improve you as a person and a teacher, and that's enough.

I suggest you wait awhile and digest some of this material before going on. Though the rest of the book contains easier exercises, you may need a short break. Something I find particularly useful for myself after a tremendous amount of new information, is to go to the earlier portions. See how simple they look in retrospect. Then think how much you have learned. Congratulations!

CHAPTER 5

CHAIN LINKS, WEAK & STRONG

Chains are really quite simple. As was discussed in Volume II, they are just states (4-tuples) linked together by anchors. The first state *is* the anchor for the second, the second for the third, and so on. As such, installing a chain in someone is as simple as eliciting states and using anchors. The only thing we need to know first is *what order* to link *which states* together in. There's that word "order" again. Keeps cropping up so I guess we'll just have to get used to it.

Your Own Chains, Experiment #1

Step 1

I thought I'd start by going back over some old territory. In fact, you have already completed most of this first exercise. We are going to use the states we identified in Chapter 2, in the exercise entitled: Your Own States, Experiment #3. That is the one in which I asked you to identify and play with four separ ate states. We also used them in Your Own States, Experiment #4. These states are:

number 1: utter, total confusion
number 2: mild confusion
number 3: sort of understanding
number 4: complete understanding

You'll recall I asked you to save your notes from that experiment. Get them now.

Step 2

Next look over each of the four states. Remind yourself of how you got into each one during those earlier experiments.

Step 3

Next you are going to anchor each state, one at a time. But I want you to do so in a specific way. Remember it is possible to use any rep system to anchor with. For this first experiment, I want you to anchor each one kinesthetically, with a simple touch. The best way when you are learning to use chains is to have them close together, in a row.

Again, any touch can be an anchor for something. The trick is to "pair" it with the state you want anchored. You do this by touching when the person, in this case yourself, is at the height of the response. That means strongly experiencing that state.

By close together, I mean something like an inch apart on your arm. Let's say that each anchor is a touch with your forefinger on each of four spots. For the first you might touch the back of your left wrist with the forefinger of your right hand at the moment you are sure you are in state number 1. For the second, it could be the same touch, one inch higher up on your arm, during state number 2. The third, state number 3, could be one more inch up your arm, and the fourth one more. Very simple. During training workshops we suggest doing this on the arm or leg because it is easy to remember the exact spots, close together, all in a row.

Or as another alternative I have suggested before, (See *Meta-Cation*, pages 102-104) touching the tip of your thumb to the tip of one of your other fingers. Four anchors, four fingers (isn't math wonderful). However you must also remember to use different anchors than you normally do all the time. If you generally use your thumb touching one of the fingers on that hand as an anchor, don't use it now. Even if this is just a common touch, say out of habit, don't use it. If you do, you'll "contaminate" the new anchors with responses from the old ones, or just as useless, anchor nothing at all.

Step 4

Take a few minutes to test each anchor. You want to be absolutely sure that they work quickly and noticeably. I want you to know when you have the response, and when it is the strongest. The easiest way for most people to tell is when the intensity of their feelings is the greatest. Remember to take a break — to break each state — between tests. We don't want to contaminate the responses here either. You are finished with this step when you have four distinct states, each anchored easily and separately, that match the original four states numbers 1-4.

Step 5

Now fire the anchor for state number one.

When you feel the response reach its height, immediately fire the anchor for number 2.

When you feel number 2 reach the height of its response, immediately fire number 3.

When number 3 reaches the peak of its response, fire number 4.

Experience state number four for a couple of minutes, then break the state by getting up and walking around.

Step 6

Now sit down again and fire the first anchor, for state number 1, again, and release it. What happens in your experience? This is the test for the chain.

There are two varieties of possible responses at Step 6. The first variety includes the following:

The first is that you went into state number 1, and that was all.

Another is that you found that you went through a couple of states, but that you ended up in either number 2 or number 3.

A third is that you seemed to go directly to state number 2 or 3, as if you fired off the anchor for that one instead of number 1.

Possibly, you noticed no effect at all.

If any of the first three has occurred, go back and repeat Steps 5 and 6 again. If you noticed nothing at all, try it again and make sure. If you still notice no effect, test each of your anchors again. Go back to Step 4 and repeat the remaining steps.

The other set of possibilities includes the following:

You actually felt yourself going through each state, one at a time, quickly. Perhaps they seemed to flow, one to the next.

Another possibility is that you only noticed that you were all of a sudden in state number 4.

In either case, the chain effectively worked as it should have. Either way is fine. Now that the chain is there, it should occur automatically each time you go into state number 1. Try it and see. And if you experienced the first of these above choices, it will gradually turn into the second. This will gradually occur over time — more so each time you go through the chain. This is because the initial three states will not serve any *apparent* function. We usually stop noticing things that don't, fairly quickly. It doesn't mean they stop happening, just that we don't notice them.

The form of this chain represents the simplest way of constructing one. This is based on the inherent logic in having a chain. The reason chains work is that each of the states following the one before it represents a relatively small change in experience. Therefore the same is true of consciousness. I have talked before about making jumps from one state to a vastly different one, with nothing in between. It can be a jarring experience to the person going through it, as well as those around him. Such a giant leap seldom makes intuitive sense. If it turns out to be a useful and smooth jump, it usually also turns out that several not-so-apparent things happened between the first state and the last.

So the above chain was purposely constructed to make the jumps small. Total confusion, number 1, is an unusual (for some people) state. But it is not too far away from a slight confusion, number 2. It seems too big a jump to go from total confusion to an even partial understanding state, number 3. It doesn't make sense. It happens sometimes, but not as often or naturally as the jump from number 1 to number 2. The same goes for each of the other steps. Slight confusion is not that different from slight understanding so this is a logical step. The same from slight understanding to total understanding.

Now I can almost hear you say with some irritation, "But these are really just words. Haven't you been telling us for three volumes that bantering words about like this, without knowing their meanings, is dumb? We could mean vastly different things when we say words like 'slight understanding' than you do!" Well, yeah. That is why I had you use states you had thoroughly identified using your state sheets. That way *you* know what you are talking about when you label the states. What I mean by the labels is not as important as what you experience. *You'll know by comparing the submodalities, especially the critical ones, how close or far apart each state is from the next.* Also, you'll remember that I gave more descriptive examples of those states when you originally elicited them in yourself than in just about anything in this entire series. That was not a coincidence.

Also remember that words, themselves, are anchors. The

only states I asked for were confusion and understanding. Then I added modifiers to these to make them "big or little" so to speak. Try something inside your head for a moment. Say the word "confusion" and find out what you experience on the inside. Then say "slight confusion." See if the experience is less intense. Then say "total confusion" and discover if the experience is more pronounced. They may even be the same experience, as far as content, just more or less intense. This pattern of choosing states that are similar, but slightly modified, is a good one to ponder for a while. And do so deeply, for effect.

Next we are going to pick states that seem intuitively close together, and work from there. These will also be a familiar chain. This is one I described in Volume II when I talked about successful people and some of their characteristics. It goes:

Feel anxiety
Focus attention inward
Remember to breathe
Chuckle at our reaction
Feel renewed self-confidence
Feel motivated

Before we go about giving ourselves that one, let's think about what we already have. All of us feel anxiety at one time or another. And we respond to the feeling in some way. How we respond, and where it gets us, is what chains are about.

Remember for a moment the last time you felt really anxious. This could be an experience from your home life or work, it doesn't matter. Run the experience forward as a movie, slowly, enough to get a sense of where you began and ended. Make some educated guesses about what states you went through in the process. I don't expect you to be able to do this perfectly. As in a strategy, there will be parts that are outside of your awareness. Filling in all of the missing pieces can be interesting for you if you wish to spend the time and energy. But for our present purposes, I just want you to make some general observations about the kind of chain you go through in response to anxiety.

Perhaps you go through no discernible set of internal events, identifiable in this form. It is equally possible that you stay in the anxiety state for a time until outside events take over and alter your state for you. If so, be aware that the environment has control over you during this time. That's OK with me if it's OK with you.

The goal of this thought experiment is to discover how you handle anxiety, now. If you find that this is something you have no problem with, congratulations. You are doing better than most. If, on the other hand, you could use a new choice about responding to worry and anxiety, this next experiment should provide just what you need.

Your Own Chains, Experiment #2

Step 1

Get out several of your state sheets. You'll need as many as 6. Now get into that same state of anxiety you just ran the internal movie of. This time, though, make sure that the movie stops somewhere near the beginning so that you can stay in that initial state of anxiety. When you are really in it, anchor it as you did in the first experiment. Don't use the same finger and the same wrist, but get an anchor somewhere that can be the beginning of a series. Again, an arm or leg is the easiest way to do these kinesthetic anchors for chains.

Step 2

Now fill in the relevant portions of the sheet. These would be, at least, descriptions of the critical submodalities for each rep system while you're in that state of anxiety. This way you'll know what you have anchored.

Step 3

The next state is one of internal focus and attention. If you have ever meditated, taken yoga classes, or done any kind of sensory awareness exercises you know what I mean. If not, imagine being completely aware of your physical state on the inside. The point is to know how you're breathing, where your muscle tension is, if you're hot or cold anyplace, etc. Consciousness of kinesthetics is the key.

Again, anchor this state in the next spot you have chosen. Fill in another state sheet for this one. You may want to remember this state clearly in the future. It is particularly useful for many things.

Step 4

The next state is one of responsiveness to your own physical state. That is what the awareness is for. All the awareness in the world wouldn't help you much if you didn't use it. Think of it as a state of internal care-taking, another vastly important state.

There are several good examples. Many of us will get heavily involved in some task, to the point of contorting our bodies. We may be hunched over a typewriter, desk, or workbench while performing some task. We may be leaning over one pot to get to another on the stove. Perhaps we have bent over to look for some nearly invisible thing we just dropped in the shag rug. Often we'll engage in whatever we're doing to the point that we notice a pain in our back, a twist in our face, or a hold in our breath. The awareness of this is what we were after in the state in Step 3.

If we are smart, as soon as we become aware of whatever ridiculous posture we have gotten into, we'll fix it. Otherwise our bodies will escalate their complaints beyond all reason. Then we'll really be sorry. It is this "doing-something-about-what-we-just-noticed" state that we want at this step in our chain.

Usually we know what the response should be. A deep breath, for one, never hurts, unless we are in the presence of poison gas, or the cooking of a particular friend of mine. Both of those being, thankfully, rare occurrences, taking a breath would be a nice start. Along with that, a straightening of our posture, or at least regaining our balance, is a peachy idea. Beyond that, relaxing any muscle tension will usually get us into a healthier state than continuing to strain. These are of course only optional examples. If you don't want to consider them, it's your body.

For many people, the state of noticing and the state of doing something about it, seem to be one step. It's as if the two were inextricably linked together, so that the response automatically follows the awareness. In this case it simply means the two are *already* chained together. I know as those people read my above descriptions they thought to themselves, "Who wouldn't respond immediately to their own physical needs?" The answer is simple: everybody else.

If you are one of those fortunate people who already has these states chained together in sequence, fine. You get to skip this step and go on to the next state. If not, you need to get into this responsive state and anchor it. You have several above examples that should help you remember, or conjure up, the appropriate internal responsiveness to your physical needs. Use the next anchor on your arm or leg for this state. Fill out a state sheet describing this state.

Step 5

The next state we want in this chain is one we should all use more often. It's the one in which we laugh at ourselves. Certainly we do enough ridiculous stuff to warrant it. Besides that, it makes an especially useful addition to this chain.

Laughter, especially at ourselves, often *is* the best medicine. Especially when we need to relax and appreciate our own foolishness. It reminds us to salvage whatever humility we have left, and at the same time helps us to give others a break for their foolishness. It is one of the best friends a teacher can have. Its ability to help combat the ravages of stress can't be overestimated.

I'm sure you can remember times when you did foolish things and laughed at yourself. If those are too few, start laughing at some of the things you missed the opportunity to laugh at when they happened. That's why we have memories. Also, it is far easier to laugh at ourselves in hindsight, especially if no one is looking. You may want to practice this. Then again, you may not — that doesn't make it any less of a good idea.

Perhaps it occurs to you now that you have no sense of humor. Maybe you can borrow one. If you are truly humorless, I'm sure you can find lots of other people who have been laughing at you for years. Perhaps they can teach you. Then you get to do it first, before they get the chance. Something about the last laugh seems to be lurking about in the back of my mind...

The purpose of this at this point in the chain is to help us get back that perspective of who we are and what we're doing. Noticing that we are contorting ourselves physically is a great lead-in for this. It really is silly to do so when our bodies work so much better in a balanced and relaxed way. If you think about that, from an outside perspective, it is kind of funny. And it is a very logical next step beyond the last one.

When you have gotten into a good representative example of this state, anchor it in the next spot you have chosen. Then fill out another state sheet.

Step 6

This next step in our chain is a recovery from laughing at ourselves. Again this is quite logical. If you think back on the times you have acted foolishly, and laughed at yourself, you will probably notice a nice pattern. Once you have that humorous perspective, and are relaxed and aware, it is easy to do better at whatever you are engaged in. That is one of those "truths" that I am willing to put money on most of the time. I know I improve when I follow those steps and have observed most other people doing the same. It is as if the pressure to avoid looking foolish is gone. That's because we already did, and survived. Then we can "get on with it."

A good music teacher or athletic coach will always teach this. If you miss a note, don't stop the song, keep going. It is important to finish and you can't go back and get the dropped note. The same goes for sports. If you missed the shot, dropped the pass, or tripped over your own feet, there is still no way to undo it. You need to concentrate on the next shot or pass. And all you can do from the ground is get back on your feet. In any case, the only way to go is up.

Remember a time when you had this renewed self-confidence. A time when the pressure to perform was past. You had good perspective on the situation, you were relaxed, and balanced — in every sense of the word. You felt as if there was nothing to do but go on. Anchor this state in the next spot and fill out your sheet.

Step 7

The last step in this chain is motivation. Some people have this step already attached to the last step of renewed self-confidence. Some don't. Check yourself carefully and if you find that you do, again, congratulations. It is one that ought to be there.

Many people, however, don't have these connected. I know lots of athletes who never made it to greatness, even though they were good at recovering from errors. That's as far as it went. Once they recovered, they just plodded along without the initial enthusiasm that got them going to begin with. Many a runner has gotten up after a fall with the idea of "just finishing." The ones who have that motivation to win connected to their recovery step, get up off the ground and try even harder than before to win the race. That is the attitude we want at the end of this chain.

Get yourself into whatever strongly motivated state you think you need. This is a state we have talked about on and off for three volumes, so you should know it well. When you get into it, anchor it in the next spot. Fill out your sheet for this state.

Step 8

Now you have all of your states mapped out and anchored in

a row. How many that is for you depends, of course, on which ones were already anchored together, or not. Before installing the chain, take a look over those state sheets to see what you have. Do they make some sense to you in this order? Think about why this chain might be so natural and effective as you look over the state sheets.

Test each of the anchors again. Remember to take a break of some sort between each one to keep them separate and un-contaminated. When you are sure each is well anchored, go on to the next step.

Step 9

Now it's time to install the chain, just like you did with the last one.

Fire the anchor for the state of anxiety.

When you feel the anxiety reach its height, immediately fire the next anchor. This is the one for your inward focus of attention.

When you feel this reach the height of its response, imme-diately fire the next anchor.

As this one reaches the height of its intensity, fire the next, and so on, until you have fired the last anchor in your chain.

Again, experience this last state for a couple of minutes, then break the state by getting up and walking around.

Step 10

Now sit down again and fire the first anchor, for the state of anxiety. What happens in your experience? Remember all of the possible outcomes we talked about in the first experiment and treat yourself accordingly. If you need to go back and check your anchors, or go through the chaining once more, go ahead.

Now I want to spend some time thinking about the different ways chains could be useful for you in the classroom. If you think about your job as a teacher, several possibilities should present themselves immediately. Teachers do many things. One of the most important of these is answering questions. Sometimes the questions can be a bit "off the wall." Sometimes, in fact, they are really challenges to the teacher. How each different kind of question is handled will determine the quality of the learning going on at that moment. The dialog between teachers and students is so obviously important that I feel a little silly in mentioning it. But I have seen so many people just answer questions without considering the impact of the answer on the *thinking processes* of the other person. Often, giving a direct answer is the least useful response. If you think in terms of learning by discovery, this becomes self-evident.

Wouldn't it be nice to have a chain that would get you to a state in which you could best determine the way to respond to any question or challenge? I think it would. This is one of those chains that may seem to be as much a strategy as a chain. Sometimes the line between the two gets a little blurred. That's why we have experiments.

For this next one let's look at a few of the processes that go into the task. First, you need to hear the question and understand it. Then, your understanding of it has to be put in context. What I mean is that the question has to be judged in terms of whatever is going on in the classroom. Also, it has to be considered from the viewpoint of the individual who asked it. That means you must know something about the child and how he thinks. In addition, it is a good idea to know how the child relates to you, and vice versa. In other words, the context of the relationship you have with this child is central.

Perceiving this context takes a good bit of awareness. It also takes a genuine interest in the child and his learning. It takes motivation and creativity to provide the most useful response. It takes continual perceptiveness to notice what the child does with the response. Most of all, perhaps, it takes a continued willingness to use the child's response to enhance rapport, and continue to build new interest and learning.

If this all sounds like a tall order, good. It is. That is why we have some states that are especially useful for certain abilities. It's also why we can go through sequences that will bring all our abilities to bear, in the right order, to get the best outcome we can manage.

Now we can imagine some of the states necessary to be able to do the above things. The first and most crucial, for me, is one of adequate preparedness. Anticipating possible questions or problems ahead of time is always a good idea. Though you can't do it perfectly, at least you can give yourself some idea of the direction you want to go in and how you might gracefully guide the class. For example, do you have prepared answers for likely questions? Better still, do you have some general ways of handling *any* questions? Will you ask anyone who has a question to wait, and ask it again later? Will you answer with another question or perhaps set up an experiment? Would you refuse to answer altogether, hopefully on some relevant grounds? I discussed some of these in Volume II in the chapter on language, and I suggest that you review the myriad choices you have again.

A second state I believe to be invaluable is curiosity. This is a good one to have most of the time when you are teaching anyway. A way to understand what I am talking about is to pose *yourself* a question: "How is it possible for this child to ask this?" If you ask yourself, "How is it possible for this child to ...?" each time you don't quite understand him, it will help you in your teaching immensely. In fact, a similar question anytime you get stuck at anything will make your life simpler and more productive.

Another good state to have while engaging in the activity of responding to children is a good resource state. In this particular one, it helps to be disassociated and looking down from above. This "surveying" position will help give you the perspective you need to view yourself in relationship to the child and the rest of the class. If you can do this, calmly and with all of your good judgment, decisiveness, and compassion, it will help even more.

Once you have achieved that new perspective, you need to add the appreciation of that person's individual needs. This takes a real interest in the child for who he is, not who you expect him to be. Then you need the motivation to get the child whatever learning or understanding you think will most help him. This is different than the quickest answer to get him to leave you alone. We all know what that is like. We get to the point sometimes when we would just like to be able to dole out the information and not have to worry about it anymore. Get a computer, they work perfectly for that. As long as you are working with children, however, individual needs have to be kept in the forefront of the process.

Next you need to have a bit of an experimental nature about you. After these books you should have more than you did. What I mean here specifically, though, is the willingness to try out your answer and find out what happens. Think of yourself as performing an experiment each time you give another person information. That really is a good description. You are trying to find out what he will do with what you give. This takes more perceptiveness and willingness on your part. You have to notice what the child does when you respond, and you have to respond to his response. This brings you back into a similar state to the first one. Sort of a lead-in to it, really.

In this sense this chain is a kind of a loop, provided that you go in the order I just described. The entire process gets you back to a questioning, and prepared, state in which you can respond effectively to the next need.

Your Own Chains, Experiment #3

Step 1

You'll notice that I gave you a great deal less of a description for each of the above states than before. Also, I gave no examples to aid you. I want to give you the chance to design your own chain, within limits.

Start by coming up with your best descriptions and examples. Decide what you think would be adequate at each step. I have only outlined what I think are the necessary ingredients to get the job done. Perhaps you have more ideas. Also, as we did in the last experiment, find out if you have some of these states already chained together where you need them. You may also notice you have some chained in ways that *don't* work. Be aware, and use your good sense in the design.

Step 2

Next, look over the order I have vaguely outlined above. Decide if this is what you think would work best, for you, as an individual. I'll give you the same benefit of uniqueness I expect you to give the children. Make whatever changes you think are necessary.

Step 3

Next, go through the process of eliciting, anchoring, and describing with your state sheets, each step in this chain. It is up to you how to get to the state and anchor it. Your choices abound. Remember to make it easy for yourself by arranging the anchors in convenient locations. I suggest you take good notes with your sheets, since this is your first real chance at participating in the design of one of these. Look over your sheets — by now you may have found some useful personal patterns that you can try here.

Step 4

Test each anchor. Remember to interrupt yourself between each one to break the state.

Step 5

Now install the chain in yourself. You should be getting comfortable with the procedure. Remember to let each state get to the height of its intensity before firing the next anchor.

Step 6

Test the chain. Fire off the first anchor you set up and find out what happens. You know all of the possible outcomes and what to do in each case. Review the previous experiments and your notes to help you.

Step 7

Spend a little time contemplating what you have done. Are you satisfied with the steps you chose? Was it as easy to install as the earlier ones? Would you make some changes in the chain? There is nothing to stop you from making a new one if you want to! Pay attention to your responses to the children in class. Notice any differences.

This was a bit of a stretch for you. I generally try to be quite explicit in my instructions when I give you an experiment. This time I was purposefully vague to give you a chance to rummage around in your own experience. This was still much more direction than you will have when you are on your own, of course. Using your logic and good sense you should be able to design lots of workable chains for yourself. You will need to practice, but you'll find it to be worth it.

As you might expect, the next step is to do this with your students. It is very easy. Based on what you know about your own chains, you should be able to explain your experiences and the processes to the children with some fluency. Also, the task itself involves nothing you have not already done with the children. It is only the combination of eliciting states, anchoring them, and firing the anchors. For these reasons, again, I am going to give you somewhat less instruction as we continue.

Chains in Children, Experiment #1

Step 1

Let's begin with a chain you are familiar with. It is the

second one you installed in yourself.

Feel anxiety
Focus attention inward
Respond to physical needs
Find humor in self/situation
Feel renewed self-confidence
Feel motivated

I am sure you can find a child who could use this chain. Gather this child up and tell him you want to help him with handling anxiety. Remember all of your necessary prerequisites for working with children in this way. Choose your words and explanations carefully so that the child will understand what you are doing. Remember not to explain too much. Be systematic and sympathetic in your approach and tell the child only as much of your experience as you think will help.

Step 2

Next take the child to each of the states on the above list. You have been in each, in this order, yourself, so this should help you. You will have to pay close attention to what you see and hear from the child to know what kind of state he is in. When the child appears to be in the state you are looking for, anchor it. The same guidelines apply here as they did for you. Have each anchor be a touch, easy to reach, fairly close to the one before it.

Use one of your state sheets to gather whatever information you think will help you and the child. Gather, at least, the critical submodalities and a brief description of the content of the child's experience for each of the states. You may want to jot down a note about what you see in the child when he is at the height of the state, so you can recognize it later.

Step 3

Test each of the anchors. Remember to have the child get up

and walk around between anchors to break each state so that they are uncontaminated. Spend a moment looking over your notes on the sheets while the child is taking these short breaks. See if you notice any patterns that you can use, or learn from. Make a mental note about what to look for as the child goes from one state to the next. You will need to be aware of these since you won't have time to look at your notes when you install the chain.

Step 4

Install the chain, just as you did with yourself. This time, obviously, you will have to use your eyes and ears to know if the child is at the height of each response before firing the next anchor. If you have paid close attention, this should be clear.

Step 5

Test the chain by firing the first anchor. Again, you will know by watching and listening to the child what the outcome is. Ask whatever questions you think are relevant to gather the information you need. Remember the possible responses that we listed earlier. These are all just as likely for this child as they were for you. The necessary steps in each case are also the same. Here are the possibilities again:

The first variety includes the following:

The first is that the child went into state number 1, and that was all.

Another is that you found that the child went through a couple of states, but ended up in either number 2 or number 3.

A third is that he or she seemed to go directly to state number 2 or 3, as if you fired off the anchor for that one instead of number 1.

Possibly, you noticed no effect at all.

If any of the first three has occurred, go back and repeat Steps 5 and 6 again. If you noticed nothing at all, try it again and make sure. If you still notice no effect, test each of your anchors again. Go back to Step 4 and repeat the remaining steps.

The other set of possibilities includes the following:

You actually noticed the child going through each state, one at a time, quickly. Perhaps they seemed to flow, one to the next.

Another possibility is that you only noticed that he or she was all of a sudden in state number 4.

In either case, the chain effectively worked as it should have. Either way is fine.

Step 6

As another semifinal test, discuss something with the child that normally causes the kind of anxiety the chain is designed to alleviate. In other words, attempt to get the child back into the state of anxiety. Watch and listen for the results.

Step 7

Discuss this procedure with the child as much as you think will be useful. This is more complex than he is likely to do on his own. But you can still describe sequences for him that you think he might try. Sometimes a descriptive suggestion is all that is needed.

The final-final test, of course, will be in the classroom. The next time you see him in a situation that would have, until now, brought on anxiety, you'll be looking for his response. Then you'll see and hear if he handles the situation better.

I hope that was as fast and easy as I tried to make it sound. If it wasn't yet, it will be. You can always repeat it with another child until you are comfortable with the procedure. This is such a nice chain that I'm sure you have lots of kids you'd like to share it with. You have probably noticed that each time you repeat one of these experiments it gets easier to do. That is mainly because you get more used to the procedure and find out that it is really straightforward. That is the point of NLP. If a procedure works the way the brain designed it, it should be fast and natural. Practice usually gets us past our tendency to overcomplicate what is easy.

Next I want you to have the opportunity to design another simple chain, but for a child. This time we'll use the first form I showed you. It will begin with the present state, that is, the one you want to get rid of. Then it will go to a milder version of that state. Third, it will change to a mild version of the desired state, the one you want the child to have. It will finish with a more intense version of this desired state. Remember for yourself you installed the following sequence:

number 1: utter, total confusion
number 2: mild confusion
number 3: sort of understanding
number 4: complete understanding

Rather than use the same chain, though, I would like you to use a new one. That way you will get to learn more about states and chains. The process is really simple if you think about it. All you have to do is pick a particular state you notice some child going into — one that you think she'd be better off without. Then decide the one you think should replace it. If you imagine "opposites" it should be easy. Anxiety vs. relaxation, boredom vs. interest, embarrassment vs. self-confidence, seriousness vs. humor, and several others come immediately to mind. I am sure you can think of many more.

Chains in Children, Experiment #2

Step 1

First choose the child you would like to help. Decide what to call the present undesirable state. Then choose what you would like to replace it with.

Step 2

Now sit down with the child and tell her what you want to help her with. Remember all of your skills at this step.

Step 3

Next get her into the present state, just long enough for you to be able to identify the state and anchor it. Remember that you will need to know, just by watching and listening, when she is at the height of this state.

By now I think we can make the state sheets optional. If you are more comfortable using them, do so. But it is important not to dwell on this first state too long since it is undoubtedly not much fun for the child. You should have time enough, though, to gather a couple of critical submodalities. Make sure you know what to do with them to adjust the intensity of the feelings that go with this state. Go directly, and quickly, from here to Step 4.

Step 4

It should be a simple matter, just by adjusting the critical submodalities, to convert this state to a milder form. So take her to this second state and anchor it. Remember to set the anchor in a convenient location near the first one. Then take a short break.

Step 5

Then go to the desired state. Describe what you would like for her to have instead of this problem state. She has probably been there before, so just the memory of it should be enough for you to help her into this desired state.

Then make sure you have a mild and an intense version of

this state just as you did before. Adjust the critical sub-modalities and anchor each one carefully. Test your anchors. This should be child's play by now.

Step 6

Now install the chain, the same as you have each time before. Watch and listen closely to her responses. Test the chain by firing the first anchor. Find out what happens and respond accordingly. I am sure you are thoroughly familiar with the possible outcomes and what to do about each one by this time.

Step 7

Next, try to get her back to the original undesirable state. Do this just as you did in the last experiment, by talking with her about something that would have produced it before you installed the chain.

Discuss the results with her as you see fit. Remember to watch in the future for more situations that would, before, have caused the original undesirable state.

This should have been quick and easy. If not, it just shows you need a little more practice. Maybe if you practice enough, you'll run out of kids with problems and have to start looking for ways to make good things better. Wouldn't that be interesting? Come to think of it, that wouldn't be a bad idea for an experiment.

Chains in Children, Experiment #3

Step 1

We have all encountered people who seem to do great up to a point, and then ... I am sure you have seen plenty of children do that in the classroom. It is almost as if they are torturing themselves purposely. My dad used to call it "snatching defeat from the jaws of victory." Some people never seem to have learned how to finish things.

Pinpoint a child you have noticed this self-defeating pattern in. Come up with three or four good examples you have seen him do — ones you would feel comfortable discussing with him.

Step 2

Round up this child and tell him what you have in mind. Describe the pattern as it appears to you. This is one he may be well aware of. He may even have some insight into how it works. Tell him you want to know, in detail, step by step, how it works.

At this point, see if you can figure out the steps he already goes through. This may take some guesswork on your part. More to the point would be some good questions. This is like eliciting a strategy, except that you want to know the sequence of states he goes through instead of internal representations. You are actually eliciting his already existing chain.

Step 3

At each step, find out the critical submodalities that you might use to make a difference. Don't anchor the states yet though. Remember, the first few steps in this chain probably work just fine for what you want. You can assume that at some point in the chain, one of these states leads him in a lousy direction. That is the one you want to find.

One of my instructors used to use the image of a line of old-time firemen fighting a fire. Imagine you are passing buckets of water, all in an organized way, one person to the next. You are working along just fine. Then someone, instead of a bucket, hands you an anvil. It can be a bit disconcerting. You can imagine that this is something like what happens inside this child. It may be less dramatic, though.

Let's look at a hypothetical example of a chain that starts off fine and then deteriorates. Imagine a child who responds well to challenge. With each new challenge he immediately becomes curious. Then he gathers his internal resources together and gets himself feeling confident. Next you notice that he immediately generates enthusiasm for learning something new. This motivates him to search out more information. He then gathers information and starts to make generalizations and comparisons to what he already knows. He finds some things that don't quite fit together. Now he gets mildly confused. Then he gets worried about whether he can solve his dilemma(s). Next comes mild, but growing frustration, followed by anger at himself or others, due to the building frustration. This leads him into a downward spiral... Let's look at this rather lengthy disaster again:

Feels challenged
Becomes curious
Gathers internal resources
Feels confident
Generates enthusiasm for learning
Has motivation to search, gathers information
Makes generalizations and comparisons
Perceives inconsistencies and discrepancies
Becomes mildly confused
Becomes worried
Frustration grows
Becomes angry
Goes quickly down the tubes (technically speaking)

Look familiar? As we look at the list, it clearly starts off fine. It also, just as clearly, ends up rotten. The point of departure may not be so obvious though. Looking at the steps logically we see some things that can't be avoided. Making generalizations, comparisons, and other interpretations are all natural processes. We wouldn't get too far without these mechanisms. Perceiving inconsistencies is just as natural. Those people who don't are missing something, usually an awful lot. Discrepancies are found just about everywhere we have information. They're a part of life.

What about confusion? Well this is a matter of opinion. I

have already stated my preference. I think confusion is a good logical process. As I said before, it is useful *as long as it leads somewhere worth going.* That is why we have chains. I would think, in the above chain, that the confusion step is the last *inherently* useful one. Unfortunately, it doesn't lead anywhere I'd want to go, but we can fix that. Worry, to me, is where this chain goes downhill. I see that step as the weak link. I would want to interrupt this example between confusion and worry.

Now you will have to look at the logic of the chain you have found in the same way. Remember that you have the knowledge to be able to change the direction the chain goes in. In that sense, it almost doesn't matter what steps come between the beginning and the end, as long as the chain works. But you will find that the more useful each step is, the better the eventual outcome will be. Wasting energy is not good practice.

Step 4

When you have found the weak link in the chain this child goes through, stop for a couple of minutes. Look at the steps that lead up to it. Then look at the ones that ruin the finish for him. See if it makes sense in terms of the examples of his behavior that you discussed with him. This can be a very enlightening lesson on human behavior, for both of you.

Now you want to figure out the best way for the chain to end. You may need only a couple of new steps. Design the chain using the knowledge you have gained in the previous experiments. The trick here is to *use* the parts of the chain that work well, up to the step *right before* the one that begins the downfall.

Step 5

You want to anchor the last two steps that work well. This is the one just before the weak link step, and the one before that one. In our example above, it would be:

Perceives inconsistencies and discrepancies
Becomes mildly confused

Step 6

Then you want to elicit and anchor each of the new states you have constructed to finish the chain with. You'll do this just as you have in each of the preceding experiments. Use whatever critical submodalities you need along with all of your other knowledge and skill.

In our above example, we would want to have confusion lead to something likely to keep him on track toward learning from the challenge. That "experimental nature" I spoke of before, in the last chain you installed in yourself, would be good. The state in which you can't wait to try something new just to see how it turns out. Then perhaps the state following that one in my description: of perceptiveness and willingness to accept and build on the results. I might want to finish a chain like this with a sense of a need for completion. A real drive to keep going until the problem, or dilemma, is solved.

Step 7

Once you have finished these steps, you will have a new series of anchors. You have the last two from the working part of the original chain. You also have the new ones you have constructed. That is all you need.

Now then, install the "patch" to this chain starting with the second-to-last working anchor from the original part. Then the last anchor in the working part, followed by your new additions.

In our example the sequence would look like this:

Perceives inconsistencies and discrepancies
Becomes mildly confused
Gains a sense of experimentation
Has a willingness to use results
Feels a need for completion

Step 8

Now you need to test the chain. Start by firing off the first anchor you used: the second-to-last working step. Watch the results, using all of your sensory acuity. Then you need to do the other test, especially carefully. Get him back to the original state that began the first chain. In our example above it would be: Feels challenged. See if he goes all the way through the chain, as you would expect, to the new conclusion.

If the chain is as long and involved as the example I chose, this may be a little bit difficult to be sure of. This is one of those times when it is good to set up a test you can count on. Give him whatever triggers this chain. In the above example, I would give him a difficult assignment and tell him I expect him to finish it, and give a reasonable time limit. And I'd make it a *real* challenge. Why test your work halfway? I'd know if the chain was installed correctly when he finished the assignment, or not. Then it would be a matter of doing whatever needed to be done, like always.

Chains are so simple and so powerful they can be almost deceptive. As I said at the beginning of this chapter, they are nothing but states held together by anchors. So the tendency is to start chaining things together all over the place. Remember what you have learned, while you're doing that. In general the simplest chains are the best ones to practice with. You can easily tell if someone is going through three or four steps. When you get up to six or seven, or even more, it can be trickier to tell what is happening inside the other person.

One of the reasons I gave you such lengthy examples was to let you experience the simplicity and complexity simultaneously. That's another one of those semi-paradoxes I am so fond of. But I think you know what I mean. As you practice these sequences you'll get more and more comfortable organizing your thinking in these ways. Then you'll start to notice patterns occurring over and over again. This will give you the chance to test your skills of logic against what you perceive. When you really see the logic, and understand how and why things work the way they do, it will give you a sense of confidence in what you're doing. Then you'll get that inevitable urge to look way beyond the things I have shown you. Or even suggested. I know that with time and exploration you can take these ideas much further than I have, toward your *own* sense of completion.

CHAPTER 6

EXPERIMENTAL CONCLUSION

When I was a kid I dreamed of being a doctor. Ben Casey and Dr. Kildare were my idols. I just knew everyone who wasn't like them had some sort of character defect. If I couldn't do brain surgery I was sure I would turn to scum. As a result of this aspiration, when I got to high school I was told I would have to study German. My advisors had me thoroughly convinced that a major portion of a medical student's, and indeed a doctor's, time was spent in reading and translating German scientific journals. This was because, as everyone in the know could tell you, German was the language in which most of the important scientific work was published.

The worst part of all this is that I actually *believed* this drivel. I was impressionable and innocent. I never understood why when I went to the doctor's office and, knowingly, told him I was in on the German scoop, he just looked at me like I was crazy, excused himself, and took my parents aside for a chat...

At any rate, I had a terrible time trying to learn German in high school. It was the hardest task I had ever undertaken in my life. In fact there were times that I was sure it would cost me my life, or at least any hope of salvaging my career and avoiding the scum parade. Yeah, I stayed pretty dumb all the way through the ordeal.

However I did have a very interesting experience one day in

German class. It was near the end of my second year studying the language I knew would seal my destiny. I glanced over to one side and noticed one of the first books we had tackled, sitting over on a shelf. I remembered it being a story I actually enjoyed — at least the parts I understood. I picked it up and started to read it — yes I already had my reading compulsion, I just didn't like it back then. Halfway through the first page it dawned on me that I understood the story! In fact I was reading it almost as easily as I would have if it had been written in English. I knew every word. What a shock. Up to that point I was convinced that I knew absolutely nothing about German. It had never dawned on me that the material was just a jump or two ahead of me all the time. Now I could actually read last year's stuff, almost effortlessly. I was dumb struck.

I thought about that experience for a long time after that. It was one of the few times in high school when I actually felt capable. Years later when I looked back I thought how sad it was that I had hated that class so much. I wondered how it would have been if someone had just *shown* me what a thing of beauty the language *could* be. Or how valuable studying any foreign language could be, simply for the variety of thought processes it engages. Anything instead of all the condescending crap. How sad that the real reasons for learning a language were kept hidden from me by a veil of lies.

Still, there was that one beautiful and lasting experience I did get from the struggle. I knew, even then, that the most important lesson I learned had nothing to do with German.

Often people who really don't know ask me if "this stuff really works." When I tell them it does, they usually want me to show them. I do. But always with the insistence that the only valuable lessons will be the ones they give themselves. This is an outgrowth of an old problem I once had. I think I have it pretty well licked now. I used to be one of those people who went around rescuing everyone I could find who was in trouble. It was a real drain. And after a while I realized it let all those people off the hook for having to learn how to help themselves. The worst was in helping other therapists by taking over their "impossible cases." I would end up really angry at them for giving me the client rather than learning something themselves. It also got *very* boring. So I decided to refuse to help them any more. Now I am only willing to teach and train others. It's a relief. It also allows me to write and teach much better. Moreover, I get the distinct pleasure of hearing *their* stories. I really feel great when I learn about the wonderful things my students have done. Often they do much better work than I would have, given the situations they describe. This invariably reminds me that I can indirectly help many more people by teaching than by doing all the work myself.

Mostly, of course, I get others to learn by doing experiments. The discovery method. So often I hear people tell me things they have found on their own that I never could have told them. It gives them a sense of ownership of their own knowledge. It also gets them to make up their own experiments to learn more. This is especially nice when they tell me about the things they have done with couples, families, groups, classes, or organizations. When they realize they can do most of what I have taught them with a group of people just as easily as with one person, they're almost always amazed. I am not really sure why. This is another one of those things that always seemed so obvious to me.

Most of the people I have taught, as you might expect, are in business helping others to solve their problems. A brave few have taken that giant leap forward into advancing our knowledge. These are the ones who interest me most. They figure out how processes work, even if they don't have anyone around to copy. Then they construct ways to get things done based on whatever pieces they can find, or manufacture, that make the puzzle work. I think we call that creativity. It's just as important as solving problems. I am still looking forward to having a lot of our social problems disappear because they can't work anymore. If the nice things in life can malfunction, why can't the lousy ones? That is where our best creative minds need to be concentrating. Making the nasty parts of life just fail.

Many of the same things are true outside of education as well as inside it. Business, government, medicine, and media are, of course, run by people trained in our educational system. They act like it too. Rigid. Doctrinaire. Remedial. The difference between leaders in those fields and leaders in education is usually in rhetoric, clout, and deception. Everyone knows what kind of shape education is in because it is right in front of us. Crystal clear. These other social systems are right there as well, but they're strangely diffused through our awareness. It isn't that they aren't as visible. Just that we are less likely to know what we're looking at.

In education and the rest of society, though, learning how to learn is still only a dream, talked about and hoped for. Some people still think they can learn how to teach first and how to learn later on. More diffusion. This is especially sad since the technology for learning to learn is already here. Fortunately, in some industry and educational circles, people are beginning to come around. They are studying NLP and some of the other new ideas that are out here, just for the asking.

It is too bad that it generally takes 15 to 20 years before good technology filters down to the people who need it most. It means a whole generation has to suffer through problems that already have existing solutions. That is one of the reasons for *Meta-Cation*. Rather than having to wait for teacher education to catch up with what we know, people, meaning you, can take what is here and apply it now. That is, provided that you're willing to take what is on these pages and put it into your brain and behavior. The only way I know to do that is to experiment.

And, please, give some of it away to someone who needs it. The good gestures like that will always come back to you. I'm not talking about rescuing everyone who walks by. I just mean do what you think ought to be done to help others. If you can't tell the difference, ask someone who can.

People who have been around NLP a while go through some interesting progressions in their learning. When they begin, they are usually like kids on Christmas morning. They can't wait to go try everything. Then they get past the initial stages and become somewhat competent. A bit of a lull sometimes sets in, a fall-back into previous routines, though at a higher level of efficiency and effectiveness. It is easy to just go about your business. Especially if things are generally OK.

Often a little later they will run into some other NLPers someplace, perhaps at a convention or meeting. It renews some of the original spark. If they keep it sparkling for a while they start looking around them again. Usually they have solved most of their major "problems" by now, but they want to make life more interesting. They already have the most powerful techniques ever developed for doing that. Then the realization comes that the only way to make things different and more exciting is to act differently and more excited. An interesting experiment indeed.

Life needs to be thought of as a continual string of experiments if it is going to be fresh and new. That is the only way it moves forward, really. With the learning we have gained, in retrospect, it is easier to recognize patterns throughout our existence. Some of those patterns work, some don't. Those that don't provide an immediate opportunity for experimentation. Those that do just take a little longer. You see, just because something works doesn't mean you *can't* fix it. It only means it doesn't have to be done today. A lot of what is "acceptable" really *could* stand some improvement. Even NLP, though it's the best there is right now, is still far from perfect. Go make it better.

APPENDIX
PHOTOCOPY PAGES

APPENDIX I

WORK SHEET FOR IDENTIFYING STATES OF CONSCIOUSNESS

Give a content description of the situation and any images you notice inside. In other words, in a couple of sentences describe what the pictures and sounds are in your head:

Under each of the following sections, make whatever notes you will need to guide you through the changes you want to make.

Visual Submodalities

Color	Shape	Size	Distance
Location	Brightness	Contrast	Clarity
Focus	Movement/Speed	Direction	Depth
Slides/Motion Picture		Associated/Disassociated	

Auditory Submodalities

Sound/Words	Voice/Whose?	Internal/External	
Location	Distance	Direction	Volume
Pitch	Rhythm	Tempo	Duration
Tone	Timbre		

Kinesthetic Submodalities

Internal/External		Tactile/Proprioceptive	Intensity
Location	Size	Shape	Moisture
Weight	Pressure	Temperature	Texture
Duration	Frequency	Movement	Rhythm

This is a description of your state of consciousness at this point in this situation. If you pay attention to the feelings they will help you know if the visual images and sounds are what you want. Systematically changing the visual and auditory submodalities will, of course, help you change the feelings until you have them the way you want them. It is always a good idea to have an anchor for any state that is especially pleasant or useful.

APPENDIX II

VISUAL THRESHOLDS

Color Increase the intensity of colors until they "bleed" into each other and the image is no longer identifiable. Or decrease to black and white and then all the way to a dull, even, gray slate. Decreasing seldom turns out to be very effective, but try it anyway.

Size Increase until the picture is so large that you can't see enough of it to identify. Or decrease it until it disappears. Decreasing is seldom effective.

Distance Bring it so close that it seems to go through or past you, losing its identity as it does so. Or move it so far away that you can no longer see it, though this too is seldom effective.

Brightness Increase it until the picture turns pure white. Or decrease it until it fades to black. Decreasing is only sometimes effective but definitely worth trying.

Contrast   This can only be decreased until the picture
                fades out of resolution and becomes indistin-
                guishable. The same is true for clarity and
                focus. Try and see.

Speed   You can only increase the speed of the motion
                until it becomes a blur and is indistinguisha-
                ble. Slowing down to a still shot may change
                the feelings but that is not the same as going
                over a threshold.

APPENDIX III

AUDITORY THRESHOLDS

Sound/Words Changing a sound into words can be fascinating. For some people, the particular sound, especially if it was unusual, never comes back again. The reverse is possible but unlikely.

Voice Changing a voice so that it matches that of some other person (or duck) is sometimes very effective. For some people it seems to stay that way for good.

Internal/ External Moving a voice from the inside of your head to the outside may help, and actually remain changed. The same is true of the reverse, but in both cases people can usually change them back again.

Distance Again, you can only move the voice so far away that it disappears. This is sometimes effective.

Volume You can make a sound so loud that it becomes just a meaningless roar. By the same token, you can soften it so that you can no longer hear it at all. Softening is seldom effective for the reasons mentioned above.

Pitch   You can either increase or decrease the pitch so that the sound is a high squeal or a low moan, neither recognizable as the original. For some people this one will work either way.

Tone   Both this and timbre can be changed so that the sound is no longer recognizable as the original. It sometimes helps to think of the sound of one musical instrument gradually changing to that of a vastly different one.

APPENDIX IV

QUESTIONS FOR DETERMINING COMPLETENESS OF STRATEGIES

1. Do you know at exactly what point the strategy begins? In other words, what is the *first Test* that starts the strategy going?

2. Do you have all the steps that you think constitute the *Operation* phase?

3. Does the strategy make logical sense? Would this operation work to accomplish this task? Can you justify each step as a necessity? If not, do you know where the extraneous ones are? Do you know why they are unnecessary? Can you surmise any that *must* be there that you have not so far detected?

4. Do you know what the *second Test* is? What is it for this strategy and how does it work to make the strategy effective?

5. Can you map out this strategy so that you know, step by step, how it gets from the beginning to the outcome? Can you write out the sequence so that it is understandable to you?

6. Do you know the important submodalities, especially the critical ones at each step in this strategy?

7. Do you know what submodality changes cause the strategy to go from one step to the next? How each threshold works?

8. Can you go through this strategy and get it to work for you as well or better than the child? That is usually a good check on your logic.

9. Based on the answers to these questions, do you need to ask the child to do this a few more times for you?

APPENDIX V

SOME GENERAL TIPS ON READING STRATEGIES

1. Speed in reading comes from a combination of things:

Moving your eyes across the words faster than you can say them. If you hear each word in your head, the way you were initially taught in school, you won't be able to read faster than you can talk.

Being able to fill in enough of your images with fewer words, i.e. seeing whole scenes flash by quickly, without having to fill in all the details. This requires some sort of filtering out to get the nouns and verbs first, and the other words only when necessary.

Having the turn of the page be a part of the strategy, rather than an interruption. Many people can speed read for two pages, then the turn of the page itself anchors in their old slow strategy. Some speed reading courses teach you to turn the pages in a different way than you used to.

Not having to be perfect the first time through. Many speed readers will tell you they scan the first time just for the general idea. Then they go back for as much detail as they need. Often they will read something five or six times to get what they need. This will depend on how much they want, how technical the material is, and how well it is written. *No one* really speed reads a chemistry text full of formulas and gets it all the first time, with the exception of certain people who *really* have total "photographic" recall. Even they usually don't have the concepts, either. They just know how to get the information back from their brains so they can figure it out later.

Being able to speed up or slow down at will. This is a plus if you can read quickly when you understand enough and slow down when you need more detail. It will allow you to go through in fewer passes.

2. Comprehension also means more than one activity:

Making your movie with enough accurate detail. This means including enough details as well as not adding your own if they change the meaning. Creative license is admissible only when reading for your own pleasure, not someone else's.

Being able to relate one internal movie to another. Sometimes switching to visual still shots helps in comparing images, like in our discussion of children's strategies. This can also mean holding a still shot while running the new movie along side it as you read. This may include a memory of a similar piece you read previously, that you mentally refer to in making sense of the present piece. I don't have a better explanation than that, but if you try it I think you'll know what I mean.

Reading the words in a logical order when you have trouble. Just as with speed, start with nouns. These will give you still pictures. Verbs will add motion and relationships between the stills, bringing them together, and making it into a movie. Adjectives and other words will add in the other crucial submodalities for you.

3. Enjoyment comes from several things on several levels:

Physical comfort.

The right submodalities in the internal movie, visually and auditorily. This is, of course, a personal matter. But a review of a list you have seen before should help you understand. Any of these will detract from your comfort and enjoyment.

  Too many images in a small space (or field of vision)

  Images moving in different directions, too fast, or at different speeds

  Images that are too close

  Images that are too large or too bright

  Sounds that are too close, loud, or shrill

  Too many sounds or voices at once

  Sounds or voices of unpleasant tonalities

In addition to these, in reading, not enough can be as bad as too much. When people don't understand something they tend to make themselves uncomfortable. I think we all know where that was most effectively anchored. Be that as it may, pictures with "holes" in them, or lack of clarity, are common when we don't quite get what we are reading. You have probably figured out by now that if we just worked on repairing those submodalities it would make us more comfortable. But remember we want to fill in the gaps with accurate information. We want comfort *and* learning.

A sense of reading for its own sake. This is my opinion but I really like to learn. I also like enjoyment. I have the belief that I will get both from just about anything I read. So I automatically go into a pleasant state of consciousness whenever I read. It took me a long time to get there, though. I had a lot of old anchors and memories that connected reading and drudgery. I had to overcome those before I could enjoy it. If you have some old anchors like those, you might use what you have learned to do something about them. You might do the same to remove old unpleasant memories about reading for some children as well. Or at least don't give them any new ones.

APPENDIX VI

GUIDELINES FOR CREATING TEACHING EXPERIMENTS

1. Make each experience you set up *possible.* It is not useful to embarrass kids with impossible tasks for any reason. There are better ways to get them to shoot for excellence.

2. *Gear each experience for success.* Kids should be able to do something right that you can compliment them on during each task.

3. Make sure that *each person involved* in the task *learns something.* This is aimed mostly at tasks that involve kids working together. You might include yourself in this as well (though that is only one of my never-ending list of suggestions).

4. Openly state something that you expect them to learn or find in each task. This is your *overt purpose* in having them do it.

5. Save at least one hidden thing you also expect them to learn. This is the *covert learning* I mentioned earlier that should be built into all teaching. This is the part you want them to discover for themselves.

6. Make sure that each task *stretch*es the students' abilities at least a little. Make it a challenge.

7. Make the learning lead to some new learning that will come later. This is called *heuristic* learning. The essence of the idea is that answers are most useful when they lead to new, better, and more interesting questions.

Printed in the United States
63151LVS00003B/13